Follower of the Seasons

A Onethology in Symphony

by Oscar Gutierrez Peñaranda

Eastwind Books of Berkeley

Follower of the Seasons
A Onethology in Symphony

Published by: Eastwind Books of Berkeley

Berkeley, California USA

www.AsiaBookCenter.com
email: eastwindbooks@gmail.com

Eastwind Books of Berkeley is a registered trademark of
Eastwind Books of Berkeley

Published 2023. First Edition

Printed in the United States of America

ISBN: 9781961562059 (Paperback)
ISBN: 9781961562066 (Ebook)

10 9 8 7 6 5 4 3 2 1

Contents

Foreword — viii
Preface — ix
Introduction — xi
Acknowledgements — xii

Key: F (Fiction), E (Essay), M (Memoir), P (Poetry), S (Skit)

SUITE #1: The Bridge — 1
The Bridge (M) — 1
Bayani's Tune (P) — 2
Lover's Leap *by Presco Tabios* (P) — 2
Passengers of The Wind (E) — 6
The U.S.-Philippines War (E) — 11
The Prisoner of Balangiga (F) — 25
An Tuba ha Balangiga (P) — 31
A Reunion of Strangers (E) — 34
Lumpia, Super Bowl, and the U.S.-Philippines War (M) — 36
Maria (M) — 37
Pancho Villa and Emeryville (E) — 38
Left-handed Lover (P) — 38
Golden Boy (M) — 39
Manila Goodbye (F) — 40

SUITE #2: The Voyage — 43
The Awakening (M) — 44
On Liwanag (the fire last time, and the emerging Filipino American sensibility in literature) (E) — 45
Serf (M) — 51
The Funeral (P) — 52
To Manny, at His Wake (P) — 53
The Courting (F) — 54
The Catch (M) — 58
The Toilet Bowl (For Steve Arevalo) (P) — 59
Kai at Two (P) — 63
The Gift of Davian (P) — 64
Babaylan In Playland By the Sea (F) — 66
Sapagkat Ako'y Makata (P) — 72

The Forgotten Present (P)   73
Day of the Butterfly (F)   74

SUITE #3: The City   87
Prelude To A Gig (F)   90
Drought (P)   96
The Fairmont Suite *(Balato)* (F)   97
Birdman of the I-Hotel (P)   112
Ode To A Fire Hydrant (P)   115
The Asshole of Chinatown (M)   116
Ang Lakad ni Rosa Rosal (P)   118
Dance is in the DNA of the Universe (and the Filipino) (E)   119
Carding the Storyteller (in search of a listener) (SS)   123

SUITE #4: The Alaskeros   125
Highway 99 Across Delano, California (P)   127
Eyes of a Century (P)   129
Alaska (M)   130
Migrants Roll Call (P)   133
Pieces of the (Midnight) Sun (M)   136
A Mechanic For the Second Season (F)   147
Lust Among the Ruins (M)   160
The Visit: At Tess' Place (Skit)   168
The Summer of '72 (F)   174
Va. Beach (P)   177
Thursday (E)   178

SUITE #5: The Cure   179
Saved by the Book (M)   181
Ibong Adarna (F)   182
Marcos Balikbayan Proclamation (E)   186
Ancestors Part One: A Barugo Reunion (M)   187
Ancestors Part Two: El Hijo de Genoveva (M)   194
The Believers (F)   200
The Lousiest Salesperson in the World (M)   204
Kearny Street (M)   206
A Valediction (P)   208
The Hijacking of America (E)   210
Prayer (P)   219
Acquaintances with the Night (F)   220
Sinigang Queen (P)   230

Queen of the Night (F) — 231
The Diamond Hotel (F) — 236
Happy Ending (F) — 238
Hubert the Hummingbird (P) — 239
The Distant Relative (novel excerpt) — 240

Epilogue - A Jewish Tale — 247
Author Biography — 251

For
Philip Norman Jayo

Foreword

Oscar Peñaranda: A Bridge, Unabridged

The function of a bridge is to connect. It connects one side to another—opposites or what we perceive to be opposites. A bridge facilitates movement, is the go-between, if you will, between here and there. Of course, there is space between either side of a bridge, the area of pause, a gray area, an area that needs to be filled. There are times when traversing a bridge when one knows not if they are coming or going. One can walk across a bridge or stop at any point of it and look out at the expanse and reflect. I see a man on the bridge as I make my way through the fog. As I get closer, I see that it is Oscar Peñaranda, "Mr. P" to his many students. He stands on the bridge—in this case the Golden Gate Bridge—looking outward at the city—the city of contradictions, of laughter, of tragedy, of legacy and history. I think the bridge is the perfect metaphor to describe the vision, work and humanity that is "Mr. P." As a Filipino American who, for a long time, didn't know he was Filipino American, Oscar bridged the gap between myself and the Philippines, guiding me on my first journey to the motherland in 2006. From this bridge we can see the expansive waters of San Francisco Bay as well as the water of Manila Bay, Bristol Bay and Moro Bay. Oscar is a bridge into our depths, our deep consciousness as Filipinos and Filipino Americans and Filipino Canadians and Mexipinos and Friscopinos and Blackapinas and Blackapinos etc. Oscar Peñaranda is a bridge—a teacher, a guide who is ready to take you on a journey through poetry, story or history no matter where you happen to be—on a bridge or thumbing a ride on the side of the road. He is a gambler, farmworker, cannery worker, pool hustler, prize fighter with a 0-150 record; a bartender ready to listen to your saddest of stories, kali practitioner, actor, teacher—BRIDGE. Come take a walk across this bridge. He is your guide. Take his hand and leap into the cool waters of yourself, your history, your struggle, your pain and finally, yourself. Listen to the tune that Bayani sings as you stand on that bridge with Oscar. Behold the blueness of possibility that awaits you.

—Tony Robles

Preface

What you have in your hands is a masterpiece waiting to be read, a collection of Oscar Peñaranda's writings that resemble a dining room table filled with colorful and delicious Filipino food waiting to be eaten. The vibrant colors of the food mirroring the richness of each intricate story. The poignant smell of the food invoking vivid memories of the people he has come across and lived life with.

I still remember being an 18 year old kid figuring out who I was as a Filipino American. I was lost and searching for that something that was always inside of me. I was that scared, yet hungry, activist yearning to reclaim my culture and heritage. I was a first year college student and Oscar Peñaranda was my professor. It was my first in-depth conversation, *kwentuhan*, trying to connect my activism with activism of the past. I asked who the Katipunans were, and he gladly shared the history of the Filipino revolutionaries that fought bravely against Spain and ultimately won. It was in that *kwentuhan* that I knew who I was in the timeline of our stories. That the lineage of the Kataastaasan, Kagalanggalangang Katipunan ng mga Anak ng Bayan [Katipunans] ran through the veins and bloodline of Oscar Peñaranda and, hesitantly, myself. That k*wentuhan* changed it all for me.

In one of many of our profound *kwentuhans*, Mr. P, (as I and many others dearly call him) were discussing how the Filipino American experience narrative has recently felt curated, and that it somehow continues to paint pictures of momentous dates and historical figures in our community but lacking the depth of each story. It's been feeling like we are watching the same movie over and over again waiting for the subsequent sequel to add more depth to our storyline. Oscar Peñaranda's *Follower of The Seasons* adds that extra spice, *bagoong*, to it, diving deep into the humanity of the characters and mere dates in the past. These historical moments of time and people are not just important placeholders but, in his writings, time is paused and stretched providing us a story of our people and how and why that date became part of our Filipino lifeline of existence. Oscar Peñaranda's *Follower of The Seasons* resuscitates life into these dates and figures that we yearn to learn about.

Oscar Peñaranda is a living legend in our community. His life mirrors indicative moments in Filipino American history. He had a hand in some way or another in the development and the creation of self-journeys from within that tell our stories. We can always trace back the lineage of impactful moments of the Filipino community to Oscar Peñaranda somehow. By happenstance or by spiritual convergence, he was always there at the right moment in time to push our community and be reminded of the beauty our community possessed. Every time I bring his name up in conversations, it conjures the utmost respect and smiling faces. From students learning Tagalog, teachers revisiting the ideas of racism and social justice, artists creating new works, friends playing poker and shooting the shit, family member's sala talks, and other people he has encountered along the way have been impacted by his person. God has given him a gift. A gift of being. Being a human that affects lives and changes the world we want to live in.

Oscar Peñaranda's *Follower of The Seasons* chapters are linked into different suites. When I think of suites, it reminds me of Pilipino Cultural Nights (PCN) with different chapters of the dance and theatrical performances or I think of large room suites in an elegant hotel. But both of these have similar energy. Because in each suite, you will be transported into a moment of time reliving the characters and feelings of that moment. As a glimpse into each suite, I share with you these. In Suite 1, the remembering of the controversial backdrop of the U.S. Philippines War. In Suite 2, the ice cream photograph with his grandson, Kai. In Suite 3, Sam's asshole attitude serving the best Chinese food around. In Suite 4, Golden Boy Sige-sige and the "awat" incident. In Suite 5, Mara, Queen of the night and her flirtatious adventures. It is in these magnified glimpses that shapes a larger story. A story of the interconnection of life.

Readers will get lost in the compilation of writings tapping into obscure emotions and complex humanities of those that he writes. Throughout the book, I caught myself remembering community leader Steve Arevalo, soulfully crying for Bayani and Ellie, laughing at Charles Mingus paying off his debt to Yaw-yaw, dancing to the words in *DNA of the Universe*, and reminiscing about the song of Ibong Adarna.

Before you pick up the book, sit in a dimly lit living room with a cup of tea in your hand listening to jazz softly playing in the background. Imagine Oscar Peñaranda sitting next to you smoking a bowl, anticipating a story being told. Pick up the book and as you turn the pages, stop at an intriguing title and immerse yourself into that one specific story. Put the book down, take a sip of your tea and ponder what you have read. Sit there . . . sit there pausing and contemplating until you're ready to read another story. Then, repeat over and over again. Oscar Peñaranda's *Follower of The Seasons* is not meant to be read in one sitting, it is meant to be read in varied times and spaces of comfort. So, let's begin...

— Dr. Anthony Abulencia Santa Ana, Phd.

Introduction

One of the most important figures that defined a generation and movement, Oscar Peñaranda has produced a body of work that chronicles the labors and leavings of Filipino and Asian American lives. Capacious in scope and intentionality, this long-awaited new collection of poems and prose — with its motley crew of balikbayans, tourists, sex workers, drummers, bums, the unhoused, the unnoticed noticers, and the *manongs* — illuminates the many ways in which our lives bear upon each other. Peñaranda weaves through time and landscapes with nuanced characters, exploring interiors, vernaculars, memory, and shared history, to bring us closer to kapwa: "Pakiramdam yan. Kutuban. To feel unspoken clues is one of the first things we learn to learn." Perhaps the most indelible image is the birdman of the I-Hotel whom the narrator observes with such insight and tenderness: "Come by later/ And take these crumbs/ And put them in one of your bags/ For your morning walks, / Manong." Seamed with grit and grace, this book is more than an essential collection. It's what we are to each other, and all the ways we have become a country and community in diaspora.

—Aileen Cassinetto, 2021 Academy of American Poets Laureate Fellow

Acknowledgements

The San Francisco Art Commission granted the author finances that helped make this book possible. SOMCAN provided invaluable guidance and support.

Not mentioned within texts were the following important works:

"The Believers" first was published by Bamboo Ridge in a slightly different version and under the title "Village of the Faithful". Three last words were added.

"Lust Among the Ruins", "Pieces of the (Midnight) Sun" first appeared on positivelyfilipino.com

"A Reunion of Strangers" first appeared in positivelyfilipino.com and *The Pilipinx Radical Imagination Reader*, edited by Anthony Abulencia Santa Ana and Melissa-Ann Nievera-Lozano

"The Funeral" first appeared in *Full Deck, Jokers Playing,* T'boli Press, 2004

"Babaylan in Playland by the Sea", also appeared in *Growing Up Filipino 3,* PALH, Santa Monica, ed.Cecilia Manguerra Brainard

"Day of the Butterfly" *from Seasons by the Bay,* T'boli Press, SF., 2004

Some sections in "Acquaintances with the Night" from *Reflections in Light and Shadow,* Sunshine Place, 2023

"Dance is in the DNA of the Universe" first appeared in the fall issue of *In Dance*, 2022

"Prelude To a Gig" appeared in *Field of Mirrors,* PAWA, and *Graphics*, Manila.

Suite #1
The Bridge

Baker Beach in SF with view of Golden Gate Bridge. ca 2021. Photo credit: Author.

When people look *at the Golden Gate bridge, they do not see what I see. I see Bayani and Ellie, jumping to their deaths, a lover's pact, uncle and niece. Witnesses said they kissed, held hands, and jumped together. I see Rod's mother who did the same thing three decades earlier. Her epileptic fits were getting worse and worse. I see the first person who crossed that bridge. It was not the white banker who financed it, as is reportedly known, but a Filipino, his driver, who test drove it before the owner. I see Pancho Villa, née Francisco Guilledo, first Filipino boxing champion of the world, with Miss San Francisco of 1925 photo-opped from a newspaper with the bridge looming large in the background. That bridge tells me of the Presidio, where thousands and thousands of U.S. troops were housed, embarked from (The Embarcadero), to go to* *the Philippines and kill Filipinos and squelch the first and fledgling republic still standing in the history of Asia.*

Bayani's Tune

your guitar
leaning on
someone's porch fence bathed
by the rain that
slowly melted your dreams away from clenched fists
clutching on, chanting, remembering
the dream more
painful is the one left
unpursued
and no-song is better
than a thousand bad ones

Lover's Leap

(by Presco Tabios, from Without Names, Bay Area Pilipino American Writers, Kearny Street Workshop Press, 1985, 1997, ed. by Shirley Ancheta, Jaime Jacinto, Jeff Tagami)

we'll park over to the other side
if we change our minds there'll
be no toll.
Blood lines run like cords on a guitar
me, the daughter of your brother,
you, in the palm of my hands
the cable on this bridge will make music
here, uncle, lend me your wing
over this rail

NOT FAR FROM another bridge, the Bay Bridge, lived Cesar Majul, historian and scholar expert on Muslims in the Philippines, the title of one of his many books. He lived in San Pablo, half an hour's drive across the San Francisco-Oakland Bay Bridge, the longest, almost ten miles, of the seven bridges.

"Sabil", Prof. Cesar Majul once told me, was what the Muslim Filipinos called what the Spanish and lowland Filipinos called "Juramentado". They would take their fast, which by the way, was also the provenance of bahal na before it was negativized by colonization and other distortions. *Bahala na* comes from the word *bathala* which means Supreme Being, Creator, God, or at least, a top god. Warriors would go to their imminent deaths uttering this deity's name. It became a battle cry. It would likely not take the equivalency of today's interpretation as "Whatever". Imagine a warrior running into the fray of battle screaming "Whatever!" as his battle cry. In Sabil, the individual would fast and work out in balanced practice. He would anoint himself with holy oil, gird his loins as tight as possible, say prayers, and then stay calm and collected. In other words, they would prepare. Under today's popular interpretation of *bahala na* as being fatalistic, things being left to "whatever", would not be the true virtue and interpretation of *bahala na*, which is preparation, preparation, preparation first, and then acceptance of whatever results. So partying all night, then saying "*bahala na*" going to your exam the next morning is a distortion, an exploitation and an excuse for the expected failure. *Bahala na* is for the strong, *malakas ang loob*, not for the weak and the rationalizers. She was 24; he was 28. Unlike most people looking at that Golden Gate Bridge, I hear things. Whisperings from his home in eternity, his voice soft as the guitar he played.

"Someday, not right now, but someday, in the fullness of time, you can write about us, because I know some will criticize, so that perhaps the world may understand how a man had come to love. It is not an easy thing that we do, to know that we will not see another sunrise..."

This was his note, along with doodlings and memorabilia of their love that was in his pile of writings in a brown paper bag that he had dropped off my place in the Mission district and given to my son Beau the day he jumped from the Golden Gate Bridge with his lover-niece. She was 24; he was 28.

He considered himself a late bloomer, in sports, in playing the guitar, in love, in camaraderie with peers, in many things. As were his muslim companions in boyhood. He was from Mindanao, a mere boy when he came to San Francisco.

Who is the luckless, I wonder?

People who have lives, hang on to their lives, but they cannot love or are not allowed to love or will not love whom they want to love, yet must carry on and go on living? Or I, who have my own true love at long last and on our terms. We dictate and declare our love to the world. How many of you still living can do that? Tell me, who is the lucky and who is the luckless.

Who is the coward?

You who put up with all the insults of reality in your life and yet decide to keep on crawling bereft of the dignity of being fully human? Or I who am fully human TO THIS MOMENT I AM FULLY HUMAN and decide not to suffer the slings and arrows of outrageous fortune, but what slings and arrows can one suffer from if one is with one's beloved? To die with your beloved is not cowardice. And I swear to you what I do is no easy thing, to know in your heart that you will not see another sunrise.

Who is the faithless?

They who doubt their worth and keep on living beneath their worth, or I who know my destiny, and welcome what awaits me. If we just ran away, our names would be soaked with filth. They would think it was concupiscence alone that drove us to our end.

Who is the desperate?

We who sail the light or you who flail in the darkness of living?

Who is the deathless?

You, whose lives will be forgotten in the dust not long after you become the dust yourselves? Or we who have made a statement of our dying, and therefore live in our deaths. Counter to you who die with your deaths. Who is eternal?

It's been eons, and it seems like only yesterday the sun had risen.

THAT BRIDGE HARKENS back indigenous voices of ancestors where there is a story told in these parts where the Miwok Indians lived way before the Golden Gate Bridge was built. There is a folklore of a native local princess marrying a brown man from the "tall ships". The Manila-Acapulco Galleon Trade, which traversed the Pacific Ocean from the Philippines to Acapulco, Mexico, at least once a year for 250 years! skirting the coast of California before terminating in Acapulco. It was a story Domingo Felix's great grandson told in a legal dispute in the Point Reyes Light (Spring 1990) about his property. Filipinos and their descendants have been in the Bay Area longer than one might think. Altar paraphernalia and metallurgical religious instruments from the Philippines can be found in the old Mission Dolores Church, the oldest part of San Francisco.

Passengers of The Wind

THE STORY OF Asians migrating about 40,000 years ago over (what is now the Bering Strait), the land bridges that connected Alaska and Russia, is often told about the peoples that became the indigenous tribes of the Western Hemisphere, now called the Native American Indians. That could arguably be said to be the first migration. But the first immigration of Asians to the Western Hemisphere--specifically the areas of what is now the West and the Southwest of the United States, and numerous areas in and around Mexico--began in 1565 when from what is now Mexico, Miguel Lopez de Legazpi went to the Philippines (Filipinas) to be its first Governor. Both the Philippines and what is now Mexico were being colonized by Spain at the same time. The Philippines was in Southeast Asia and Mexico in North America, about 8,000 miles of what is now called the Pacific Ocean between them. Spain had, so to speak, her right hand on one end of the world and her left hand on the other. Both colonized peoples would eventually wrest their independence by revolutions. This shared history generated similarities in many words, foods, and customs, and it persists today. One's education behooves its study when looking at the conflations of Mexico, Philippines, Mexican American, and Filipino American.

By June of 1565, Legazpi had already built ships in the Philippines to launch the maiden voyage of a trade route that would last for two hundred and fifty years! 1565-1815)--the oft-neglected, yet colorful, Manila-Acapulco Galleon Trade.

Forty-four years earlier (1521), when Cortes was taking Tenochtitlan (Mexico City now), a Portuguese sea captain, Ferdinand Magellan, who was working for the Spanish Crown landed on a bunch of Southeast Asian islands and claimed them for Spain and Christianity. Cortes killed the native leader Montezuma in Tenochtitlan. But in the Philippines, the script was flipped. The natives and their chieftain, Lapu-Lapu killed the Portuguese Magellan, and sent the would-be invaders home. This voyage home of the now "captainless" expedition was the first of its kind to actually sail around (circumnavigate) the world.

The "white men" would come to those Philippine Islands in three more forays and would be rebuffed three times. In one of those forays, the Villalobos expedition, the islands would be named after the then prince Felipe, the nephew of King Carlos I, (Charles V of the Roman Empire). However, on the fourth try, in 1565, they came to stay. For almost four centuries. This time in the person of the aforementioned Legaspi, who had come from Mexico, fresh from the spur of the stories and tales of his contemporaries and his predecessors. He came to Filipinas (Philippines) in the beginning of the year and by June the first ship,

The San Pablo, sailed from Cebu to Acapulco which began the Manila-Acapulco Galleon Trade for 250 years! It would get there around Christmas.

The galleons were large and could hold two hundred hundred people, some more, in them. Who were in them? They were a majority native Filipinos, and Spanish who lived in either Mexico or Filipinas, American natives, and the rest a mix of middle eastern, Chinese, Hindu, European, and other nationalities of the world at the time. (National Geographic, Sept, 1990). The main object of the long six-month voyages was to bring the silver and gold, (actually a lot more silver than gold) and other raw materials of the Americas to sell or trade in Filipinas, where the Eastern and Asian and Mediterranean traders would bring their wares of porcelain and silk and cinnamon and other spices. From Mexico, the Spanish would go the other way, that is, eastward, straight to Europe, and home to Spain or Portugal, the Iberian Peninsula. Filipinas and the Americas was a perfect left and right launching pad for the Spanish Empire. The establishment of the Manila-Acapulco Galleon Trade was arguably the first global venture that literally connected the world, carving a passage for trade, commerce, and social interactions.

The native Filipinos were not called Filipinos at the time. In the records of Spain and Mexico, they were called "Luzon Indios" or "Chinos". Luzon, the largest island in the Philippine Archipelago was where almost all the ships sailed from, although the first few years was in Cebu. It is where the Port of Manila was (and still is) located. They were called "Chinos" (which means "from China") by some because the ships that docked in Acapulco, where the exotice goods were to be unloaded, came from China way or Asia. It would not be till the middle of the 18th century that there would be documentations of some real Chinese from China coming to the shores of what is now California. This may confuse some today, but if a "Chino" was named Antonio Miranda Rodriguez in the Galleon Days, one can safely assume that individual was not a native of China, but a native Filipino.

Most of the Filipinos, though not all, did the hard work on the ships. They were experienced with sea vessels and the high seas. Their ancestors were great sailors and sea people. Some say that some of them had gone all the way to Polynesia and Hawaii. No doubt the Spaniards used their talents. One Filipino, however, probably did not do much "physical labor" because he was a master craftsman. The Spanish employed him because he was specially skilled at building armors and guns, and other metal crafts. His name was Antonio Miranda Rodriguez, and his story will be told shortly.

There were also women aboard these galleons. The women, unless they were Spanish family members, were also Filipinos (Filipinas). They were either the servants of these families, or concubines (harem, slave girls) of Spaniards on the ship. For them, the long voyage was an unspeakable nightmare. Some, when they were found to be pregnant, were forsaken in Acapulco or other ports off the coast of Baja California, left to fend for themselves. (*Eloisa Borja, Filipino American National Historical Society journal*)

Filipino dissident leaders, rebels of Spanish rule in the Philippines, were also put on these ships. They were exiled to New Spain (Mexico) to stop them from inciting more rebellions in the archipelago of the Philippines. An interesting subject to research is whether the Spanish authorities did the same thing in reverse with Mexican dissidents, that is, exiled them from Mexico to the Philippines.

With these three components (able-bodied men, women of childbearing age, and community leaders), the Filipinos in the "New World" would be able to build their own communities, if they wanted to, if space and situation allowed them to interact. Until today there are pockets of Spanish speaking Filipino-looking communities in some places of Mexico, especially around the Acapulco area.

A galleon was scheduled to take a trip once a year, on rare occasions twice. But as the years passed, the Spanish started to realize that all the hazards, hassles, and expenses–numerous shipwrecks, pirate attacks, mutinies, diseases–of taking the long voyage, got too risky for the powers at the time. Consequently, they did it at about the average of one every year and a half.

There were about 65 to over 100 Filipinos each trip. Needless to say, none of them (the concubine, the ship laborer, nor the dissident native rebel leader), was exactly overjoyed at the situation he or she was in. So, every opportunity he or she saw, the Filipino would jump ship--disappear and never come back to the boat. There are stories told of Manilamen Cajuns around New Orleans about their ancestors jumping ship. On scouting assignments some Filipinos would never come back. When these Filipinos landed on shore, most were not anxious to return to their ships. What would be waiting for them there? Here were wide open spaces to start a new life, a new beginning perhaps, brown skinned women like home, for most of them were young, or else the Spanish would not have conscripted (draft) them in the first place. Most were naturally adventurous and were willing to build dreams. They would rather take their chances with the new land. Those who arrived after the first fifty years of the Galleon Trade found other Filipinos already living in California and Mexico.

They would adapt to and befriend the native population and cast their lot with their people and their families. Some Filipinos, however, found themselves living relatively close to each other. Though most Filipinos intermarried/mated with people of different races, it is not inconceivable that some of them married within their ethnic group, an estranged community of other Filipinos, one of the first immigrants of the Americas after the Spaniards.

On October 18 of 1587, At Morro Bay near San Luis Obispo, California, the first documented presence of Filipinos was recorded in a ship's log. This was twenty years before the first established English settlement in Jamestown, Virginia (1607), and thirty-three years before The Mayflower touched Plymouth Rock (1620). As mentioned, Filipinos mostly intermarried with the American Natives of the area. A California Indian tale tells of a native American princess marrying a brown stranger from the big ships. One Native American claimed that his ancestors, the Miwoks from around Marin County (across The Golden Gate Bridge from San Francisco), descended from a Filipino man and a Native American woman.

On expeditions or on disasters of expeditions (shipwrecks, ambushes, lost trails) the hard-pressed Filipinos would take every opportunity to escape the harsh treatment they were getting from the Spanish. Sometimes they would band together after their escape and try to stay together within their new found place. And as mentioned, until today there are pockets of Spanish speaking Filipino-looking communities in some places of Mexico.

The earliest documented Filipino settlement (where a community was established) in what is now the United States was around the mid 1700's, in the bayous near New Orleans, Louisiana. It was later called Manila Village and the people in it called themselves Manilamen. Whether it was designed or not, there were no women in Manila Village. Every member of the original settlers in Manila Village married out of his ethnic group. Some married French, French Canadian, Cajuns, Native Americans, creoles, mestizos, and blacks.

Many of the Filipinos were with the Conquistadors and explorers when Mexico and the U.S. West and Southwest were being explored and settled by Spanish Expeditions. By the late 1600's and early 1700's, according to Church records, California had three main ethnic populations:, first the Spanish, then the Native Americans, then thirdly, the Filipinos. They proliferated throughout Mexico, California, Louisiana, Texas, and Florida. What is now part of Texas and Louisiana was once called Nuevas Filipinas--New Philippines.

Let us now look at Antonio Miranda Rodriguez. William Mason (deceased), Curator of the Natural History Museum of Los Angeles, claimed that he had stumbled upon the name, with the word "Chino" after it. That word, used along with such a name as Antonio Miranda Rodriguez, could only mean that the individual in question was a native of the Philippines. Mason said that he had come upon the name when he was looking at a list of the founders of the city (in September of 1781) of what is now Los Angeles. Rodriguez was the 12th person on the list of 44 families that was sent on an expedition from Loreto, Mexico, to start a settlement by the Porciuncula River. They called it Nuestra Señora la Reina de Los Angeles de Porciuncula--present day Los Angeles.

There was a bit of a mystery involved because Rodriguez' name never showed up in the list of founding families during the official inauguration. Upon closer research, Mason found out that Rodriguez' daughter was deathly ill of smallpox at the celebration of the founding, and that he had to go back to Loreto, Mexico, to see her. So, he actually missed the historical event. His daughter Juana shortly died after, and Rodriguez went back to California, alone and bereaved. He died in 1784 in Santa Barbara, a member of the Guard in Charge Of Weaponry in their Presidio. This is the first recorded burial of a Filipino in what is now California.

"Entry No. 7: Buried this day of May 26, 1784, in the Church of the Royal Presidio, Antonio Miranda Rodriguez, a widower of Sinaloa of the Company of Leatherjacketed soldiers, without sacrament, due to sudden death, by Father Vicento de Santa Maria of the Mission of San Buenaventura."

"Sudden death". It seems that one mystery, upon reaching a solution, only opens up into a deeper one. How did Rodriguez die? What situation or suddenness of death could prevent the administration of the last "sacrament"?

In 1815, the Galleon Magallanes made the last run in the Manila-Acapulco Galleon Trade. It seemed that a cycle had been completed. The ship was named after Ferdinand Magellan, the first white man, a Portuguese sea captain working for Spain,who had set foot upon the Philippines in 1521, and which, like Mexico, was eventually colonized by Spain, for over 330 years.

THE BEGINNING OF modern, official U.S.-Philippines relations began ignominiously with the U.S.-Philippines War.

The U.S.-Philippines War

When the United States Armed Forces arrived in the Philippines in May of 1898, the Filipinos had been fighting a War of Independence against Spain for two years. Their revolution against Spain started in 1896 and by June of 1898, a Declaration of Independence, a revolutionary government, and a provisional constitution for a republic had been established by the people. The elected President of that republic was also the leader of the revolution. He was a fighting president because he waged war as a general and commander-in-chief of the Philippine armed forces against the Spanish. His name was Emilio Aguinaldo. He had to serve in office and fight the Spanish for independence at the same time!

The person most responsible for the writing of that Philippine Constitution in the earlier years of the revolution was Apolinario Mabini. He wrote many letters and arguments to the Spanish and U.S. governments defending the Filipino people's right to keep their sovereignty. He made efforts to mediate many quarrels that the Filipino generals and their followers had among themselves.

How then did the U.S. Americans get into the picture of the Philippine Revolution against Spain? Let us go back two years.

In late August of 1896, Andres Bonifacio, a founder and the third president of the secret revolutionary society called the Katipunan, stood in front of a large crowd in the hills called Pugad-Lawin, Hawk's Nest, surrounding Manila. In defiance towards the Spanish authorities, he tore up his I.D. card, called cedula. Others did the same, and the Revolution against Spain was de facto underway.

On December 30th, 1896, Jose Rizal, an educated Filipino doctor and writer from the Ilustrado (Filipino Elite) class, was executed by the Spaniards because of his "subversive" and "incendiary" writings of reform. The Filipino Revolution then caught fire among all classes of people—rich, middle class, and poor. Jose Rizal, in his essay "The Philippines, A Century Hence", had warned the United States that the Filipinos would defend their freedom if they (the U.S.) might have intentions of taking it over. Though not corroborated by solid evidence, some say he was married in his prison cell on the eve of his execution. That was also, it is said, when he wrote his last poem, "Mi Ultimo Adios", "My Last Farewell".

Meanwhile in Cavite, 30 miles south of Manila, the aforementioned Emilio Aguinaldo, a young mayor, also took up arms and led a group of rebels.

In May of 1897, because of an ugly rivalry that developed between the followers of Bonifacio and Aguinaldo, Bonifacio was executed by Aguinaldo's men. Meanwhile the revolution against Spain continued to rage and Aguinaldo emerged as its sole chief and leader.

After months of fighting, neither side could claim a victory. A stalemate developed in the war. On December 25, a truce was struck between the two forces. This truce or treaty was called the Pact of Biak-na-Bato. Aguinaldo with some leaders allowed themselves to be exiled to Hong Kong in exchange for some promised reforms and money.

It was during this exile in Hong Kong that Aguinaldo and other Filipino leaders met with some U.S. officials to negotiate a combined effort to oust the Spanish from the Philippines. This was the time (1897-1898) that the United States started preparing for war against Spain. Cuba had also taken up arms against Spain. During this period, influential people like Teddy Roosevelt, the newspaper magnates Pulitzer and Hearst, started fanning the flames of war on the United States' home front. War sells more papers than peace.

If there was one event that sparked the oncoming war, it was most likely the explosion and sinking of the U.S. battleship The Maine on its way to Havana Harbor, Cuba. This happened on February 15, 1898. Until today, no one knows for sure the cause of the explosion that killed two U.S. officers and 264 men. The explosion was from the inside of the ship. But that event was used by U.S. war hawks to convince the American government to declare war on Spain. The day after the sinking of The Maine, February 16 (February 17 in Southeast Asia), U.S. Commander George Dewey arrived in Hong Kong. He had left San Francisco December 7th, 1897, about a month and a half before the sinking of The Maine.

Now we have in Hong Kong the principal characters that would later decide the fate of three countries: Spain, the Philippines, and the United States.

Teodoro Agoncillo relates the Aguinaldo experience in Hong Kong quite movingly in Malolos, Crisis of the Republic, U.P. Press. While the Filipino revolutionary leaders were planning to continue their struggle against the Spanish, they were "electrified" in March of 1898 by the news that a flotilla of the American navy had arrived in Hong Kong on its way to Manila. "Their surprise knew no bounds when a Captain Wood, commander of the American ship the Petrel, acting on behalf of Commander Dewey, sought out Aguinaldo for a conference". The two had a series of meetings, the last one being held on April 6. Captain Wood urged Aguinaldo to return to the Philippines in order to once more lead the revolution against Spain. The Captain furthermore assured Aguinaldo that the U.S. Americans would supply him with the necessary arms. Aguinaldo inquired into the policy of the United States following the expulsion of the Spaniards from the Philippines. "The United States," answered Wood, "is a great and rich nation and neither needs nor desires colonies." Aguinaldo suggested that the understanding be put in writing. Wood agreed in principle but said that he had to confer with Dewey.

In April of 1898, while Aguinaldo was in Singapore, Agoncillo continued, another stranger sought an audience with him. Howard Bray, an Englishman, who lived a long time in the Philippines, told Aguinaldo that the American Consul E. Spencer Pratt would like to talk to him. They did, with Bray as interpreter.

Pratt told Aguinaldo, "As of the other day, April 19, Spain and the United States have been at war. Now is the time for you to strike. Ally yourself with America and you will surely defeat the Spaniards! America will help you if you will help America.!"

"What can we expect to gain from helping America?" Aguinaldo asked.

"You need not have any worry about that. The American Congress and the President have just made a solemn declaration disclaiming any desire to possess Cuba, promising to leave that country to the Cubans after driving away the Spaniards and pacifying the country. Cuba is at our door while the Philippines is 10,000miles away!"

Pratt cabled Dewey in Hong Kong. Dewey's answer came the next day: "Tell Aguinaldo to come as soon as possible.' Pratt told Aguinaldo that Dewey promised the "United States would at least recognize the independence of the Philippines under the protection of the U.S. Navy." Aguinaldo again asked for written assurance. Dewey said he could not speak for the government. Eager to return to the Philippines and renew the struggle, Aguinaldo promised to help the Americans. (Agoncillo, ibid.)

Meanwhile in the Philippines, the Truce of Biak-Na-Bato, born from the stalemate of the fighting which exiled the Filipino revolutionaries in the first place, was not faring well. There had been a change of Spanish governors and this current one was not honoring the concessions that his predecessor had agreed to with the rebels. The rebels at home therefore again took up arms. And the exiles in Hong Kong used the money given them to buy arms.

George Dewey and his fleet arrived in Manila Bay May 1st 1898 and fired on the Spanish Navy, defeating them in a rout, on May 17. Commander Dewey became Admiral Dewey during these victorious encounters. Aguinaldo arrived from Hong Kong after about five and a half months of exile, on May 19. Upon his arrival and before going ashore to meet with other Filipino revolutionaries, he had a conference with Dewey and was again reassured of Philippine independence if the Filipinos would help the U.S. (Agoncillo, ibid p. 134). At home, within three days of his arrival, the former leaders of the revolution enthusiastically surrounded Aguinaldo's headquarters to offer their services. And when the shooting died down, The American Consul in Manila reported that the Filipinos "have defeated the Spanish at all points...save Manila" (p137-138, opus cited). Here, the Spaniards, fearing the shame and humiliation they would suffer if the Filipinos defeated them, started negotiations of surrender with the U.S., unbeknownst to the Filipinos.

Not only did the U.S. accept the Spanish surrender, they also prohibited any Filipino troops within miles of the walled city! This was the first event that dampened Filipino-American relations and made the Filipinos suspicious of the United States' true intention. The Filipinos beat the Spaniards to a corner of the city, yet they (the Filipinos) were not allowed (by the U.S.Americans) to march in victory on the streets of their own capital city! When the Spanish flag was brought down from the fort, the U.S. stars and stripes were hoisted up in its place. Nowhere was the Philippine flag seen flying.

More and more restrictions were placed on the Filipino people as the number of U.S. Troops landing in the Philippines increased. The Spaniards had surrendered, yet more U. S. soldiers continued to land on shore. Things went from bad to worse.

On December 10, 1898, the Treaty of Paris was signed to end the Spanish-American War. One of the provisions of the Treaty was for Spain to receive $20,000,000 from the United States for (the former's) "ceding" the Philippines, Guam. Puerto Rico and some smaller Islands to them. Philippine Ambassador Felipe Agoncillo, present in Paris, was not even admitted to any of the meetings or proceedings.

Reluctantly, Aguinaldo and his revolutionary compatriots started to prepare for war with the United States. They had just finished fighting a bloody and costly war with a waning world power (Spain), and hated the prospect of taking on a rising world power, the United States.

Apolinario Mabini, the aforementioned lawyer, repeatedly wrote treatises and arguments to the U.S. government urging them that of all the peoples of the world they, the citizens of the United States, advocates of freedom, self-government, democracy and independence, should not even think of colonizing the Philippines. He urged the U.S. which had recently revolted against and repudiated colonialism itself, to help the Philippines in achieving their sovereignty. He pointed out that officials of the U.S. government (George Dewey, Admiral Of the Naval Fleet, E. Spencer Pratt, American Consul-general in Singapore, and Rounseville Wildman, American Consul in Hong Kong, for examples,) made promises to officials of the Philippine government (Aguinaldo and other Hong Kong exiles) of the U.S. decision to not take over the Philippines. Mabini appealed to U.S. officials in the Philippines. In addition, Felipe Agoncillo, the

Philippine Ambassador to the United States, appealed to the U.S. government not to betray the Filipino people. Clemencia Lopez, from a prominent and prolific family in Batangas, went to Washington and made a passionate appeal in her speech to Congress asking the United States not to colonize the Philippines.

Though their words went largely unheeded by government and military officials, a large faction of the American people believed that the U.S. should leave the Filipinos alone to govern themselves. They were called the Anti-Imperialist League and the whole country seemed to be split in half in its opinions as to whether the United States should take over the Philippines or not.

The reasons for taking over the Philippines were many, according to the Imperialists and "expansionists" in the United States. One, it would secure a strategic military foothold for the United States in Asia. Two, it would provide a global market and distributing sector for U.S. goods. Three, it would provide the U.S. the resources that the Philippines had plenty of—goods and labor. Four, the U.S. would "civilize" and "christianize" the people (even though the Philippines had already been "christianized" 250 years before the United States even existed!) And five, the U.S. would gain new colonies to better aid the country in competing with the other growing imperial powers of the European world, such as Great Britain, Germany, France, Belgium, and Holland.

Ironically, it was primarily the influence of North American, Latin American and French Revolution ideals that fanned the fires of independence in the hearts of many Filipino patriots.

On February 4, (the 5th in the Philippines), 1899, shots were fired on the corner of Sociego and Silencio Streets, Sta. Mesa District, Manila. Thus, the U.S.-Philippines hostilities officially started as Aguinaldo had to declare war immediately. Back in the United States, the day after the shootings started in the Philippines, the ratification vote for the Treaty of Paris was counted: 57 yes and 27 no. One vote more than the needed two-thirds to pass. Thus, Philippine-U.S. relations officially started in military hostilities and bad feelings between the two peoples.

Most U.S. Americans and the world actually thought this war would last for only several weeks. But tens of thousands of U.S. troops kept landing in the Philippines. At one point in time there were close to 78,000. A total of about 130,000 U.S. soldiers went to the Islands. Though atrocities were committed by U.S. troops, the Filipinos under the able supervision of General Antonio Luna, could not be defeated. In fact, the Americans were losing lives, money, time, and prestige much more than they had expected. U.S. General Lawton, who was famous as an "Indian fighter" in the States, and who had captured

Geronimo, was killed in battle by a Filipino contingent led by, irony of ironies, Licerio Geronimo.

However, the Filipinos were unable to continue fighting. General Gregorio del Pilar—one of the Hong Kong exiles, was with Aguinaldo during all the conferences with U.S. officials Pratt, Wildman, and Dewey, and had heard first hand all the latter's verbal guarantee of Philippine independence in exchange for helping the U.S. oust the Spaniards. He kept and commanded Aguinaldo's rear guard and held at a pass called Tirad the U.S. soldiers at bay for over a day. Finally, the 60 almost all barefooted soldiers at his command were overrun by General March's 400-(some say 900) troop outfit. There were six (some say 8) Filipino survivors. That was on December 2, 1899. General del Pilar had just turned twenty-four the previous month. Because of this last stand of del Pilar, Aguinaldo was able to wage the revolution against the U.S. for more than a year longer.

In March 1901, Aguinaldo was captured through a ruse by General Funston. The Filipinos and their leaders fought on as one by one their compatriots were killed or captured. The last officer of Aguinaldo's Revolutionary army did not surrender until over a year later. He had been left to command the islands of Samar and Leyte. In 1902, on June 19th the day after his twenty-fifth birthday, he surrendered to the U.S. Officer in Baybay, Leyte. It was told that the young Colonel had surrendered under the condition that when his men and women march down the street towards the Plaza to lay down their arms, there be no chains or bonds among their persons because they were not bandits, but patriots, who were fighting for their country's independence, much the same way as the people he is surrendering to, the U.S. Americans, had at one time done. The young Colonel's name was Florentino Peñaranda. Three months after he surrendered, in September 1902, Theodore Roosevelt finally declared the Philippines as "pacified", though many more Filipino patriots fought and continued the resistance.

Commentary

1. Any significant, comprehensive, or serious discussion of Filipinos in the United States cannot be complete, (at the very least prefaced) without an essential understanding of the U.S.-Philippines War. The modern Filipino experience or predicament or situation in the United States must be anchored in solid, basic fundamental knowledge of this War. Otherwise, it would be like talking about the United States as a nation without talking about the Declaration of Independence and the

Revolutionary War for Independence. The understanding of this war is vital to any in-depth discussion of Filipinos in the United States and in the Philippines itself, because official relations, records, and attitudes began to be developed and formulated at this time. Ramifications of these perceptions apply to this day. Many of the racial slurs inflicted upon the Filipinos in the U.S. during the hate crimes of the 1920's to 60's originated in this war. Names like "goo-goos", "gook", "monkey", "brown niggers", etc., were part of the campaign and vocabulary used by U.S. troops in the Philippines. Many of the U.S. soldiers were veterans of the wars against Native Americans that were fought just years earlier in the United States, with some still being fought. They (the U.S. soldiers) transferred that psychological and sociological hatred to another people of color and enemy at hand—the Filipinos.

It must also be remembered that the Filipinos fought their War For Independence against two World Powers—Spain and the United States. It was no small feat. Though short-lived, The Philippines became the first Republic still in existence, in the thousands of years history of Asia.

2. Though the name of this conflict is slowly changing, most of the U.S. and Philippine textbooks and historians call this War an "insurrection", the Philippine Insurrection. This is a gross misnomer. No insurrection took place in the Philippines during the U.S. occupation. One of the most referred to documents of this war is J.R.M. Taylor's Philippine Insurgent Records, five volumes. However, The Filipinos were not insurgents in this War. They were patriots fighting for the independence of their motherland. An insurgency is when a group of local people rise up against an established government (one that is already in existence). The Filipino people already had a government established, their officers elected from president to more minor officers, a standing army, a tax collection system, and a constitution. The Filipinos did not rise up against a government that the U.S. Americans had established in the Philippines. They (the Filipinos) had the government built already, their own, and were in a war with the Spanish when the U.S. entered the scene in May of 1898, asking for the Filipino government's permission to enter Philippine waters in order to "help" them (the Filipinos) liberate themselves from the Spanish. The Filipinos had already established their own government in June 1898, only a month after the U.S. entered the Philippines. They had an initial constitution established in Biak-na-Bato in 1897, a year before the U.S. came into the picture. When war was declared against the United States in February of 1899, the Philippines declared it as a nation

against that of the invading U.S. Armed Forces. Thus, "Insurrectionist" as applied to the Filipinos is a gross misnomer. Ironically, the U.S. American "revolutionaries" were a lot closer to the meaning of "insurrectionists". They did in fact rise up against an established government of the British colonials. It is the United States "Revolutionary" forces who were much closer to the tag of "insurrectionists" than the Filipinos. But of course, the U.S. people will never, not even let it enter their minds, describe their so-called revolution as an insurrection. It trivializes their revolution. But when it is against the U.S. that a country like the Philippines wants to free herself from, the U.S. would trivialize the Filipino's sacrifices and acts of courage and heroism by calling their war for independence an insurrection. The U.S. is quick to put that label of insurrectionists on another country, especially if that country is wrestling its precious freedom from the U.S. itself. The Filipinos did not want to be called insurrectionists because the connotations of that word belittle their cause of independence. Insurrectionists imply irresponsible people bent on destroying and wrecking orderly institutions and governments, instead of cool, deliberate, intelligent, socially conscious people deciding a country's government without any outside interventions. Also, the U.S did not want to admit or even let its citizens think critically that as a country, by this act, it has gone against its own precept of governing only with the consent of the governed.

3. Women's role in the Philippine Wars against Spain and the United States was crucial. They hid documents and weapons under their clothes. They organized, managed gatherings and "parties" to camouflage secret meetings of the revolutionaries. They were healers, transporters, messengers, protectors, feeders, and executives. They also served as inspirations to many. Many women were warriors and dynamite smugglers who fell in battle and other assignments with the best of men. Several women were generals.

4. Unspeakable but documented atrocities were committed by the U.S. during the U.S.-Philippines War, there were U.S. orders to kill everyone over ten years old. Commands in the spirit of "the more you kill and burn, the more you will please me" were widespread. Uses of torture such as the "water cure" were common. Cordoning off and zoning off the population resulted in mass starvation and separated families. There were about 4,000 U.S. troops killed in this war. No one knows for sure how many Filipinos died. U.S. records claim 440,000. The real figure, according to other sources, however, is close to a million. One out

of every eight or nine Filipinos died in this war, women and children included, compared to one out of every 34 who died in the second world war. The statistics corroborating this were gathered from both American and Filipino sources, from noting the populations of towns before and after the war.

Many call this war "the first Vietnam."

German officers present in the Philippines at this time took notes of such American tactics as "concentrating" and "zoning in" citizens and used them later on in their country. Hitler and U.S. President Franklin Roosevelt employed many of these techniques during World War II. History knows them today as Concentration Camps.

5. By the time the Treaty of Paris was ratified, the United States had acquired all the following territories: Hawaii, Guam, Puerto Rico, and the Philippines. Only the Philippines rose in organized and methodical armed resistance, and fought at length the United States for their independence.

6. The practitioners of the martial arts in the Philippines are called Eskrimadors, and though they were called this Spanish appellation, the martial arts they practiced were ancient and had been used by Indonesians and Malaysians and Borneans long before the Spaniards ever set foot on their native shores. When a sector of the population of Native Filipinos, the dissident leaders, were exiled in those Galleon ships that plied the Pacific prolifically between the years 1565 to 1815, from Manila to Acapulco, that also meant that those leaders' martial arts would go world-wide, so to speak. The Spaniards would capture and imprison dissident community leaders and exile them into far away lands of their other colony across the Pacific, New Spain or Mexico. One thing those community leaders brought with them was their art of fighting, their martial art. Many of the Community leaders knew of the secret art of the warrior and that would be one thing they would have brought with them, and that to be a community leader one would have proven oneself in battle, most likely.

The Katipunan and the Philippine Revolutionary Army were taught by some of the best Eskrimadors of the land at the time, legendary in stature. It is a fact that Eskrimadors fought the Spanish and the U.S. Americans, and that after the latter's seizure of the Philippines at the turn of the twentieth century, some of those *Eskrimadors* like many of their countrymen and women, found their way into the United States. Most stayed and worked and started a new life, all the while practicing and honing their skills as martial artists, in Hawaii and California and Washington mostly, but eventually, virtually all over the United States. And it was in these places that the Filipino martial arts, secretly at first, found a spawning ground, until now, and it has almost blossomed into notoriety, mushroomed into fame. The names for these martial arts are usually given as Kali, (the mother ancient art). Escrima or Eskrima, and Arnis de Mano. In the beginning of the Second World War, The first and second Infantry *Laging Una* and *Sulong* had many brilliant Eskrimadors, and they taught some of their techniques to non-Filipinos, and they in turn taught it to others.

To trace these Eskrimadors' coming to the Americas is truly to trace a very unique event, truly Filipino American in development. For this marks the beginning of the internationalizing of the Filipino Martial Arts, the globalization of it, so to speak. They built a home base in the United States and were determined to leave the legacy of the fighting arts and spirit of the Filipino people in their new home. It was the art used, centuries ago, to drive the first foreign western invader (Lapu-lapu's killing of Magellan) away from native shores. Traditionally and historically, it has been an art that always stood for family and community—justice and resistance to foreign invaders.

7. This war was also peculiar as far as establishing its end. When exactly did this war end? According to some U.S. Americans, (they themselves have several dates on the end of the war,) it ended in July of 1902, some in September of the same year. Some declared it when Aguinaldo was captured in Palanan, Isabela in March of 1901. Yet others say that Aguinaldo's proclamation (issued in captivity) to the people to lay down their arms was the official ending of the war, for the U.S. But the Filipino's war for their independence was a lot longer. Macario Sakay of Luzon was hanged in 1907. Revolutionaries, libeled and labeled by the U.S. occupying regime as "bandits", fought into the teens of the new century. Theirs is a story yet to be fully told. The Moros in the south were still fighting in the teens as evidenced by the U.S. massacres of Bud Dajo (1906) and Bud Bagsak (1913).

Many think that the U.S. conquered the Filipinos and ruled them for fifty years, (1902-1946), when the Philippines finally got its postponed and promised independence (see the Tydings-McDuffy Act of 1934). Some say the U.S. ruled up to until the toppling of the Marcos regime in the mid-nineteen eighties. Some say up until the removal of the U.S. bases in the early nineteen nineties. Some say that the Spaniards conquered and ruled the Philippines for 330 years. But that commentary can only apply to the Christianized, lowland Filipinos. These two colonizers conquered only part of the Philippines; they subjugated only some Filipinos, not all. The indigenous Filipinos, like the Ifugaos and the Kalingas, along with the Moros were not defeated. Unlike their Christian, lowland brothers and sisters, these Filipinos were never vanquished by any foreign invader.

8. The reason that the U.S. Americans did not get an actual date on the ending of this war was because they did not want to call it a war. There was therefore no official declaration of war, so there could never be an official termination of war, a sort of a Treaty to end it, as the Treaty of Paris did with the Spanish American War. But this was tenfold more of a war than the Spanish American War ever was. The U.S. Americans called it an insurrection, an "uprising". Yet their (the U.S.) struggle for nationhood and independence they called a Revolutionary War, a War for Independence. Though they did not call it a war, the U.S. government and many of its officials did in fact, in writings, proclamations, correspondences, and certainly verbally, called it a war. If it was not a war, they certainly acted and treated this event with a remarkable imitation of one. They sent troops to a foreign land to fight and kill the people of that land who advocated and supported independence, be they military or civilian. But the United States realized that their global and self (national) image would look a lot better if its citizenry and those of the world, can perceive the event as an "uprising", or "insurrection". The U.S. government could not declare war on another country who did nothing wrong to the United States. (In fact, the Filipino leaders had nothing but admiration for the United States and its ideals, until the latter betrayed them.) This way the United States can say that they were just in the Philippines to help keep peace and get them prepared for independence—in due time; when the United States government deemed it the proper time. That is why most United States institutions, until today, do not want to call it the U.S.-Philippines War. They would rather call it the Spanish American War in the Philippines, (which actually lasted only four months, in reality, less than one) or the ensuing Philippine "Insurrection". They do not want to give their government a bad name, and at the same time, they do not want to give credit to the Filipino people and their leaders who were true patriots.

9. Though invented earlier, the Colt .45 Revolver became infamous because of this war. With a lot more power than the .38, it was modified

by the U.S. Americans to physically knock down or backwards targets on impact, like the Muslim Resistors in the south. The Moro "Juramentado", as the Spaniards and their U.S. American heirs called it, would tie their genitals extremely tight so that no pain or body reaction might immediately follow any damage done to them by their enemy, be it bullet or blade, then anoint themselves for their last day on earth. Then, they would say their prayers offering their bodies, their forthcoming deeds, and their souls to Allah. They would then insert as many sticks of dynamite they can to the strappings around their waists. Calmly they would light the dynamite as they rushed towards a group of U.S. soldiers and start hacking anybody that gets in their way. The enemy would shoot at their fanatic attacker, but he would keep on coming even after he was hit by their .38 caliber revolvers. To stop the Moro in his tracks or to bring him down or knock him backwards, they needed a more powerful-impact handgun. Thus, during the Filipino American battles between U.S. Americans and Muslim Filipinos in Mindanao, the Colt .45, which was invented earlier for the Wild Wild West, was modified and made more powerful for this purpose. The Wild, Wild, West it seems was not wild enough for the Filipino Moros in Mindanao.

10. Unheralded though they were because of the colonizer's hegemony, censure, and censorships, there were many Filipinos who continued the legacy of the Katipunan. They took that legacy into the new century, the twentieth century, continuing struggles for people's sovereignty in various forms and in various eras (early U.S. "Benevolent Assimilation", the Commonwealth Years called by Samuel Tan "The Critical Decade", the pre-war Years of Communist/Socialist Consciousness, WWII, the Huks, and the present National People's Army) throughout the years after the U.S. takeover of the Philippines. Unrests and protests, rebellions, and uprisings, along with other forms of nationalistic movements plagued the years of U.S. colonization. Though popular uprisings in these times are well documented, they are not at all well studied and publicized, and is sadly missing in many a coverage of both Philippine and U.S. history and Filipino attitudes and sentiment at the time.

11. This war also revealed global connections between the struggles of peoples of color against Western oppression. Because of the racism and bigotry at home, many African Americans joined the war so they may prove their worth in battle and therefore perhaps gain the respect and acceptance of whites in their own country. However, not long after they set foot on Philippine soil, many African Americans immediately

realized that the Whites' attitudes toward them will never change. Just by observing the U.S. treatment of Filipinos and by hearing racial slurs prodigiously hurled upon the natives, many African Americans saw only too well that the country they represented was treating the Filipinos pretty much the same way they and their kind were being treated back home in the U.S. Atrocities and racial slurs and native-demeaning songs abounded and were pretty much routine in the campaigns throughout the Islands. Court martials, interrogations, and senate investigations of ordinary soldiers as well as the highest-ranking generals proliferated even as the war was being waged. Several African American soldiers defected and joined the enemy Filipino revolutionary forces. One, David Fagen, was reputed to have become a captain or a general under the Filipino revolutionary forces. And as an indication of how class and racial solidarity went beyond international boundaries, a bicycle thief in San Francisco at the time changed his name to David Fagen, according to the documentary "Savage Acts".

12. The United States reportedly spent 300 to 600 million dollars on this "insurrection". One could say, with morbid humor, that the United States bought the Philippines from Spain for 20 million dollars only to spend 600 million dollars more to keep it. It really was a debacle.

    But the cost to the Filipino people was much more expensive and expansive. It went beyond the one to two million dead. What it did to the Filipino people was astronomically and atrociously more costly, the vestiges of which are still evident up to this day: self-hate, colonial mentality, obliterated achievements, suppressed and supplanted history, bereft sources of pride, manacled intellects, omissions, distortions, outright lies, and, of course, the loss of sovereignty and self-determination.

Some resources on the US-Philippines War

JRM Taylor's *Insurgent Records* (Five volumes)

Leyte, a Colonial Odyssey (Reseña de la Provincia de Leyte by Manuel Artigas y Cuerva) translated and edited by Rolando Borrinaga and Cantius J. Kobak, OFM

The Balangiga Conflict Revisited by Rolando Borrinaga

Roots of the Filipino Nation (V. 2) by O.D. Corpuz

Malolos, a Crisis of the Republic, by Teodoro Agoncillo

A Past Revisited and The Continuing Past, by Renato Constantino

Bandoleros, by Orlino A. Ochosa

The Tinio Brigade, by Orlino A. Ochosa

Sakay (1993) Film, dir. Raymond Red

The Prisoner of Balangiga

In the ripeness of their youth, their manhood sprouting, were Tennessee Ernest Stokes (buffalo soldier) and Florentino Peñaranda (Filipino Independence leader) to have met in the Balangiga Uprising in Samar, September 1901, during the U.S.-Philippines War, they would surely have been on opposite sides.

The prisoner after cleaning the jail yard walked towards his cell behind the gallows. Other men with bayonets surrounded him. They tied his hands securely with a strong vine behind him and he bravely looked up at the scaffold where the rope and a hangman were waiting. The meager procession had just finished. A small black dog dashed into the crowd playfully as if in a game. How is wrongness destroyed by more destroying? Some, including the prisoner, might have asked. Guards were checking the fearful edifice, shaking it and trying to jerk it loose, hoping that this structure of death would hold true for the execution. The young Colonel was quietly making his rounds checking and eyeing the framework when, from the bamboo gates of his makeshift headquarters, a horseman approached him. He had not completely halted yet when he started to speak. When he spoke, the animal was still neighing and settling down.

"It is time, Colonel. We must make our move", he said, pulling the reins as he descended, a boy out of nowhere taking the animal away. "They're right on our tail". And he walked straight to the barrel of rainwater under an awning, dipped a wooden ladle of water from it and poured it to his face while drinking from it. He was an older man, perhaps a generation older than the young colonel.

"Are you telling me to postpone the execution of this prisoner, Tiyo Pepe?"

"Absolutely, my Colonel." He pointed to the direction where he had come. "They're hot on our heels. Just across the river. We must hurry! The choice is really unworthy of making the effort--the Republic or one man—and a black one at that," said the elder one alluding to the prisoner.

"We have to destroy everything and leave. The U.S. Americans are right around that mountain. Now . . . Sir."

"As you say, Tiyo. Halto. Stop everything! Let's pack up and leave. Baldo," he told his assistant, "Announce it to everyone!"

"And the black prisoner, what do we do with him? "The messenger, the older man, Tiyo Pepe, asked rather annoyed.

The Colonel looked at his uncle with all the reverence he could muster and said, "Of course, we'll take him with us. Weren't you the one who taught me principles like that?"

Thus, the young Colonel procured the black prisoner as his hostage.

In the mountains, and on the hills, and in the caves, and in the middle of the forest, as the Colonel was being hunted down by the U.S. Americans, or operating guerilla activities, conversations with the Colonel and the prisoner would emerge. They would speak in a cacophony of tongues: English, Visayan Waray, Spanish, Tagalog, and at times Chinese and Japanese. Tennessee Ernie Stokes got pretty good with his languages (because he was pretty good with the people). The young Colonel picked up fast, too. They became at ease in conversing quite quickly. Both grew very patient with each other.

"What were you doing in a white man's Company?"

"Might as well ask what I'm doing in a white man's war."

"What? What was that? I did not hear you."

"Nothun. Jus' mumblin'. I'm in transit, sir. They were transferring me to another Colored company of soldiers via Tacloban. Insubordination. Punishment, they thought. "I was in that Company of Negro soldiers for about 4 months. Before that, with my original company, I stayed for only two months."

"Why can't you stay with it?

"I guess I can't stomach it."

In the middle of this conversation, a messenger entered the room, the same Tiyo Pepe, who came to him and interrupted, whispering something in the young Colonel's ear, showing him a note.

"It seems you have a knack for timely interruptions, Tiyo."

"This is no joke, Colonel. They want you to follow the rest and surrender."

"It might not be a joke but it's nothing new. Can't be that alarming if nothing new."

There had also been letters from his single mother asking him to reconsider his position. Many of his people would try to convince him that this was her way of asking him to come down from the hills. But he pointed out that his mother never said "surrender" but "reconsider". Like her brother Pepe, she had taught him some principles, too.

"I just heard news that Gen. Vicente Lukban, who was captured just last month in Samar where it was said that the General offered his young captors inside shelter from the relentless rain in the forest, had signed the oath of allegiance and was set free. You are now the only officer left, Colonel, nephew. I think it is time to come down from these hills and caves. Look at your people. Surrender can be the noblest of choices. A selfless act though often misunderstood. I think I know what you're going through."

"Of course, you do. You taught me these principles that bring about these confounding, conflicting decisions!" And the younger man laughed. "And I thank you for that."

He looked at his people's ragged faces, their conflicted positions, families barely eating, men wounded and sick, with little to no ammunition, no time to enjoy the beauty and the bounty of this beautiful land that they are defending. "Maybe it is time for peace," he mumbled. "Let the chips fall where they may… in peace now, no more in war."

He was on a precipice somewhere in his hidden fortress in the Amaldawing Mountain range overlooking Leyte, reading a letter from his mother.

"They even have an alleged note from Nanay urging me to come down from the hills and lay down our arms. It's futile, she said." The young Colonel turned to the black prisoner, picking up the conversation from where they left off, without missing a beat. "Why did you join up again?"

"I didn't know war. I didn't know the White Man."

"How did you get out without a scratch from Balangiga?"

"I don't know. Somehow, I thought they were purposely sparing me. I don't know."

He had just "escaped" from Balangiga, Samar, September 30th, 1901, of which he (in transit) was a part of the U.S. troops there when he was taken prisoner by Florentino's men who were at the outskirts of that town and who brought Stokes to him. Was Stokes fleeing for his life or deserting? In fact, he was present and witnessed the attack itself. The Filipinos, for some reason, spared him during the attack, he told the Colonel.

"Your people, that is, the U.S. government, will counter very hard. We must prepare for hard times ahead, again."

"Not if you surrender," interrupted Tiyo Pepe. "General Malvar, the last general, has already surrendered. They have burned Batangas to the ground, hijo, I mean, Colonel. Not one living creature left! No dog, cat, chicken, cow, carabao, pig, nor horse, left. Nothing," said Tiyo Pepe to his nephew. Tiyo Pepe was his mother's youngest brother.

He turned to his black guest/prisoner. "Please excuse these interruptions. As you may have noticed, my uncle is a master of interruptions." And added, "You, you are just my prisoner. I, I am a prisoner of my own land. I have a feeling I have a longer sentence than you."

"But it seems your own people are selling you out."

The Colonel was looking far into the mountain mist outside the mouth of their hidden cave.

"From the common criminals posing as soldiers to the elite who put their self-interest first," mused the youthful Colonel. "I know this truth and feel it deeper than most, believe me."

"I know the same or similar truth."

"Indeed, we are brothers. Maybe both our own people, each to each, are selling out," said the Colonel whose rayadillo uniform looked impeccable in the mist around the campfire.

"Maybe." They both said and toasted another drink of tuba and downed it.

"I have a woman I left at home."

"Oh, really? How sad. It is sad that the war is on my land, close to our hearts, but it is sad for you because you are far from it."

"Yeah, at least, your women are close by…She won't be there when I get back, if I get back, that's fo' damn sho'."

"Maybe you should stay here?"

"It crossed my mind a few times, especially when I think of its attractive features like malaria, dysentery, cholera, and such. But it's a great place, you're right." The two were beginning to laugh.

"It's the people", continued Stokes, the black Yanqui, as Tiyo Pepe called him.

"Must be," laughed the young officer. " And I will turn in after this," as he toasted another cup of tuba.

"Do you read Spanish, Mr. Stokes?"

"I'm trying to learn as much as I can, sir. I'm fascinated with languages!"

"It's a beautiful language. These are my colleagues' letters urging me to surrender. All from various friends and family. Now this from my mother. 'Come down for your birthday, she says. It is useless for now. It is time to plant seedlings.' She knows I like planting big trees, like Acacias. I like knowing that the shades will be enjoyed by my grandchildren."

"My colonel, these are posts asking you to surrender," interrupted Tio Pepe again. "These others are posts for your promotion to general. My Colonel may a proud uncle indulge a bit, my heartfelt congratulations, my nephew. But alas," he turned to Stokes, "there are no more generals in the field to promote him, for only a higher rank can promote, and the generals as you can see from these letters, have all been captured, killed, or surrendered."

"Never mind, Tiyo Pepe. That seems to be the story of my life."

"The story of the Filipino's life," said the unshaven, illiterate elder.

"Human beings never cease to amaze me. Our deepest secrets we reveal to complete strangers. Is it the same in Spain, I wonder? The same in the United States?"

"I think it's pretty much the same all over, sir," said the black Yanqui. "Sometimes the best home for a deep secret is a stranger's ear."

"Look at us. Complete strangers, as you say, yet pouring our hearts out to each other. And enemies at that!" The Colonel paused. "I myself was born out of wedlock. A bastard. I'm illegitimate, as they say. So I know how it feels to be on the outside looking in." And they both laughed hesitatingly. "Yes, I suppose surrender is the best course. They will have my word of never to take up arms again, and work for peace, if and only if...may I read you some of it. Perhaps you can correct my English."

"Don't come to me for correct English. Ain't my language, either." And they both laughed again.

The colonel gave the letter for Stokes to read. "You're good at languages. Can you please..."

"Yeah, but English ain't one of them."

The young colonel continued reaching for Stokes to take the paper from his hand.

The black man started reading . . . "never to take up arms again and to work for peace, and when our men and women who will come down from the hills and out of their caves in the mountains to surrender, including myself, let them be free of chains or shackles of any kind. For, we are not slaves." He paused and looked at the Colonel. "Nor are we bandits, despite your convenient branding. On the contrary, we are patriots, who served only in the interest of the people, and who fought to the last, however mighty are the giant footsteps of U.S. Imperialism." Stokes scooped a wooden dipper and drank the rainwater from a huge drum container.

The young Colonel extended his hand. "It was an honor to have met you, sir." Aside to his aide, "Send that in to Baybay," handing him the note of surrender. He lifted one side of the tent to let the messenger and his prisoner exit then he followed. "And I will walk with you a bit. Who is the prisoner now, you or me?"

The Colonel's men took Stokes for a long ride, his head hooded by a burlap sack, until they were in the middle of an open field in the forest, and there made him drink herbal brews, and then left him lying on a meadow, quite open but safe, alone in the middle of rice paddies surrounded by gigantic coconut trees. He could smell the sea just beyond. There on the wild grass, Stokes was just beginning to get conscious from the tuba and herbal tonics. The rope around his hands had been cut.

He walked back to their Headquarters to greet his U.S. comrades but he saw as he was coming down a distant hill those same comrades were busy killing, firing squad style, lines of Filipinos, some looked like mere children. But down they went, mowed like rice fields in the wind. Balangiga. Horror, then sadness overcame Stokes. And his stomach began to heave and turn and he could not stop it. He turned around and ran the opposite direction, like a prisoner trying to escape.

The young colonel did not surrender until 15 months later. And the two never met again. Except through their grandchildren. In the winter of their lives, the grandchildren of these two, the granddaughter of Tennessee Ernie Stokes and the grandson of Florentino Peñaranda, very far from Balangiga, met and worked with each other in the San Francisco Bay Area of the United States under the shades of big trees of organizations of their communities, their people, and their countries.

An Tuba ha Balangiga

(Kan Viscuso ngan Doc Rolando)

Inin tuba ha Balangiga
Hilarum gud an tinikangan
Tikang ini ha usa nga babayi
Na namamaligya hin tuba
Hadto pa
Han tiempo pa han mga Amerikano
Na istasyon dinhi ha
Bungto hin Balangiga
Ha Samar
Hadto hadto pa
Tiempo pa han mga Amerikano
Natikangan na an amun pag-ato,
Pagdumut

That tuba I know
in my guts
my grandfather had drunk plenty of
and compared it,
as people now still do,
to Barugo's (his hometown and mine)
in Leyte, reputed to have the best of that joyful libation
and which proved
lethal to Company C of the U.S. Infantry.
In Balangiga that fateful feast-day of St. Michael the Avenger

For in Samar
is where my grandfather fought most of his campaigns
in that unspoken War,
the mere utterance of which
clamped silence among the people

Kay yana an tuba han Mga Waray
An rasa ay ira la gud
Inin tuba ha Balangiga nakahuhubog
hin mga istorya

pag ato, pag cariño, pagbulig, pag andam, pag respeto,
ngan pag bilin ha mga masunud na henerasyon

Inin tuba ha Balangiga
Hilarum gud an tinikangan
Ngan pamati ko
Harayo pa an ma-aabtan.

The U.S.-PHILIPPINES WAR and the birth of Philippine Independence were still fresh in the minds of everyone when my father was born in 1904. In our hometown of Barugo, Leyte, my father's generation only remembers those days silently. My grandfather was a revolutionary leader who was reputedly the last of Aguinaldo's officers to lay down his arms. His son, my own father, never spoke about those days to me. I had to find out for myself how life was during the U.S.-Philippines war when I decided to teach the subject for the newly-formed Ethnic Studies Department of San Francisco State College (now University).

Silence was the source of many historical gaps, like the story of Philippine Independence, upon whose principles my lolo and many other Filipinos like him, fought so fiercely.

Twenty years ago, Abe Ignacio, colleague, historian, author and librarian, called me out of the blue and told me that he had just seen on eBay, a Filipino flag dated 1899 with the name "Peñaranda" written on it. He thought that was my lolo's flag, captured by the U.S. Americans during his battles against them, and that I should bid for it before someone else gets it. I had never heard of this flag or any stories related to it from my lolo.

Last year in Dumaguete, Negros Oriental, this flag and I had a rendezvous with destiny.

A Reunion of Strangers

The gathering, of course, was not planned at all. We all notified each other and arrived in front of the Florentina Hotel of Dumaguete within five minutes of everyone. In the company were Nonoy del Prado the hotel owner, Edo and Annabelle Adriano, Jose Manuel Villegas ("Dong"), Alexander Bautista Bayot France, and myself. I had met Alex France a full 48 hours ago, Dong not at all, Annabelle and Edo last year, via text by a mutual friend Krip Yuson, and Nonoy, the kind of person you thought you met before but not quite sure from what occasion. Alex had never met any of them.

Alex, a Filipino martial arts master and teacher had moved to nearby Sibulan three years ago. A Caviteño by origin, he had lived in the States almost all his life and had come to retire with no apparent link to the area. I came to see about an appointment at Silliman University for next month, January. I too am a student and advocate of the Filipino martial arts. Come to find out, Nonoy had taken some form of martial arts in his youth and was very interested in taking it up again, along with his son Ramon, who had taken the "stick" fighting arts before but stopped because of Dengue fever and had been looking for a way to get back into it. Right then and there, Father and son verbally enrolled themselves in a private class with Alex.

I told the group of how about 15 to 20 years ago, I missed a bid on a certain invaluable family item on eBay, a then new, bidding auction online, because of my incompetence with computers. And I paid a heavy price that only I bore for that shortcoming ever since. It never really left my mind. The item was a Filipino flag dated 1899 with the words "Peñaranda" handwritten on it, an obvious item identifier by whoever retrieved the flag. My heart jumped. My grandfather Florentino Penaranda (also my father's name and my middle name) had fought the U.S. fiercely for Philippine Independence at the turn of the 20th century and was arguably the last officer of Aguinaldo's Regular Army to surrender, a year and a half after Aguinaldo himself, after Lukban, after Mojica, and after Malvar. But alas, not knowing how to bid on eBay, I could not procure his flag, a symbol of his legacy. I, however, wrote the seller and eBay people to tell whoever had bought the flag that I am the grandson of Peñaranda and that my family would be forever grateful if the buyer would contact me. But I had no response.

As mentioned, I am a student and advocate of the Filipino martial arts. I am also an educator of language, literature, history and culture. Fast forward decades later, when one of my fellow educators found out about my going to Dumaguete. He suggested that I contact his friend Alexander Bautista Bayot France. The name rang a bell. The previous year that I was in Dumaguete when I met Edo and Annabelle, I had walked along the Boulevard one Sunday morning and while I was eating at the Bethel Hotel for some Filipino food, I spied a group of stick-fighters practicing by a gigantic tree along the Boulevard. I approached them and the instructor talked to me. He said that his name was Leonardo de la Luna and had told me that a colleague of his was also from the States, like me, but is now living in the Dumaguete area, one Alexander Bautista Bayot France. He gave me his card. That was just last year.

When Ray Cordoba, a fellow educator and martial artist, asked me to hook up with a mutual acquaintance Alex in Dumaguete, everything fell into place. When Alex (who was also from San Francisco, though I've never met) picked me up from the Dumaguete airport and we were having a late lunch, he said he knew Leonardo quite well and that he also wanted to talk about another topic. It was then that he broached a question to me that caught me off-guard. "What do you know about the Peñaranda family?" he asked. I said I knew about our private family history and my Lolo's role in the fight for independence, though it was hardly in any history books. I thought he was interested in a business proposal of some sort. He said, "I know about your Lolo. I believe I have your grandfather's flag. I was the one who outbid everybody to get his flag on eBay twenty years ago". I was floored. A mountain was lifted off my long-burdened heart. "I put all my month's salary (without telling my wife, of course) to make sure that I outbid all those war memorabilia collectors," he said. "When I was bidding for that flag, I was thinking that since the U.S. Americans had taken that flag from the Filipinos, I was going to liberate it from its American captors." He also said that serendipity had it so that an acquaintance who had owed him a long-standing debt of a thousand dollars had, out of the blue, paid him within a week of this purchase.

I said that one of my missions here was to put up a plaque in the typhoon ravaged Baybay Municipal Building where my Lolo brought his people to surrender, June 19, the day after his 25th birthday and made his final and gallant speech as a last hold-out of that gruesome war. A friend of mine, Joe Robles, another Filam now retired in Baybay, will help me, I told Alex. "I know Joe quite well," he said. Good man." Another surprise. I did not know he knew Joe. But the Philippines is the country of small worlds. "When you and your family get that plaque built, it will be my honor to give that flag to your family. For then, at long last, it would have found its true home."

By the time we meandered our separate ways home past midnight, we felt like old friends. We probably were. That is, our souls were like flitting butterflies hovering around our destinies before we ever physically met. But it took Dumaguete to introduce all of us to each other and to discover our past lives.

Dec. 6, 2013, Dumaguete, Negros Oriental

Lumpia, Super Bowl, and the U.S.-Philippines War

I had just moved from my sister's house in Daly City to San Leandro across the Bay. First and only house I bought. I was about 52 years old. I was enjoying the space in the newly bought house by relaxing and watching the Superbowl. My wife was in the bedroom, and I was frying lumpia to top the stress-free feeling with beer. The game was on Feb. 4, and that was the day the U.S.-Philippines War started about a hundred years ago, a war forgotten by almost all. I was alone watching the game, and in my mind, was trying to relate that war and the 49ers, somehow. The U.S.-Philippines War, the city of San Francisco, and 49ers were somehow allegorized as characters. The City, the Team, and the War floated around in my head. San Francisco was where almost all the US troops embarked to go to the Philippines when that War raged some from 1899 to 1913 and beyond. Between imaginative meanderings and the excitement of the Super Bowl, I forgot about the lumpia I was frying in the kitchen. It was the strange, menacing shadow that was formed by a large glow from the side vision of my left eye that jerked my legs leaping from the couch. The lumpia and pan were aflame, and it was creeping above the stove and its walls. I rushed toward it not knowing what to do. I quickly took the flaming frying pan off the stove and in one motion went for the backyard door to dump everything on the ground. That one motion turn proved tragic, painfully tragic. That one motion action produced a swish of the burning oil that landed on the front of my naked left foot! I felt it burning and as I rushed to open the sliding backyard door, I found it had a screen. I had to open the screen first. I am right-handed, so I held the pan with my right hand and had to open the screen with my left hand. Meanwhile, I was feeling my foot burning like crazy. Panic, the best friend of tight stressful situations, was ready to rule. I got the slide AND the glass doors finally opened, and in one motion again, dumped the burning pan on the grass. Immediately, I rushed back to the kitchen to check on the damage. Whew, luckily the walls were not marked by the fire. The aluminum top and side of the stove was a bit blackened but not burned. I could brush that off. My wife came out of the bedroom and asked me what the hell happened, what's goin on? I explained. Very frustrated she said she was going back to the bedroom, "It's a good thing you didn't burn the house down! We just moved in." I went back to tend to my foot. I have the marks until today.

Maria

It's an old story and it didn't take long to recognize it was happening to me. You like someone and that someone liked someone else. And that someone else in turn liked somebody else, too. She liked me but she liked more my friend Bill Orlando, Bob's twin who was already living with someone else. That's where and when the hurt started and it spread like a cancer in our friendships and throughout our *barkada*. She wounded up with an individual, who dealt drugs more intensely than the rest of us. Maria was a dancer. She spread her wings everywhere and galloped like a racehorse in the winds of North Beach. I didn't know what kind of tribute to give her but I know she deserved one. She traipsed on the streets of the City with her four sisters with such a joy for living that the tragedies festering in her families being played out by destiny were hidden from the public view. But I knew. Her mother was Waray and her otherwise languid movements would perk when she saw me. She hungered for the language so that her eyes would light up when I came for a visit. Maria had a son but she was not married to his black father who ran around calling himself the prettiest man in 'Mo. She said she liked me visiting them because I listened to her sisters' and her mother's stories and I always made her mother laugh. She was a beautiful and kind and pure soul and many men took advantage of her, abused her, and left her depressed and longing. One day that joy of living left her permanently and never came back. She lost the will to live and those close to her could not touch her anymore while those who harmed her could no longer hurt her, as well. Too fragile for this uncaring world that she left too soon, though broken in pieces, still she gifted us with her whole and wild and graceful spirit as now she rides the wind and dances across these painted city skies.

WHEN I SEE the Golden Gate bridge, I see the city Pancho Villa tasted when he photo-opted an ad with Miss San Francisco of 1925. I see the small city east of it, Emeryville, just across the bay where he met his fatal fight in a non-title bout. He had an abscessed tooth but would not cancel the fight because so many of his *kababayans* had gone to the arena from their respective *campos* all around the west coast, to see him fight, Francisco Guilledo of Iloilo aka Pancho Villa, my carpenter uncle Tio Rupin's favorite boxer, the first Filipino world champion, who fought forces inside and outside the ring.

Left-handed Lover

Today is not a good day for hats.
But it's a good one for kites.
For the wind is a left-handed lover
She'll kiss you with a soft breeze,
then
Left hook you with a bad flu
The next day.

Golden Boy

At their fifty years reunion, at the Beach Chalet, Frank Naraja greeted Freddie Madayag with a couple of body punches, and a left hook, "Golden Gloves, *putang ina*, Golden Gloves, man," said Frank as he fake pummeled Freddie with a barrage of combination punches. I did not know till then that he, Freddie, was a golden glove boxer. He played bass for the Wanderers and did background vocals. That's how everyone knew Freddie. Falsetto singer who looked like a gangster, but his high-pitched voice always caught people off guard, the way he caught me off guard fifty years ago on that nothing-to-do afternoon in the Avenues, which were the flatlands of San Francisco.

Just because Freddie was my height, Carl and Pat, during our teenage years once pitted us together for a boxing match down in Carl's room in the basement that his father built. I thought I was pretty good, and we started feeling each other out, boxing, jabbing, a combination here and there. Then somewhere in the second or third minute, I pissed him off somehow. He started to swing with solid and accurate punches. I hardly had time to cover up, when he started pounding again. Then I realized, man, this guy is pounding the shit out of me! Did I say something? It was not like that in the beginning. Or was the time for feeling out over and now time to box, or did I hit him in a sensitive spot that he started wailing on me. Nonstop. After a while, Carl and Pat asked me if we should go another round? I wanted it to stop but, of course, I couldn't say that. I shook it off. "Whatever," I said. "Up to him." "Okay, then, one more round," said the boys. Okay with them. It wasn't them getting pounded. Then he really unleashed on me. Everywhere I turned his punches found me. I could not even open up for a peek. I backed up into Carl's father's vice grip that was clamped on the worktable. It rang hard. "Ok, that's enough!" I heard someone raise his voice. Needless to say, I was relieved. But it took me fifty years to realize that Freddie Madayag, bass player and vocalist in the Wanderers, was a golden glove champion. That's when I remembered seeing a picture of Pancho Villa, first Filipino World Champion boxer, with some U.S. promoters, and it looked like he was carrying a violin case. Golden Boy. Boxing, dancing, music, with Filipinos, they're all one.

Manila Goodbye

Things were just beginning. He had to go back home, put on some decent clothes and see about Leanore. This particular Sunday, he had found out that she was one of the players acting in a play and they were rehearsing. He hung out around his school, Philippine Normal, where, on a sidewalk under an acacia tree, he listened and talked to and watched Aling Idad the Santol Lady peel her globed fruit in one long continuous motion. Not a break! He watched the long curly-cued line of peel dangle closer and closer to the ground without ever touching it, all the time telling her stories. She always amazed him.

He did not know whether he should count his third grade teacher Miss Trinidad as his first love but what he remembered clearly was his crush on his sixth grade classmate Leonore. He remembered two or three other classmates in Philippine Normal School Elementary who were prettier and initially more attractive but Leonore was like a Christmas card. She had something in her carriage, so lithesome, so confident yet always conscious of others' needs. She must be an "Ateh". Must be somebody's older sister. Older sister, mother, crush, sweetheart all-in-one. And the way she moved, subtle and graceful, especially when girls were playing that high jump game Luksong Tinik, where part of the unspoken game is showing how graceful one was in jumping high and yet keeping her dress down by placing hovering hands over her billowing skirt. Her face was not a striking beauty but her skin was cinnamon spotless and at times she wore her hair in pigtails and at other times, in a ponytail and yet at others, left long and loose.

That year would be his last year in the Philippines. Though that was not really foremost in his mind at the time, it had some impact on his last actions before leaving the place where he was born and raised, the only place he has ever known in life, so far.

One day, after school, he decided to follow Leonore to her home in Pandacan. From Ermita to Pandacan was not a stone's throw. A couple of jeepney rides for most. Well, "follow" may not be the right word. Some may say "stalk" would describe his actions more honestly.

Leonore jumped the luksong tinik with ease and grace deftly holding down with both hands her skirt a-flaring in the gust of uplifting air as she cleared the bar of outstretched, alternate palms of two other playmates facing each other, measured palms, pinky to thumb, on top of each other, and her feet landing on the ground skipping lightly, head up and already talking.

"Oh, what are you doing here?"

"Well, I followed you,"

"What?"

"I followed you to church. Skipping ditches and stepping around and under stairways. I followed you from church, too, to where the jeepneys stop by the bus terminal and I've been following you everywhere." He had to tell her. It was now or never.

"What?" Her pigtails hit her face softly as she turned to him

"Yes, I'm so sorry, Leonore. Now I know the jeepney you take to your home here in Pandacan."

"Well, I hope you have money to get back home. It's going to get dark soon." The shadows and the soft light of the afternoon filtered through the trees of the avenue they were walking on.

"Don't worry. I don't pay. I mean, I get off before paying. Not for me. Things will be bright for me for a while."

"I know. You're going to America, ha?"

"Well, yes. But that's not what I mean."

"When?"

"Soon. Before we know it." It's now or never. He must tell her. "When I saw you coming down the stairs so delicately with your bakya wooden shoes into the mean tight streets of your neighborhood, I knew it was you, and I felt like your home became my neighborhood. . ."

"What steps? Bakya? Tight streets? What on earth are you talking about?"

"I guess I am trying to say goodbye, Leonore."

"I see. And you don't know how. I heard about you going to America before pa."

She came closer and hugged him. He hugged back. "Tighter now," she said like a big sister, and whispered, "You'll be back, this much I know."

He came back all right. She was right. Nineteen years later and at least nineteen times after that. But he never saw her again.

Suite #2
The Voyage

The "Wanderers". Author is tallest person in the back row on the right. Photo credit: Romeo Celestial. ca 1963

When we first moved to San Francisco from Vancouver, Canada, where we lived for 5 years, it felt like a linguistic oasis to me. In five years, (1956-1961), it was the first time I saw other Filipinos beside my Dad's officemates' families on special occasions. First time I heard and spoke Tagalog again. We spoke Waray at home. It was refreshing. It felt good. The language provided the first real tug at my distant and severed heritage. And I was reunited with a boyhood family neighbor in the Philippine Consulate where my father was just assigned. This would be my home from here on in. Another city by the bay. The other three bays, so far, being Carigara Bay by Barugo, the town of my birth, Manila Bay, English Bay (in Vancouver, Canada), and San Francisco Bay. The other Bay would be Bristol Bay in Alaska. That would come when I reach 21.

The Awakening

Ed de la Cruz was a couple of years older than I and he was drunk again so I had to drive him home, just the two of us. He lived at the bottom of Twin Peaks, Haight-Ashbury District. When we were going along Lincoln Avenue by the park, he got violent in the passenger seat and started vandalizing my car while I was driving. So I had to fend him off and at the same time drive the goddamn thing. He was ranting and raving," Oscar", he seemed to be in pain looking for words profound…"You fucking asshole…are such a waste! Such a waste! Goddamn it. Piece of shit!" and tore off my rear-view mirror that hung limp above the windshield inside my car for the rest of its natural life. I thought that might have been a turning point in my life, in many directions, along with community involvement and admitting to oneself the not-so-pretty truths about one's situation. I was beginning to write; that was good enough for me. Not for Eddie. And some folks, like Ed de la Cruz, had such strange ways of communicating their golden hopes and vision and frustrations. I don't believe we ever mentioned that incident again to each other or to anyone else. At least, I didn't. Until now, of course. But I never forgot that day Ed de la Cruz in a drunken stupor straightened me out and pointed me to a path in life from which I have never veered. Drunk or sober, he saw more in me than I did at the time. Kuya Eddie. All City, ex-Marine, City College, Lowell High School, sharpest community person I knew. *Mano po.*

On Liwanag

The Fire Last Time (the emergence of a Filipino American literary sensibility)

In the counterculture decades of the 1960's and the 70's, a Filipino/U.S. American sensibility in literature emerged. This came in two publications: *Flips* (ca. 1971) and *Liwanag* (1975). They hit the West Coast scene at the cross-roads of many intersections: independence and anti-colonial global wars, the Vietnam War, ethnic studies in the schools, racial unrest, gender issues, and cultural developments, which included Filipino-U.S. American literature.

The writings of Filipinos in the U.S. before *Liwanag* were substantive, starting in 1904-6, with the Pensionados. Though not rare, these writings were not plentiful, but coast to coast, California to New York. Soon, publications in forms of student papers, community news, features, and op-eds proliferated in Filipino communities, especially in the West Coast. However, the sensibility of a literature that *Liwanag* and *Flips* ushered in during the 1970's proved to be, in hindsight, indelible.

That sensibility differed from the Filipino writers previously writing in the U.S. These writings came from Filipino established writers on a visit to the U.S. or by Filipinos in the U.S. via the aforementioned newspapers, magazines, journals, and school programs. The most renowned exception would be Carlos Bulosan, who came to the U.S. not as an established writer, but a laborer who, an avid reader from the start, became a writer while in the U.S. But his juices as a writer were still steeped in the Filipinos' sensibility in writing from the Philippines.

Two years before *Liwanag*, *Flips* had come out, a brown paper bag covered booklet of 11 mostly San Francisco Bay Area poets edited by Serafin Syquia and Bayani Mariano. "*Flips*" at the time was an English derogatory slang, somewhat counterpart to "nigger". Just from its title, the reclamation of that word *Flips* as a positive force was a bold statement. The writers elevated that word, and themselves along with it, by proudly putting their voices and images "out there." *Flips* was reissued in 2015, through the efforts of Juanita Tamayo and others. *Liwanag* is being reissued as of this writing. There is also a *Liwanag* 3 in the offing.

Liwanag, Literary and Graphic Expressions of Filipinos in America was a much more expansive and inclusive offspring of *Flips*, and it would include graphic artists. Among its editors were Emily Cachapero, Bayani Mariano, Seg Belale, Luis Syquia, Dan Gonzales, Dan Begonia, Al Robles, Richard Likong, Judy Talaugon, Reggie Macabasco, and Presco Tabios.

In some ways, *Liwanag* helped forge a kind of Filipino American literature by forcing us to define ourselves, along with others' parallel journeys, into a new United States, a new world, and a new identity, like Al Robles' parabolic trek to Ifugao Mountain where sometimes to find the way to the top, one has to dig deep.

Liwanag heralded ideas, voices, and images that highlighted, or at least, emphasized or accentuated a call to question definitions and layers of identity, and proclaimed the naming and claiming of our history in the U.S., expressed pride in our heritage and indigenousness, exposed U.S. imperialism, took sides on civil and gender rights issues, illuminated (*ipinaliwanag*) the marginalized, and raged and reclaimed the militancy of the oppressed, but all throughout, there was a thread of both the lamentation and the celebration of humanity. The spirit of *kapwa* in all its cycles, persists and prevails. In "Pilipino Party Time" and "Going To the Country", Juanita Tamayo nostalgically depicts her childhood memories of family trips, event preparations, and intergenerational interactions. These festive practices would become a hollowed and enjoyable tradition of the *Manongs* and the *Manangs*, their version of their fiestas in the Old Country.

From the very first image, the viewer encounters one whole page of the *Baybayin*, the ancient script of Filipinos, an experience of wonder in language and vision. Then, a glossary of the many ways the meanings of *Liwanag* can be gleaned. From the preface onwards, one can feel that the posture in the writing had changed from that of the writings before them. The writers and artists cry out: **'No longer are we sojourners, but settlers and locals,** and we claim this land as much as any white man. Only the Native Americans are the true hosts of this land. This nation's future includes, calls for our vision, as well as other third world people's. Our attitude has changed and our stance, our *paninindigan*, has shifted critically. This *paninindigan*, or conviction, was born out of the cauldron of conflict and unrest in the country and the world at the time. This *paninindigan* whose provenance is a core homeland value, had re-located itself and transformed an identity into the realm of what Filipino American literature would be.

Eschewing the assimilationist ideal that was prevalent with the generations before them, *Liwanag* boldly claimed in the introduction, that they do not have to assimilate, *"rather, it is by being whole, by retaining consciously, what is Pilipino...by acknowledging heritage that the Pilipino-American is enabled to achieve the insight necessary to function progressively...in this society."*

The *Baybayin*, tattooing, and the proud and sometimes proliferate use of Philippine language(s), the use of "P" instead of "F", reinforced this **non-assimilative attitude,** even though the 'f' sound definitely exists in some indigenous groups of the Philippines.

The critique of colonialism and imperialism is everywhere in *Liwanag*. The grandson of a last hold-out Filipino colonel who fought against the invading North Americans in the U.S-Philippines War (1899-1913+) was among the contributors and advisers in the staff of both Flips and *Liwanag*. The learning and study of this brutal, unjust, and hidden War became a benchmark and a lynchpin in the developing literary, historical, and cultural Filipino American consciousness, a must for any kind of structural knowledge, both contemporary and past, concerning Filipinos in the homeland and Filipinos in the U.S. *Liwanag* empirically brought home the definition of colonialism and imperialism into the emerging Filipino American literary consciousness.

Many of the artists and writers in *Liwanag* **had been disillusioned by, and had lost faith in, the United States,** exposing its double-standards, inequalities and exploitations, domestically and internationally. The generation before them were grateful to the United States, but this *Liwanag* generation thought that it is the United States that should be grateful to them, their former colony, and whose ancestors they had been exploiting for generations.

Even Carlos Bulosan, though much maligned by racism, still believed in the U.S., its spirit and its ideals, so much so that he titled his now classic work America Is In the Heart. It is always interesting to compare that book with Manuel Buaken's *I Have Lived with the American People,* an autobiography and a non-fiction portrait of Filipinos in the same era.

Liwanag voices and imagists reminded us that **we walk on stolen land**, kept and held by endless deceptions. We stand on sacred ground and everywhere behold scenes and landscapes of genocide. This, along with slavery, the white immigrants from Europe who had claimed this land, must own up to and redress. This ship of a nation will never be steered aright until its passengers come to terms and reckon with the stains of **slavery** and **genocide**. If one does not pay rent or labor, nothing but profits and exploitation lie on the horizon. It is so until today. Liwanag echoed voices and images that helped build the foundation of ethnic studies and called out this bitter truth of whiteness while claiming their own people of color's place in this nation's history.

Consequently/corollarily, the **themes of sisterhood and brotherhood of peoples of color were echoed**. The **kinship** (and at times, enmity) **with other ethnicities** of color and their separation to whites, their constant rejection by the latter, and the battling of whiteness as a result of racism fed and informed this sensibility in Filipino American literature. **Civil rights struggles and solidarity were constant themes**. The solidarity of people of color as brothers and sisters, not strangers and foreigners became more and more a felt reality of a common denominator. The learning of each other's histories, especially shared histories, was practiced and advocated. *Liwanag* emerged simultaneously with fledgling ethnic studies classes being adopted in schools.

Liwanag was born during the eras of the Vietnam War and Martial Law in the Philippines. Sensibilities of **anti-war, anti-military, anti-dictatorship, and activism** dominated the consciousness of writers in the U.S. *Liwanag* was no exception.

Though the staff met at several places, the two main areas were community spaces in Central City, now called Soma, and the International Hotel, both in San Francisco. Some *Liwanag* contributors were frequenters of the newly formed Kearny Street Workshop at the basement of the then beleaguered and tormented International Hotel, with Al Robles writing some of his best poetry from the belfry of the Old St. Mary's Church by Chinatown where he worked. Kearny Street was walking distance to the South of Market. Contributors were also in contemporary publications of the times, like Time To Grease, Third World, *Aiiieeeee!,* and other harbingers of today's ethnic studies materials. Some artists were already established (albeit ingloriously and almost anonymously) in Hollywood's Disney establishments. Many will find Conan the Barbarian's illustrator Alex Niño's unmistakable style very familiar in *Liwanag.*

With some overlap and exceptions, the generation of Filipinos before *Liwanag*, around the '40's to the 60's, called themselves the Bridge Generation (documented by FANHS, Filipino American National Historical Society), and they were the first Filipinos who were born in the U.S, (not counting the New Orleans Filipinos and very few others). Like the Bridge Generation before them, *Liwanag* contributors went through **a racialized institution of education** from the earliest grades, as sharply delineated by Sam Tagatac in his poem "A Matter of TH—". And John Lanosa, Bridge Generation poet, lovingly remembers the peak of his manhood, in the exuberance of Jazz in several after-hours hangouts. One can feel the whirl and pulse of the Stockton nights of his youth in the lyrical "Stockton 1950" and "Music! I Remember You!".

As Serafin Syquia observed in *Flips*, we "done time in the same laundromat." The Filipino/U.S American literary sensibility took in the machinery of having gone through the institutions of the U.S. starting as a child. They had gone through the racist grind of structural machinery starting with elementary schools and the early bombardment of television and movie programs of nothing but white characters, white stories. Authors of *Liwanag* realized the value of stories and what narratives mean to a people. You don't have stories; you don't exist.

Moreover, *Liwanag* emphasized the rise of the indigenous and the **return to the roots**. Emily Cachapero's poetry captures this claim in both lament and celebration of history and migration in "there's a wedding in wailua" and "new women". *Liwanag's* vision was on the front page even as it heralded the publication itself with the ancient *Baybayin* writing syllabary as symbol and testament. No one, no Filipino American publication to my knowledge and looking back at it now (some fifty years later) has ever printed in an anthology the *Baybayin* before *Liwanag* and here it was in *Liwanag* in bold print as a front piece, no less, an intro to an intro propelled and fueled by mostly the young Filipino Americans of the late sixties and into the seventies.

Some contributors were also affiliated with the traveling Filipino American theater group *Ating Tao* and came up with the term "coconut" (white in the inside and brown on the outside), a term that other ethnicities have since appropriated for themselves, giving their own versions: "banana" for whitewashed Asians, "oreo" for whitewashed blacks, etc., as well as the term "Filipino American", included in an Asian American umbrella. The Bridge Generation and prior, simply called themselves "Filipinos".

Look at the images, graphic and literary, in *Liwanag*. Imbibe in the visions of artists and writers such as Al Robles, Jessica Hagedorn, Sam Tagatac, Emily Cachapero in their beginnings, and mark the weight of images and sounds in their early youths.

A pro-labor, worker mentality, too, became part of that consciousness and its legacy reverberates today. The aforementioned America Is In the Heart is still the bible for many millennials today, as it was then. The legacy of unrecognized heroism and leadership lie deep in many "Fil-Am" writers because of the *"manong/manang"* experiences, and the rage of not recognizing leaders like Larry Itliong and Philip Veracruz and the Filipino common farmworkers who first struck against the giant agribusinesses of California and sparked the forming of the now famous United Farmworkers for which only the Mexican American Cesar Chavez (who joined the Filipinos in the strike several days later) is known.

The non-idolizing of white authorities: on writers and white publishers and white editors and white schools and workshops on writings, and other institutionalized certifications, also marked the mentality of *Liwanag*. The communities they write from certify them, not The New Yorker. What the hell do they know about Filipino American stories and writers? Hardly any *Liwanag* writer took the Iowa Writers Workshop really that seriously. I for one will be forever grateful to my white teachers for introducing me to great literature and writers like Shakespeare, Emily Bronte, Emily Dickinson, Jane Austen, Walt Whitman, James Joyce, and Dylan Thomas, but I will forever not be grateful to the system for not leading me to Edith and Edilberto Tiempo, to F. Sionil Jose,

NVM Gonzalez, Ben Santos, Estrella Alfon, Aida Rivera-Ford and Jose Garcia Villa, for being a cog in that system that neglected these great writers.

Our education had introduced us to our neighbors and landlords but not to our own family. In *Liwanag*, we got to know our family. And that introduction to ourselves became one of *Liwanag's* legacy to Filipino American literature, a main vessel for knowing our stories and ourselves, and letting the world know we are here. We exist. Like the once embattled and besieged International Hotel, we are still alive, and so is our literature, our Filipino-U.S. American literature.

Serf

Serafin Syquia was the first among us who saw and was moved by social is-sues, like Vietnam, Martial Law, Black Panthers, Civil Rights. He was woke when "woke" was just being born. He wrote about the Alaskero experience before me and dated girls I liked way before me. We both went to SF State and because we were into literature and already writing, we took the same classes and had the same teachers. He had ideals and Danny, our good friend from the Mission, was however the voice of a dog-eat-dog practicality, and would always call out his idealism. Only Serf and I were into literature and writing so we did not talk about it with the rest of our friends. Parties were what was foremost in the group's minds. Even Serf and I did not really have a lengthy literary conversation then. We did not know then that we did not have much time left. He died young, in the middle of our youth. He hardly got to stretch out the years. He died when he was thirty and I was twenty-eight, young enough to dream but getting too old to believe them, as F. Scott Fitzgerald in words, and John Handy in music, had expressed.

The Funeral

When they asked me
I couldn't say that we were great friends
I couldn't even call
it friendship what we had

Nor could I merely say
we knew each other we
had more than that

And I couldn't say
we always hung out together we hardly
were aware of each other's presence in
those velvet days you
had your things to do
I had mine

All we really did was fall
with the rain
drops grow with the trees
and buoyed up by the wind's wings
breathe with the earth
and scan the soft-swept landscape at
dawn when with the flaming suns
we rose
how then should I answer how

could I even begin to
tell that you and I were just

young together

To Manny, at His Wake

Here are the four queens
that beat your full house
that story-filled poker night
and caused you
the $400 you have owed me
ever since.

Take them with you
All of them
To wherever you are going

The stunning stories of U.S. Pinoy life
that you've given me across the poker table,
with sometimes a thousand dollars in the pot,
with those stories alone, fellow-storyteller,
I think I can safely say
that we are more than even now.
Bon Voyage na lang
and sweet licks of
Flip Nuñez
sing you to your rest.

SF/2010

The Courting

The Richmond District of San Francisco are the flatlands (relatively speaking) that spread rectangularly west of the upper Golden Gate Park, and bordered by two sides of the great Bay. A group of friends grew up there in the early Sixties during the birth of Rock and Roll and Teenage Power. They called themselves "The Wanderers". They were mostly in their late teens and the brisk sea breeze from the Bay cliffs splashed their blood into never sleeping. Unless it was Saturday, of course. Then they got up, to their parents' chagrin, at about two in the afternoon.

'Tiger' Mapuso was one such person who belonged to the "Wanderers". He designed as the logo of the group, the barkada, in the back of their jackets, a balisong, a switchblade knife open with both blades gleaming. He would stroke his duck-tailed hair mechanically every now and then. He, along with every youth in that generation, would look at the mirror for hours, at times intermittently, at times in long lapses.

The oldest buildings in the City, however, are in another area called the Mission District, from which the most ancient ruins of the City would, some future day, perhaps be found. There was one boy, Dante, in that Richmond District group who lived in the Mission. He had four younger brothers and his parents were everybody's favorite, especially his mother, Aling Taling. He, of course, also hung around the Mission District because that was where he lived (in fact O. J. Simpson was his schoolmate at Everett Middle School), but Dante had just developed a close friendship with the aforementioned 'Tiger', one of the Wanderers who lived and were with the Richmond boys; so he hung around the Richmond boys, too. It was certainly a close relationship these two had developed because they went almost everywhere together. Spur-of-the-moment trips to Reno, Slovenian Hall dances, courting excursions (as one forthwith will follow), poker games, getting jumped together, and other occasions. But the strangest thing was that they were always arguing, and at times would come close to swinging blows. They fought and argued like proverbial cats and dogs. They had different ideas and tastes for beauty, for love, for dying, for patriotism (Vietnam was pretty hot then), for everything. They disagreed on almost everything. But if one was missing on some sort of gathering (and there are many in Filipino living), the other one would invariably seek him out, asking and looking for him. And on rare occasions, on not finding the other, the one would sit and be quite melancholy for spats of time. Even though they cut each other down in public, they really missed each other's company when one was absent. The wonder was not that the two were always cutting each other down but that, in spite of this, they were the closest of friends.

For they were similar in one thing. That was their love for Magdalena Domingo. She was like the Virgin Mary. What else can you ask for? Would it be sacrilegious to want for more? But Magdalena, how shall one put it, was not famous for her intelligence. She seemed devoid of wit. But she was herself the source of much wit from others. She was also devoid of malice, till malice one day came. This, of course, no one could articulate nor predict at the time. Her hair would almost always be in that bouffant or beehive or pompadour. In parties she would wear a fall wig and a long gown and she would look like the brown Helen of Troy. Her eyes were big but they were made much bigger by her false eyelashes. Both Dante and Tiger liked Magdalena but both of them knew that they were not going to get her. A sort of companion in misfortune, sometimes they would feel toward each other.

Tiger was about five-four, five-five at the most, though he claimed 5'7". His frame was small but never frail. His hair was combed towards the middle, the top of the head receiving the ends of both sides that was combed upward at the top. It puffed towards the front and slightly fell. It went well, he must have thought, with his James Dean look. And on the football field on Lake Street Park by 12th Avenue, where they played tackle, he among all of them, with his 5'4" stature, was by far the fiercest. That was the tiger in him. Small as he was, his favorite position was to rush the quarterback. No one had the nerve and heart to tell him that that position was reserved for the biggest of guys.

Twelve years later, when he was thirty years old, Tiger would walk into a hospital to check his glasses because Dante and the boys were already making fun of his taking his glasses on and off and rubbing his eyes at two or three in the morning while they were playing poker at Tiger's parent's attic on 8th Avenue, the same place where they had learned and played fifteen years ago, which would be around the time of this story, when the boys were teaching Tiger how to play, and strangest of peculiarities, he was steadily losing. They were really getting into each other's personalities through playing poker. Those were the days of James Dean, West Side Story, and Elvis Presley. Sometimes they would go on playing cards through the weekend continuously, only to borrow each other's money later on in the week.

Everyone was confident that a pair of new glasses would be all that Tiger needed to remedy such nagging and now humiliating headaches. He went to get his eyes checked and would never come out alive.

Dante that day made his way into the U.C. Medical Hospital on Parnassus Avenue where Tiger was. He would ask the information desk for his room. The woman at the desk, busy with something else, would look up Tiger's birth name in her handy Rolodex within arm's length, and she would have a hard time looking for it, and she would tell Dante, "Nope, I can't find his name", and would go on counting the money. Dante would quickly turn around to go outside, not knowing really what to do or what to think, but before he had turned completely around, he would do a double take, a second look, on the trash can that he noticed at the side of the information desk. Among the littered items of torn envelopes, cut paper, cardboards, and candy wrappers, he would see a small Rolodex card clinging to the side of the small trash can. Both holes of the Rolodex card on the garbage can were torn incomplete. The card had Tiger's name on it.

But our story got ahead of itself. The courting happened when the two boys were seniors in high school, Tiger still very much alive, everyone still very much alive, and Magdalena Domingo was for a brief moment the topic of conversation. There were eleven people who winded up at Magdalena's house that day in Bernal Heights when they came courting. Tiger and Dante were two of them. The others were mostly friends from the Wanderers.

Besides Tiger and Dante, there were three other boys in the car when they finally pulled over to the curb across the street from Magdalena's house. They didn't quite know what to do. Should they go straight to the house, or indulge some more on the conversation they were having inside the car, for it wasn't quite resolved or finished yet, (the topic was "What is your definition of love?"), or just continue drinking some more, for some felt they weren't quite ready to go in yet? In this atmosphere of drinking and thinking, smoking and joking, the smell of a nasty fart started seeping subtly into their nostrils. Though it was subtle, it steadily got very obvious and relentless.

"Oh shit! Who cut the cheese, man?" wailed Sal. Sal Anton was one of the Wanderers. He was very witty. But sometimes his wit bordered on cruelty.

There were vehement denials and no one admitted to the dastardly deed. In the middle of all the chaotic shenanigans, they saw Magdalena from up the stairs on the doorstep of her house.

"Oh shit, there's Magdalena!" Dante said. "She's waving at us. She's waving us in. Let's go, man."

"No, wait a minute. Let's finish this bottle. It's almost gone. Just wave back at her and signal we'll be in shortly," said Sal Anton. So one of the boys started waving some kind of gesture to Magdalena on her doorstep. She bent down a little, squinted her eyes (she rarely wore the glasses that she needed), and smiled. She started going down the steps holding one hand above her forehead.

"Shit, she misunderstood your fricken gesture. She's coming right at us. She thinks you are waving her in! She recognized us. Let's go in. Let's finish the bottle later." Dante wanted to open the door.

"Later? What for? What'll you do with the grass when the horse is dead?" Said Sal Anton in Filipino.

"Don't open the fucking door, Dante!" Tiger suddenly interrupted. "She's coming down. Shit, she's heading straight this way."

The rotten stench in the car was just peaking. Panic started to grip the occupants. The vehicle started moving and rocking. Some wanted to stay, some wanted to go. But it was too late. Magdalena Domingo in her kindness, ran across the street to personally greet and invite her visitors in.

"Roll up all the windows. She's coming!" More than one of them said.

"How the hell am I supposed to talk to her," asked Dante. He was in the driver's seat and Magdalena was coming straight at him. Before any satisfactory decision could be made, she was poking her innocent nose in to invite the boys into her house, slightly knocking on the window, trying to get Dante the driver's attention, who had his face turned away from her, pretending to be occupied. Dante, not knowing what to do, opened the window a little to try to say something, but although Magdalena's expression on her face changed, her smile disappearing momentarily, she controlled herself and acted quite the lady. Dante, still with his face turned slightly away from Magdalena, closed the window.

"C'mon in, you guys," she moved her face toward her house. "What are you guys doing there, drinking huh?"

"What are you doing here, Magdalena? Get back to the house. Who else is here? Better not leave them in there too long. Get back to the house, Magdalena. Aren't you cold? It's all right; we'll be right there." Dante said.

"Don't make fucking conversation. Just get rid of her!" insisted Sal Anton from inside the car. The odor was in full bloom and just about wreaking havoc. "Close the damn window will you!"

"It's already closed'" said Tiger, sitting on the passenger seat, riding shotgun. He opened the door on the other side and said out loud, yet quite casually, "We'll be right there, Magdalena. Go on ahead. Don't stand on the street."

"Yeah, I have to get back", she said. "I just snaked out."

When she had crossed the street, the boys roared out in laughter in the car, with no one, absolutely no one, to this day, admitting to the fart. "She just snaked out," repeated Sal Anton, in the middle of his convulsive laughter.

Inside the house, Magdalena Domingo was the only girl. Yes, all eleven of them were boys. That's how the courting went in those days. Poor Magdalena, looking around perhaps bewildered and wondering just who it was that was actually serious with her, or moving in on her, as they say. Perhaps not. Perhaps she knew more than she let on.

One fine day, malice came knocking at the door which was slightly opened already. It came in the form of one named Calvin who led the band called Purple Haze at the Tonga Room. No one really knew him. He was an outsider, though they heard of him and the band. Dante and Tiger and everyone in the Wanderers heard through the grapevine that Calvin came with a bouquet of flowers in his arms and was at least ten years older than Magdalena. He came courting alone. That was a bad sign. The next news about Magdalena was that she had married Calvin. They had eloped. Later, they heard she was a battered and abused wife.

Twelve years later, when Dante visited Tiger in the hospital too late that day he saw the torn rolodex card with Tiger's name sticking to the side of the plastic wrapper around the trash can, he saw Magdalena on a wheelchair, bruises on her face, and a faint but brave smile. She was being treated in the same hospital. One night, a few days later, the same day as Tiger's funeral, Magadalena Domingo shot her husband to death in an alley behind where he was playing music. He was having a smoke break. It was in the papers.

The Catch

The day of "The Catch", the afternoon that started the 49ers dynasty, when in the decades before they've been our sweet losers, I was in a hotel room in Reno watching the final moments of the game. I had bet pretty much all the money I had, three thousand dollars, half of it my mom's, without her knowledge of course, on the Forty Niners. Put your money where your mouth is, I have always said and now I was proving it. My friend Sonny, who was watching with me in the room, jumped up and shouted because he, too, had bet on the Niners. "Two hundred bucks!" He was quite elated for a supercool person. "I knew they'd come through. It's their year, pare!" Then, I showed him my ticket. "What the fu . . .?" He looked at me wide eyed (which was weird because he had squinty eyes). "What the … six thousand fucking smackers! You had that bet and you were just sitting there quietly?"

"Until the catch. Yeah!"

My mom trusted me to keep what little money she had from social security to put in my account because she did not like dealing with banks. She had cash under pillows, blankets and dishes when she died. I felt real guilty but I rationalized it by saying to myself that I was doing it for her, too. I'd figure out how later.

The Toilet Bowl
(for Steve Arevalo)

In the classrooms and hallways of San Francisco State
You roamed and rolled
like a young carabao, its horns thick as your jutting eyebrows.
Leaflets of announcements
Fliers of revolution and change
You, my youngblood brother
Would pull out papers like rabbits
from your half-dozen pockets
like a magician

Kapwa in our admiration for the Pinay woman
(always from afar, for alas, they liked someone else)

Our love for sports
How much you got on the Warriors this game? You would ask.
We were together at the airport when they won their first NBA championship in
the fourth game of their underdog sweep over the Washington Bullets.
In the days when there were no cell phones,
you would call long distance about 49er possibilities for the super bowl

And we had our own version of "The Catch"
when we played at the panhandle of the Golden Gate Park.
I threw you a long touchdown pass and with out-stretched and shaking hands,
you belly-flopped on the ground but the ball still intact within your fingers.
Touchdown! But when we came together for the next huddle, we smelled you.
You had slid into some dogshit when you caught that touchdown.

But now I smell your presence again, though with a more wholesome thought
of your deeds, your tireless, unselfish efforts despite your debilitating illness.
Steve, you'll always come out of the pile smelling like a rose, my brother,
because you have always come from a place that was pure and true. No hidden
agendas, no strings attached. Your heart and your mind and your guts were all
you needed.

But the world could not sustain a gentle warrior like you. It's so full of crap,
you couldn't help but step on it.

Credit: Freddie Mar and Mignon Geli

IN OUR FLAT on Guerrero St., in the '70's, my daughter woke me one time very early in the morning, just before dawn.
"Dad," she said.
"What is it?" I asked.
"I had a bad dream."
"Come and go back to sleep beside me and I'll hear it when I get up, ok?"
When I later woke up in the fullness of the morning, I had forgotten about it, but she had not.
"Do you want to hear my dream now?"
"Tell me," I said.
"There were people with guns who took us away. They put us in a car with them and along a deserted road they stopped and asked us to get out and there were nuns with guns and I was confused and..." She suddenly stopped... "Wait a second, don't you remember, Dad? You were there!"

All my children were born in San Francisco. Not one of them lives there now. My firstborn does not care much for the City. He now lives in Las Vegas. My first daughter, who was born in the Summer of love, also lives in Las Vegas. She's not too crazy about California in general. The crime, the grime, the cost of living, the politics, you name it. All that is there, of course. But it does not portray an accurate San Francisco. And it's not the only city with squalor. And the people sheltered from that squalor in their own cities will have the most fear reading these manufactured, cherry-picked malaise. All major cities in the country have similar problems. The viewer's bubbled world sanitizes them and prevents them from seeing, identifying with, their own similar problems. I know and have felt the problems of the city since day one.

The sources of these negative videos of inner U.S. cities have their agenda of hate, fear, and blame. But me, I always liked the place. In spite of it all! I just didn't have anybody to tell this to. She's been abused, refused, excused, confused like others have, like I have! Surrounded on three sides by the sea, seven times seven square miles of choice real estate spread among diverse neighborhoods spaced around eight subway stops, among seven magnificent hills, and with seven bridges in which to enter her. The City that broke my heart. Twice. Somewhere between Chinatown, Mario's Cafe in North Beach, and Dolores Park in the Mission. When Montgomery Clift answered Donna Reed's question in their cheap hotel in *From Here to Eternity*, when arguing she could not understand why he would want to go back to the Army right after Pearl Harbor when it was that same Army that persecuted him all his years of duty, demoting him, humiliating him, breaking him, resulting in him still being a private. "Why?

For what? The army don't give a shit about you?" she fiercely asked, and he answered, "You love someone or something, it don't have to love you back." I love her wild winds, her curvy up and down streets, her hidden and not so hidden beaches and parks, and no matter how long you've lived in that small, big city, you always run into a street you've never seen before, a city where you put your jacket on, then take it off again about three times walking ten blocks. Within those ten blocks you would have traversed the diversity of the globe from all continents. When you get on a bus, you hear a cacophony of languages, and the only one speaking English is the driver, and he's black. It's a crazy town, but with a spirit that breeds and attracts creativity, and originators that oftentimes influence the trends and the lifestyles of the times. I've had a lover's quarrel with this city for as long as I can remember. Like memory, like music, like water, it takes only a moment and the lambent light of her December noons for me to make up with her again. *Sa mga suliranin na pinaglalabanan.* In the chaotic madness of the world, she is a haven sometimes. And I'm back in her arms again. The city that broke my heart. Twice. And there is a sentimental sunset-like feeling about the place, as if you're far away and at home at the same time. This city is my city. And I am part of it as much as she is of me. There is no San Francisco without my people's footprints on it; without Al Robles' words on it, without Bill Sorro's dancing footsteps all over it, without Ed de la Cruz's spilled black coffee all over its sidewalks, without Mrs. Rapisura's strong legs climbing staircases with a fifty or a hundred pound rice sack like a Cordillera woman with a goat slung over her shoulders, without Carmencita, Annie, and the Geli sisters traipsing across the rooftops of North Beach, without my mother's singing and father's farting, and without my children's stories covering it like a mist before the fog rolls in. That is how I finally came to see the city. And how the city helped me find myself in my own voice. It's a place where memory is important because some things change so quickly.

Kai at Two

On a lawn at the edge of the soccer field
I sitting on the matt-covered grass
had you in my arms

When you held out
your ice cream cone to me
for a bite
and as I was about to indulge
I heard a click
That was beautiful, said the photographer
A fellow parent no doubt

Kai, you were always a giver
You knew too well
Your grandpa's sweet-tooth,
And where in heaven's name
is that photo now?

The Gift of Davian

A Christmas present wrapped
in infant form
a boy into which things come
a boy of destiny
a piece to the puzzle of family
first name-carrier
like his father before him

the wisdom to decide
the courage and strength
to persevere
are the gifts he brought.

Kai and Davian Peñaranda, ca. 2017, Photo credit: Oscar Peñaranda

Babaylan In Playland By the Sea

"Rosebud... A girl's name? You wouldn't think that a man in his dying breath would mention someone's name out of the blue after fifty years, would you?"

"Well...you're pretty young, Mr. Thompson. A fellow would remember a lot of things you wouldn't think he'd remember. You take me. Crossing the ferry to Jersey one late afternoon in 1896, I saw a girl with a white dress and a white parasol. Just for a second, it was. Don't think she saw me. But I bet that a month does not pass by that I don't think of her."

—Mr. Bernstein, Citizen Kane, 1941.

The stupidest thing that the city of San Francisco ever did was to get rid of Playland by the Sea, with its Funhouse Fat Laughing Lady with freckles and red hair, its grand towering Ferris Wheel, and the formidable Salt and Pepper Shaker Loop (where he, as a teenager, once discovered too late not to have anything in one's pockets because they will all fall down, coins, pens, whatever, when the ride turns you upside down violently and fearfully). Hot Dog stands steaming in the night and the carnival atmosphere everywhere and all around, the various sounds of laughter floating in the air. It was a mini-Disneyland right across the misty Pacific Ocean, the Great Highway and the Cliff House, a turn of the (twentieth) century Restaurant made of brass and dark wood. Unfortunately, Playland was swallowed up by the waves of greed. Speculation, they called it. So they closed it down, built apartments and condos instead to make more money. Joy subsided quickly like the foams from among and along those silver-crested waves. No more mermaids beckoned from the sea. Where once it shimmered in the summers of the City, the area now is a very quiet place and deserted. Lonesome winds frequent it. Condominiums and apartments were put on the site where Playland used to be. Those apartments and condominiums have never been fully occupied. In due time, desolation took over the place and no children were ever seen near it. That was the day the magic died in Playland by the sea. Songs and stories will be the only remnants of those days. This is one of them.

Priday Night Walker called his trusted friend Amador one day during prom season and told him to get ready for a double date that he, Priday, is arranging.

"You gotta go on a double date with me, pal." He said with his phony Texas

(Filipino) accent. Priday Night Walker was a Filipino mestizo whose white U.S. citizen father was in the service and found himself growing up mostly right in the heart of Texas, of all places. His father was transferred to San Francisco only 6 years ago. He got to know everybody fast. He was a very social guy as you can tell by what folks called him.

"I don't got a 'date'," Amador reminded him.

"I know that," answered Priday quickly. "I don't know why; you're kinda cute…in a sort of ugly way. Look at me…Pry-day Night Walker…"

"No thanks."

"I just don't know what it is they see in me, but…"

"Could it be that Chevy Impala? It ain't the looks, that's for sure."

"But I always got a girl, right? And seein' that I knew you wouldn't have one, and seein' that the prom is already this Sarday nat…I got you one."

He was right, the fucker. Compared to Priday's social life, Amador felt at times that he would languish in loneliness for the rest of his obscure life.

It seemed that his (Priday''s) date's parents won't allow the two of them on a date alone. Amador did not know whether the parents had heard of Priday's reputation or not. They would however permit her to go on a double date with her girlfriend, (and family trusted companion), who will turn out to be his, Amador's, blind date.

"We'll pay for everything," Priday told Amador. "I'll take care of expenses," he said.

"What about for the date?" Amador asked.

"Not the expenses that don't involve me, pare. You gotta cough that up yourself, brother. I'll just provide the merchandise; you gotta pay for the maintenance. Don't be *kuripot*, man. C'mom, you gotta fork out something. Show some class, all right?"

Amador, the ever-accommodating (in his mind) young man of seventeen that he was, said, "Yes, of course." Amador himself had just graduated. His graduation celebrations and activities were nothing to brag about. In fact, it was nothing at all, period. Just a kiss from his mother and a controlled smile from his father. He had not planned on going to his school prom, though the priest, his Saint Ignatius High School English teacher, had offered him a couple of names from his list of Mercy High School girls. The same priest had procured him one before on the Sadie Thompson Dance. Her name was Anne Farmer and her straight, long, red hair still had him remembering. The truth is that Amador had hinted to his Mom about going to the prom, but she picked up on it right away and said, "Nating doing! No money for all *dis kalokohans*. It's not enough that you go to the most expensive school in San Francisco. You have to pick the most expensive event pa!"

"Ma, this is the prom. And I didn't pick the school. You guys did.'"

"Not me," she said and cast a furtive glance toward his father who was reading the newspaper while watching the news on the television in the *sala*, as he, with his Giants baseball cap on, was listening to the baseball game on the radio in the kitchen.

"They're paying for the whole thing, Ma."

"Who are 'they', ha?"

"I guess their family, Priday's girlfriends' family, or her girlfriend's girfriend's family. I don't know. All I know is that I, I mean we, I mean you, are not paying for a centavo, Ma. *Wala. Libre lahat.*"

"Siyet," she curtly said.

And he kissed her on both cheeks, making *gigil* noises and grabbed her shoulder and started massaging it and shaking it until she wrinkled her forehead and started screaming for him to stop. "Hoy! Hoy!" And laughing, he slowly let her go.

"*Kalokohan!*", she said, regaining some control and fixing herself up.

The ride after the prom was rather quiet. He had danced with his date Maria only a few times. He should have danced more, he knew, but it was too late now. Priday pulled over by the diner with the big Dachshund hotdog on top of it by 48thAve, near the Great Highway. Priday and his prom date quickly disappeared into the Laughing Lady's entrance gate, leaving the two alone.

Amador and Maria sat down at a small eating place and as they were ordering the food, Amador started noticing Maria. And he started listening well to what she was saying, as he slowly chewed on his fish and chips with a sprinkling of vinegar. The jukebox was playing "Sally Go 'Round the Roses'' and she was humming and oo-oowing a bit. They finished their meals and smiling at each other (as the Rocky Fellers were busting out "Killer Joe "), walked outside into the light-studded mist. They walked somewhat awkwardly through parts of Playland to cross the Great Highway into Ocean Beach, passing the fat Laughing Lady, the dart/balloon games, the shooting galleries, and the cotton candy cart wagons, till they confronted the giant Ferris Wheel with all its lights and colors and slow, creaky turning. Everything must have been turning in Maria's inside, too, because she suddenly said:

"Someday, I'll have my name in lights. Keystone Korner, Black Hawk, Blue Note. You never know, right? Why not?"

"Sure, why not?" He said. "You're a good singer. I can tell by your humming you got soul. I can't sing, but I can tell soulful singing."

"To sing, I think, to really sing your own, you gotta do it with passion. But you gotta have a broken heart or two under your belt to have that passion. So they say. I don't know what I'm saying." She looked up at him smiling a bit and took his arm to cross the street into the ocean's side.

"Rumi knew exactly what you are saying. He said that for one heart to open, it first must break. Makes sense, I guess."

"I'm afraid so."

She was looking up at him and beyond him, at the sky, with white-edged clouds bathed and drifting by the silvery moon, seawind blowing, foaming waves pounding, her chiffon dress billowing with the billows of the sea.

After they've crossed, he said, "Maybe you can teach me to sing. Think it's possible? Can anyone learn? I'm pretty hopeless. I might scare away all the mermaids."

"Nonsense. Anybody can sing. My niece is tone-deaf and I taught her."

"Wow, you're a teacher, too. You're gifted."

She looked at him straight and clear and kindly. They were stepping on sand now. "You're the gifted one." She was looking through him, beyond him, into the moonlit sea of Ocean Beach. "You'll write about us and someday people will read them and someday, maybe, one will come to know someone like me. You're the gifted one."

"I guess we all have our talents."

"Yes, but it's you who will tell my story." She moved a little closer to him and walked in his rhythm, taking bigger steps. "The waves, the ocean, the sea, will wipe them all out immediately, but the spirit of our footprints will still be in these sands because you will write about them, I can tell. I know a little bit about you before from Priday and them. Research is good, right?."

"When before, or before when?"

"Before before pa."

"Wow! A budding private investigator, too. 77 Sunset Strip, Hawaii Five-O, female Ponce Pons!"

"More like Pawai Five-O. I'm Ilocana. My mother's Tagalog, though. She named me after the legendary Maria of Mount Makiling because I was born in the calm right after a storm. I like to know what I'm getting into, of course, before I jump into anything. With a practical and desperate friend like Priday, one has to excavate a little oral history on his double date choices," she smiled, her red lips accentuating her scarlet and gold shawl. "You keep writing."

"That's funny," he answered. "Everyone tells me to dream another dream, to stop writing. I'll be broke all my life, they say. No one is interested in reading about Filipinos, especially Filipinos, they all tell me. Don't know if I should even consider it now. My own family…"

"Consider it? I don't think you have a choice, young man. And you're good. I read some of your poems that you write for your friends to the girl of their dreams, or the object of their lustful affection. Some are too good to send. I hope you've kept copies."

"Yeah, some of them won't appreciate the poems, huh?"

"Oh, they'll appreciate them all right. Every one of them. A girl appreciates those things. But not necessarily for the same reasons."

"Really? Do they know it is not from their aspiring suitors?"

"Of course, they do. C'mon, they all know they came from you."

"I'll make sure to keep them all from now on."

They took off their shoes and started laughing. He tried to carry her pair but she would not let him. "It's all right. I'll carry them. They're my shoes, after all." The night was all a-splash in spindrifts brought by the wind and waves. As they strolled on the sands of the silver-ladened seascape, he noticed the moon, though not yet full, was bright and it made his gaze wander towards the horizon. It was during this gaze that a strange surge of romantic feeling overwhelmed him. It was prom night after all, and he suddenly swept Maria off her feet and scooped her up, carrying her as they both almost fell. Regaining his balance, he continued carrying her, trying to keep up a conversation. He noticed the silveriness of things as the moon momentarily got in his eye. It took his attention for a split second and then that was all it needed, because a wave, a gigantic one, rose like a monster from the sea and it was heading straight for them. Terror-stricken and instinctively obeying the most formidable human urge, that of self-preservation, he forgot everything and ran away from the great wave, toward the Great Highway. But of course, he forgot the bundle he had in his arms a few seconds ago, the object of his romanticism. He looked down at his empty arms and looked back and saw Maria squirming to get up from the water's edge like a cockroach on its back trying to get right side up. Coming to his senses, he rushed to her, shouting apologies before he even got to her and picked her up.

"Not just our footprints, now," Maria said laughing, "but my body prints, too," while brushing off the sand and water from herself. "I was shaking like a cockroach out there."

"Or a mermaid," he said.

When he had gathered her in his arms safely and things started to look right-side up again, he clumsily added,"You're a wise one. With a hell of a sense of humor, too."

"But you," she touched both his hands and turned them palm up, "with these soft hands, are the gifted one. Remember that."

"Your dress...? You're all wet?"

"Just a little."

"Wanna go back to the diner and change in the bathroom?"

"Change to what, my slip or shawl?" She said jokingly, and then she thought for a while. "Why not? I'll just put my coat over it. C'mon. No. Let's go to the Cliff House. I'll change there."

When she came out of the Cliff House, she came out all colorful and baba-ylan-like. She looked like she belonged in the opulent, classy Cliff House (by her carriage and posture), yet she did not belong in the Cliff House (by her splash of many colors), too bold to neatly fit the ambience. Biblical yet pagan. Folkloric, yet modern.

He never saw her again. And to this day, hard as he might try, he can not remember an iota of whatever happened to Priday and his date that prom night when he used him as an excuse to satisfy his (Priday's) concupiscence, bursting through lustful teenage loins.

They must have been dropped off home that night to end the date, but he has no memory of her at all after that night she came out of the Cliff House. They must have said goodnight but he does not remember if he kissed her or not, nothing, that unmentionable, for some, that dreaded moment, the prize of the prom—that goodnight kiss. No memory of it at all. Just the ocean, the beach, the moon, the wind, the Cliff House, the steaming smell of hot dogs, burnt cotton candies, and Playland by the sea that disappeared into the mist and recesses of San Francisco history, but not from memory, at least not from his.

Sapagkat Ako'y Makata

Gagawing kong bansa ang daigdig
Gagawin kong lunsod
Ang bansa't gagawin
Kong lalawigan ang lunsod,
At gagawin kong kapit bahay
Ang mundo
Sapagkat ako'y makata.
Tila mga tulay ang aking salita
Sapagkat ako'y makata
Pantay-pantay ang halaga ng kahit anong bagay
Subalit, sapagkat ako'y makata
Ang mga salita
Ng makata ay
Hindi pantay-pantay.
Bawat isa, iba-iba ang dating.

The Forgotten Present

I forgot to thank you
For the See's candies
You had brought me
But left in the car
Yesterday afternoon.
Forgive my delay in gratitude.
But not for that lapse of yours,
I would not still be tasting them.

4/2011

Day of the Butterfly

I was not there at all. I was sick from eating too many peanut butter sandwiches and had to stay behind in camp that day in the summer of '62.

It was the sort of story that I've been told constantly by participants, but in different stages of their lives in the City, at different intervals, on different occasions, sometimes from two or three of them together, sometimes individually, and though all of them told it more than once, they have never told it all together at one time in one sitting. It was the sort of story that you kept hearing parts of and at times in differing versions, so that it could not be completely forgotten. Scenes and times would change, but the story remained constant, yet elusive. So, you can see the pains I had to take to tell the whole thing coherently when pressured by the old crowd for that particular story during some once-in-a-blue-moon Get Togethers. I had to piece things together, take liberties to fill in gaps, iron out seeming contradictions, and restrain implausibilities to make sense out of the whole fiasco that was the roadside showdown on freeway Interstate 80, about 40 miles northeast of San Francisco where we were all from. And even then, it was still open for several interpretations. Though I heard about the incident in relative solitude, I was always forced to tell it in company. Sometimes I felt like a priest speaking at the pulpit about his parishioners' confessions. We were all from San Francisco, but in the summer months all worked in various fields and orchards of California.

My older brother Antonio and his schoolmate from USF, Bong, was there, and Batok, the Elvis Presley of the group, and Clarence, the smallest and the one who really started the whole thing and the one who got married first, and then went to 'Nam. He never really did explain why he did both. And when he got to Vietnam, they said he volunteered to be point-man. And then there was one more with them that day. There were five of them, they had all said, but none of them could remember the fifth man. When they told the story and when they came upon the tally of the participants, they all quickly said five. But upon request, they could only name four, the same four, and it would take for the whole story to be told before they could remember the fifth man.

Batok had definitely the best looking hair among them. He would spend hours in facial pantomime in front of the mirror, touching different parts of his head. The word *batok* is that flat area in the back of one's head between the ears. There is something very vulnerable and humiliating about that part of a person's head, especially when one gets hit there. Connotations of that word were often not too uplifting for one's ego. That is also the very place that elders hit you when getting scolded. They called him Batok because once when

Clarence was giving him the finishing touches of a haircut, Batok complained that the neckline was slightly crooked.

"How about straightening this out, boy" he said, chewing his gum. In those days in San Francisco, in every *barkada*, one or two could cut hair fairly decently. Clarence and I were the two barbers of our *barkada*. In fact, I was somewhat his pupil and he, my mentor in haircuts. Undoubtedly and ubiquitously, Clarence was the best barber even among other *barkadas* that we knew. But that day, the gift of the gods was just not with him. He must have, as the old ones liked to tease, 'forgotten to wash his hands after he took a shit'. "You ain't no good no more. Washed up. La-us!" Batok chewed his gum bobbing up and down, neck twisted, his eye straining to get a better look at that crooked line in the mirror.

"Here," Clarence finally admitted. "Sit down. That ain't nothing. I'll fix that. That's only hair. It's your face you should worry about," he added, "my preng."

"Puck you...my preng."

But Clarence straightened it out anyway. Yet upon closer inspection, Batok noticed that the other side of the neckline was lower now. Clarence had raised the right side too high.

"Hey, man. How much booze have you had? The other side is messed up now."

Clarence put down his beer and really got to work. But it was too late. By the time he took another good long look at the back of Batok's head, his neck-line had crawled up above one of his ears, a good part of the scalp on the back of his head, his *batok*, was already quite exposed. For a person whose source of pride and self-esteem was his hair, it was disastrous, and from then on, he was called Batok.

He was not really a bad looking individual. It was just that his looks were unusual—not because of his brown skin and broad nose and other outer features, but because of a boyish fire of lustful madness that gleamed occasionally from his moist lips and big restless eyes. *Malibog* was the Filipino word that came to mind. He was rather stocky, broad-shouldered, and had somewhat of a voice, unschooled, of course, and that voice he bent out of shape every time he up-tempoed it to imitate Elvis Presley's grunts and groans, his Elvis Presley hair gradually falling in bunches on his Elvis Presley brow.

From the City, Bong's family used to visit our camp by Green Valley Road near Suisun about twice a month and everyone would anticipate those visits more than Bong himself because he had a sister whose name was Maganda. They would bring Bong some Filipino food from the City and leftovers for those of us who might want some. Batok would run around crazy looking for a tree to lean on while plucking on his guitar, pretending he didn't notice her face glowing in the car that had just pulled in, "Oh hi, Maganda. Was that you guys that just pulled in?" It was an idyllic scene indeed. Save for the fact that the keenest of observers might have noticed that Batok was left-handed, and being left handed, he had to strum his romantic guitar from the bottom up, with his thumb jerking upwards at each stroke and his mouth going slightly askew as a result of it. And then he would sing. And his voice would float in the evening like a velvet veil. Batok had a beautiful crooner's voice with so much passion that it carried far into the evenings of camp life.

They had just finished high school then, though Antonio and Bong were already in college. But it was summer. It was in the dead heat of summer, in the Suisun Valley of California, just northeast of San Francisco.

We had been working in the fields and had just had a day off, after more than three and a half weeks of apricot picking. Apricot is the most brittle of trees! I have seen a puff of casual summer wind split a tree like lightning would. All it took was air—a gust, a breath. The boys had hitchhiked into town. I was left behind because I did not feel well. So, the rest of this incident was told to me. Some had bought groceries while others had stolen them, and were now walking back to camp along the freeway Interstate 80, hitchhiking. Five young, brown men, Filipinos, walking with packages and hitchhiking along the freeway between Vacaville and Vallejo.

They had just gotten off their first ride, a brand new '62 Dodge Pick-up. The driver was "a nice white Okie farmer" who had some stories himself for he never stopped talking. Bong said he was one of those "country-philosopher type Okies". He had told them about five riddles, still the most difficult ones he'd heard, then dropped them off without telling them a single answer.

"Okay, while you're thinking of that one, lemme tell you this one. Maybe this will be more to your liking." Then he would rattle off another, one more fascinating than the one before, Bong recalled, his rabbit nose slightly twitching. The Okie kept saying, after a laugh, "sometimes the essential is absent, and sometimes absence is essential." Puzzles and riddles and ridiculous statements like that got to Bong. He was smart with a lot of useless things like that. He would touch his earlobe then smooth his lower face with his hand. He was the only one that really tried to solve (or even remembered) all those problems. In fact, he was pondering them the night the cook busted in on them with a shotgun looking for his light bulb.

But this day, this walk along the highway, was their first day off in three and a half weeks, and though they would have to work again all day the next day, they could take it relatively easy because the seasons were shifting from apricots to peaches. And in many camps if one worked "by the box" (called a contract worker), one could take some time off, depending on what was prized more at the moment, rest or pocket. Working by the box meant one chose (or was chosen) to work for an employer who paid so much money for every box picked (plus bonuses, of course, if you're a good boy) of the fruits of California summers—cherries, apricots, pears, peaches, nectarines, strawberries, grapes. The dying pear and apricot season were gliding quickly into peach. I remember the burr-like fuzz that got so many people sneezing, and the smell of peach blossoms clinging to the still air and warm starry nights. Engulfing the brittle and now fruitless apricot branches, the lavender sky glowed in the twilight like a god pinching homesickness from those far away from home, and a mixture of fragrances—flowers, soil and fruit—hung heavy in the soft evenings after a hard day's work.

The counterpart of, or the alternative to, working by the box was to work "by the hour". Here they paid you for your time regardless of the amount of boxes you picked. The foreman and peer pressure, of course, kept one moving pretty fast. Consequently, the politics of survival became so that the workers with less responsibilities (that usually meant those without a family), or the worker who had a "rebellious nature," or the worker who tried to redress injustices, as well as the plain lazy in nature, for obvious reasons, chose "by the hour", and had their own interpretations to the saying 'the trick to being good is not to be too good'. Those who were new to farm work usually worked "by the hour". They would not get hired by contract. They weren't fast enough and lacked the experience in handling the tender fruits. Some had the speed and the experience but were content to get paid by the hour so they didn't have to work "like burros," as the Chicanos would say.

They were mostly single men who could afford to feel like this. They fooled around a lot and used their experience and knowledge of camp life not only to survive, but to "get over". Before one can "make it" at something, they claimed, one has to make it first. They would pack the inferior quality fruits for the company but cover them with layers of first-rate picks. The hundred per cent quality fruits they would steal and secretly give to visiting relatives and friends, some of whom in turn would, when they got to town, sell them to someone else.

So into the orchards of the Suisun Valley, we started work early in the still-cold mornings before dawn, and we clambered onwards with ladder and container in arms marching into the coming day. There was always that daily conflict on deciding whether to bring a jacket or not. For though one will be comforted from the cold and damp of false dawn, shortly after lightbreak that sun will be beating down mercilessly on your neck, and you'll be burdened the rest of the hell-hot day with lugging your jacket everywhere and eventually leaving it somewhere under some fruit-laden tree. In the long days of summer, the sun would hang around till well past 9:30 in the evening, like a nervous guest preparing to make his leave. The worst nightmare, of course, is if one should get caught wanting to take a dump when one is out there in the fields because there were no outhouses or anything like that. One worker was forced to take a dump out there because he couldn't hold it anymore and he wiped his ass using poison oak. Oh, he was in pain!

Anyway, the Okie farmer let them off at a fork on the road and were now walking with groceries in hand somewhere between Vacaville and Vallejo. They had decided to cook their own meals and not pay for those provided for them by the company. They would save more money (for gambling, of course) and not get constantly and mysteriously overcharged by the company store. Besides, the cook, a tall, lanky Filipino with a gut, was a token company man, a poor loser in gambling, a bully, a braggart, a coconut, an Uncle Tom, and just an all around asshole. They had asked him for some light bulbs for their bunkhouse before (the cook was also the utilities supplier), and he had refused, making some snide remark about how "real Filipinos are not afraid of the dark, anyway" and telling the boys to buy their own, even though such items were supposed to be supplied by the company. The cook did this, they figured, because they had beaten him so badly in their last poker game that his rage was bordering on suspecting the youths, the "young eggs," of playing partners without declaration, a conspiracy-by-camaraderie, so to speak, a practice considered unethical in poker. The cook basically accused the boys of cheating.

Clarence, one participant in "the showdown" and who had the youngest-looking face, relished this particular section of the anecdote, even though it had very little to do with the showdown itself. Over and over he told about how someone had snuck into the cook's room the evening after the showdown and had taken one light bulb, and for several hours, things were back to normal in their bunkhouse, when suddenly, in the middle of their card game, while all were huddled under that one bulb, while Bong was deliberating on the Okie's riddles between inside straights and unfilled flushes, the door flung open, and by the time anyone had time to react, the cook, with a shotgun in hand resting on his belly, spoke almost wearily, "Alright. Who took my light bulb?" To this day, no one has admitted to it.

Clarence said they had duped Batok into doing it, telling him that they had seen Elvis Presley do it once in a movie. Batok had admitted he had agreed, but that was just to pacify the taunters, *"nakikisama lang ako,"* for he had, as usual, lost his nerve at the last moment. But according to Batok, the cook was not all that much of an asshole. He claimed that Clarence always teased the cook behind his back, that's why the cook had a minor grudge against him, and well, that's just the way Clarence was. He could not keep from publicizing some of his feelings. He always brought his own brand of perversity along with him and when he came upon things already perverse, he laughed at it all the more. For laugh he must. And laugh now, because soon he would be "Going To the Chapel," as the Dixie Cups swayingly sang "sweet I really love you", and so on and so on.

My brother Antonio denied that he had anything to do with the theft. In fact, he claimed he was the one who broke up the melee, just as he had done the time he broke up or tried to break up the skirmish in the midday sun just hours before the showdown, as it eventually came to be known. From the incidents of that same day, Antonio's nickname would be "the peacemaker-with-a-grin". But all denied the theft of the light bulb then, and they would deny it more vehemently as the years rolled by.

Clarence loved to tell humorous stories and play practical jokes on people. He was about to get married, and everyone knew he was nervous about it and scared, and he was trying to coolly deflect his nervousness by making people laugh so he could make himself laugh. It was also around the same time that Vietnam was getting hot, and the draft was in full swing and Clarence (along with many others) was thinking of the not too pleasant a prospect of going to "a fucking war," not because of the "fucking war" itself, but because he would "rather be fucking his wife-to-be". The Service would drive him away from his girl and, being a fairly astute gambler, he knew his luck and it was not good. It would not stand the test of the times. The girl maybe, or him, but not his luck. One thing about Clarence, he hardly blamed people for anything. He always blamed his luck.

"The odds don't look good, kid." He was telling me in my room in the Mission District of The City one day. He looked like he'd been up a good part of the night and it was getting late in the afternoon. There was a faint smell of liquor. I was still living with my parents at the time and I don't remember anybody ever coming through our front door messed up. I guess that was one of the reasons for the back door.

"Slim to none, I'd say. Stakes don't look too good, either" I reminded him.

"You got that right." He also said that, anyway if he stayed he would have to tangle with both Uncle Sam and Raul. Raul was his wife-to-be's not quite ex-boyfriend, a Kearny Boy who always had a bolo hidden in the sides or back of his pants when he went to dances. "But it's not going to hold up, man" He was talking about his luck again; and later, running out of explanations, dismissed this dilemma as "staying pat on a ten" in lowball poker.

"I know," I said. I had stayed pat on a few tens myself and what one remembers is not so much the loss or the win, but the long, drawn out discomfort of fear and resignation, your fate completely left to the mercy of chance, for you had to wait for everybody's turn to have their chance at drawing a better hand than yours because you stayed with the hand that was dealt to you; you didn't want to replace your cards with others, thinking that you might get an even worse hand. So, you stayed at a relatively just-above-mediocre hand.

Clarence was staring blankly at my bedroom window. (It was also my brother Antonio's bedroom, but he was not there then). "It was like the time when we were hitchhiking Interstate 80 and we somehow got in a beef with those nine white guys on the side of the road." And he told me the story for the first time. "Nine of them, man!" he emphasized again. There was a twinkle all of a sudden in his eye. "Football players, they looked like. You know, no necks." Then he slowed down his talking and sat down at the end of the bed looking out the window. "Odds weren't too good then, either. Fucking and fighting, they're always bad bets..." In some perverted yet natural way, Clarence had a wisdom all his own. "You weren't there, kid. Let's see who was there..." And then, winding up for the story, he started to rub his chin. For a while, immersed in the telling, he would forget his card game with fate.

"It was in the dead heat of summer," he recalled, "I think it was the fourth of July," and they had just been dropped off at a fork on the road, so they continued thumbing toward camp, toward Green Valley Road in Suisun where their orchards were. In town they had bought about twenty dollars' worth of groceries and other sundries and stolen about forty dollars' worth. They had gone into a store in the hundred- and ten-degree heat with trench coats and jackets, Clarence recalled with a chuckle. But when they got to camp later (after the showdown) and emptied out their pockets onto the table, they rolled out three bottles of ketchup, two bottles of chili peppers, two can openers, toe-nail clippers, six jars of pomade, coffee and creamers, sugar cubes, assorted candy bars, and not one light bulb. Someone had to go and get that. Their thieving definitely needed better coordination.

Back out on the road, Clarence went on, they had been hitchhiking for some time. They were getting tired of each other's company, for some could banter better and intimidate more than others. From the same side of the road, a black Cadillac with about four or five young people in it sped by and its passengers were laughing and yelling, saying something as they passed.

"Did you hear that?" Clarence had said to Batok. "Someone in the car called you a motherfucker!" and started snickering.

"What?" Batok, seemingly in deep thought, was totally surprised.

"Sure, man. And look! He's giving you the finger now." True, there were arms being waved wildly, but the car was disappearing so fast down the road that Batok had to ask again. "There, there, look!" Clarence had shouted right at Batok's face.

Perhaps indignantly, perhaps in self defense, perhaps in total or partial confusion, perhaps intensity is just contagious, but Batok suddenly shouted at the car also. "Puck you, too!" his middle finger bold and defiant, solidly thrust upwards toward the speeding Cadillac climbing up into a hill and out of view. "Madapaka," and trailing into a mumble, "ones op dis day..."

"You weren't there, kid. Let's see... who was there . . . " Clarence kept trying to remember, pressing a finger to his lip, still looking out the window, through lime-green and red-wine still trees, between rooftops and treetops and covered chimney tops into the dis-symmetry of a skyline made up of steeples, spires, telephone wires, antennas and way, way out toward the iron skeletons of ship-yards in Hunter's Point, way out into the Bay against the eastern Berkeley and Oakland Hills and jutting out from the right corner of the horizon, the lights from Candlestick Park glimmered in the fragile gauze of falling twilight where the hometown Giants were battling out a nightcap with the despicable Dodgers from the Southland.

"You should have been there, kid. You missed out." And he would laugh again. "Well, anyway, as I was saying about this Batok and his Cadillac..." and he continued his story.

"Puck you, too, Madapaka!" Batok had shouted at the speeding Cadillac. Casually he had shifted the grocery bags that he was carrying into Clarence's arms who in turn had grabbed them without thinking; the better for Batok to say, "Here, eat dis!" with his two obscene and stiff middle fingers. "Puck you! Puck you!" Batok, and soon all of them found themselves saying it with increasing intensity and ritual. Then Batok took his bag of groceries from Clarence.

Bong said it seemed that their seething anger made the Cadillac shrink as it slipped away onto the freeway. Bong told me this, however, a year after Clarence had told me his version. He too was looking out the same window one year later. What was on the radio was the same. The same San Francisco Giants were playing against the same despicable Los Angeles Dodgers. Bong said (of the showdown) that "it was the rage of the brown man rising." He really never forgot the larger picture. "It was the rage of centuries," he claimed. Then he became even more philosophical. Some uncontrollable, nameless, nebulous and amorphous indignation started becoming monstrous inside them, first building up individually, then gathering itself into a collective ball. As the varied fruits of the seasons were shifting from one to another, so the seasons inside them were also changing, it seemed, but no one understood the changes. They were beset with larger questions that they did not want to ask, let alone answer. Sometimes it felt that some people always had the answers and others only the questions. He definitely knew which group he belonged to that time. It was a part of their lives in which something had to give, burst, given the right moment, in the fullness of time. The incident on Highway 80 triggered it.

Bong told me a lot that afternoon. I had taken over depositing the rent since my folks went back home to the Philippines to visit and he had passed by. He said he was the one who christened my brother Antonio "peacemaker... with a grin" from that day at the highway. Although he was telling me about the showdown, I could tell at the time that his mind was someplace else, as though he were using the telling of the story as a necessary distraction. Bong was looking out that same window that Clarence looked out of about a year back, though this time Bong had just recently found out about his mother. His mother died when she gave birth to him. But his father never told him this. He suspected it all along, though he kept saying, "he had to find out for himself." So one day when he had built enough courage, he visited his mother's grave for the first time. And sure enough, there it was. The date of his birth and the date of her death were the same. When he was growing up, there were more than a few times that he overheard people asking his Dad and his relatives and then pointing him out among the rest with or without gestures and saying or asking "...is that the one?" And "yes... he's the one..."

"Strike 'em out, Juan!" Bong was talking to the radio. Bong was one of those people who could devote equal attention and intensity to many things at once. That was what he was good at. The baseball game on the radio, the showdown story, and the present conversation, all these he juggled fairly well. Me, I was good for nothing. Out in the fields, I couldn't even pick right, nor fast; and I was one of the youngest. I was the rookie and I was a victim of a rookie mistake that year in camp. I overate. And because I wanted to save up money for some contact lenses so I could not only look cool but play basketball without the distraction of glasses, I ate only one thing. Peanut butter sandwiches. I thought that as long as you're full, you're ok. I got sick. I started seeing spots, double vision, blackouts, a whole range of symptoms, till finally my head and stomach revolted simultaneously. So the next day, I stayed home while everyone went to town to celebrate their first day off in three and a half weeks. That was the day of the showdown.

After the brief tense moment of the Cadillac speeding by arrogantly while the boys were hitchhiking in the dead heat of summer, and the finger posturing and loud cursings had ceased, the boys became curiously quiet. There was no conversation of any kind. They were all immersed in their own thoughts. So they did not notice the Cadillac, the same black Cadillac, coming down the freeway again, slowing down, edging onto the shoulder of the road, and heading toward the Filipino boys. When it finally stopped right by the road-side where the boys were walking, and they started coming out of the car, nine of them. "All football player type. No necks. Big, white, and ugly," were just some of the words used to describe the oncoming mass of human bodies.

"That's the motherfucker that gave me the finger." A big blond boy pointed straight at Batok and kept on moving towards him, not hurriedly but steadily. Separate groups had formed with their own conflicts, but the focus of attention was definitely on this particular white boy. He was one of the biggest in the pack.

This could very well be why Batok replied, "No, man. It wasn't me."

Clarence almost imperceptibly tried to take the groceries from Batok's arms. "Go get him, man. You can take 'em"

"That's easy por you to say, *pare*." he said, and held the groceries tighter.

"Don't worry. We'll help you out," Clarence assured him. And tried to yank the bags from Batok.

Batok slid his whole body towards Clarence this time. "Walo sila." He told Clarence in Filipino. There were eight of them.

"No, nine," Clarence retorted in English.

"Yeah, that's the little motherfucker right there." The blond boy got within striking distance of Batok.

Batok tried to stay firm in his denial. "No, man," he said, shaking his head slowly but not taking his eyes off the blond boy who had no neck, a lineman, no doubt.

"Yeah, you! You gave us the finger, right?" Batok was at a loss for words in both languages. He was in a fix and he knew it. He made some sounds, but he said nothing. At least, nothing comprehensible to anyone else.

The big blond boy seemed to be thinking. He thought for a long excruciating while. Then he said, "all right. Let's forget it." He waved his hands shaking his head. He looked around and motioned to the rest of his friends, "Let's get going." They were pretty much all in their car, just a few of the football players were left outside, some even having a pretty friendly conversation with Bong, and Batok actually shook hands with the big blond dude.

As the *puti* turned around to enter the Cadillac, Clarence said quite firmly, pointing, "Just don't think we're afraid of you."

That was when Clarence got hit. By the time Clarence got off the ground and turned around straight, there was a mob of big white dudes around him.

Antonio picked up a big boulder, held it up in the sky and started saying, of all things, "Peace! That's enough! Peace! We're all brothers, goddammit," then hurled the rock towards two or three of the football players huddled around Clarence, who in turn, kept looking for Batok. It probably shocked the rabble into silence, just like in the movies, because surprisingly, there was peace. They looked up at Antonio on some mound, like Moses who had just hurled the tablets of the ten commandments. Scurrying into a more open area, Clarence ran into Batok, who was in a worse predicament. The same big white guy had Batok backing up into a roadside cliff.

"That's the motherfucker that gave me the finger. This one." He picked up his line of contention. He was pointing straight at Batok again, who still had the load of groceries. Clarence offered to relieve him of it again by extending his arms to take it. No response, however, from Batok. Clarence started to pull on his arm, but Batok resisted. He wanted to keep the groceries so he could have an excuse not to fight and maybe the big ox would go on to the next victim. But this was far from random. "There he is. That's the one. Lemme at 'im."

"He wants you," Clarence resignedly told Batok, lightly tugging again at the bag of groceries. Immediately, the white guy lunged at Batok who somehow moved to the side, unhurt. The two Filipino boys looked at each other, and with his right hand holding the bag of groceries and his left arm held up, Batok suddenly screamed "That's enough!"

The White boy had just gotten up anew and was ready to lunge again when Batok repeated, "Don't come any closer. Please." But the white boy lunged again. But this time when he lunged, it looked like he stopped in mid-air like a frozen shot in the movies, because when he landed on the ground, he was back peddling. He had met the point of a butterfly blade in mid-air.

The butterfly knife has very little to do with butterflies. It is called *Balisong* in Filipino. Like real butterflies, the boys' cocoons too were bursting upward and onward and spinning every which way like the way Bong's '62 Impala spun around the red light by the curb of the park's edge by Fulton and 25th Avenue almost every frustrated evening after a party in the City. This was the butterfly knife that the white boy suddenly confronted in mid-air. Batok himself was surprised when he pulled it out so smoothly with his left hand, because in camp he always messed up clearing the hinged part of the handle by the front pocket overlay, and finally taking too long to open the balisong. Batok's hands were more practiced with the microphone, like Clarence's were for the barber's shears. But this time, all in one motion came the opening of the knife as it was pulled out of the pocket, then the close-open close- open action of the palm, the clip-clap of the blade and the ivory handle, and the closing grip on the flying half of the knife itself, then the thrust, all in one motion. Batok was magnificent.

The white boy stopped in mid-air about a hand's length from the blade point and when he landed, he was a good arm's length. "Hey, man. None of that shit. C'mon." Batok did not know whether he detected a pleading tone, but it seemed to him that the white boy's mouth started to resemble that of a duck's. If he were Filipino, one might have said he was pointing with his mouth. "Ppput that down..." But Batok was quiet. He circled around him so that now it was the white boy nearing the edge of the cliff and he spoke again. "Hey, c'mon, man. Put that thing down. Let's fight square. No knives."

Batok only shook his head looking straight at him and said, "No . . . no . . . no", his right arm still carrying the bag of groceries. "You have two hands while I have only one with a knife. That's fair enough, right?"

"Do you know Dominic? He's Filipino. He's a good friend of ours."

"Neber heard ob him. You think we're the only Flips in San Francisco?"

When Batok and Clarence and Antonio and Bong collected themselves, they found they were only staring at each other. There was only the white boy that Batok had cornered by the cliff that was to be seen. The other eight had all scurried and disappeared from view, their Cadillac's engine still running.

"I want you. . . I'm goona get you. . ." Batok's eyes bulged in excitement just like they looked when he sang "Remember When/To my sur-frise" by the Platters. Batok seemed more like he was talking to himself when he almost whispered, "Once op dis day. . .and dat day is here."

When the white guy realized he was alone, he said to Batok, "Listen . . . There's a party. Tonight. And next week, too. We'll give you a ride to your camp. Where are you headed?"

"Green Valley Road. All the way to the orchards," was Batok's quick reply. "You got the keys to this thing? It's still breathing."

"Yeah, of course. It's running ain't it?"

Antonio interfered. He didn't want to let it get hot again. "Well, let's go," he offered.

"Can we wait till at least one of my friends comes back?"

"Sure, why not?" Clarence interjected. "Hey white boys! Where are you? You can come out now. It's over!" He was calling people as if it were the aftermath of a game of hide and seek. Sure enough, the putis started coming back out of nowhere. They emerged out of the freeway, under ramps, mounds of dried tall weeds, behind trees, and out of low bushes. Some still had dried grass stuck to their naked chests.

"It's ok." The big white boy that confronted Batok explained curtly to the rest of the white boys. "It's ok. He's ok. They're ok. They're coming to the party tonight. and maybe next week. You all stay here for now. I'll bring 'em to their camp just down the Highway. Green Valley Road. Be back in about an hour." He turned to the Filipinos and asked. "Can I bring Red with me?" He pointed out a red-headed boy among the approaching white boys. He's my brother."

"Sure. The more the many-er," Clarence answered.

"Stay under this tree here," the white boy told the rest. "We'll be right back. There ain't no room for all of us."

Bong went to dig into some grocery bags and said to the remaining white boys, "Here. Get some drinks from here. And there's some sardines and pork and beans there, I think." And he left them a bagful of food.

All the Filipinos got inside the Cadillac. The blond drove and the redhead sat in the back. They saw the remaining seven white boys mill around the shade of the big Walnut tree by the highway and when the car dipped down into the valley, they disappeared. Inside the car on the way to the camp there was silence in the beginning. After a few tense moments of feeling each other's vibes, they got to talking like old friends with the redhead inviting them again to a party next weekend in Benecia, a town not far off.

Years later, after everyone had returned from the service, we all got together again, and this is how I got to telling this story. They insisted. I told this story to some people before, but I hardly tell it to anyone anymore. Like I said I wasn't really there, and when people find out you weren't really there, they tend to think that you are not telling the truth (as if people who were there always tell the truth), even though it was upon their insistence that I relate the damn thing. We haven't really kept in touch at all. Most got married, got themselves houses, and moved away. Some got divorced and moved away. Some planned to stay because they couldn't move away. Some of the people who stayed, stayed away from each other. Some moved away because they couldn't stay. The last time I heard from Clarence was about three years ago. He phoned one night when it was raining hard. He sounded just as excited as the weather. He was inviting me to come to an Amway party or meeting of some sort, of which he was an aspiring sales director, and that he was going to go back to the Philippines and make millions. My own brother Antonio has been living in Hawaii for about a dozen years. Batok had gone to Las Vegas after a term in jail and disappeared without a trace. Bong went to Alaska one summer and never came back.

There was a fifth person in that incident. Who was that sonofabitch . . .?" This question was always asked at the end of each telling by all the participants, and there would be a litany of curses attributed to that person whom they couldn't remember. "For the life of me I can't think of him now, not just his name. I can't think of any images of him, nor his part in the story....It'll come to me later...I could have sworn there were five of us...Are you sure it wasn't you?"

Before I was. Now, I'm not too sure.

Suite #3
The City

Lou Syquia and author walking down Kearny Street. Photo credit: Tony Remington. ca. 2022

In San Francisco, around mid-September, the days get softer even at noon. The sunlight never gets harsh, always with a certain glow like the light just before dusk. And then sometimes the rains will visit the city; but that would come softly, too.

As the rains disappear, the tennis courts and golfers and street players would proliferate. And Indian Summer would be on its way again. Hot days in September in San Francisco surprise no one. It was during these days that George Cousart and I happened to stumble in getting into the finals of a tennis tournament thrown by the Filipino students and teachers at San Francisco State University during the early days of the Ethnic Studies classes.

George Cousart and I have been playing ball for a while. Basketball. Here and there, out in the streets and on the courts. He was about five years younger than me maybe, so he grew up playing with different crowds in the city. But we heard of each other. He was what is known as a scrapper, a classic hustler all the way, no let-up, in and out, that was George, and it was always good to find yourself on his side in a street game or any game. He played hard but he always played fair, not taking anything personal even though he took and dished out trash-talking at times. If you got through him for a lay-up, he'd be the first to shake your hand. But your hand would be hurting. He was in it a hundred per-cent for a hundred percent of the time, as opposed to me who put out a hun-dred percent but not a hundred percent of the time. I would time my moments of intensity, which, I discovered, was a skill in itself.

One day, George and I found ourselves at a tennis tournament at San Francisco State College (now a university). I think I was already teaching there at the time. Sitting down together waiting for our next matches, we found that neither of us had brought a tennis racket. We really didn't plan to be in the tournament. The organizers just convinced us on the spot. So we borrowed one from the others sitting next to us.

Turned out, I won my first match, against Virgil, who is a perennial athlete, (I think he's still playing until now!), and I don't know how I won that. All I knew was that I just kept hitting the ball back and waited for the other guys to make a mistake. And they always did. There's a bigger lesson there someplace; I just did not grasp it at the time. But my body knew; my movements were wiser than my brain. Then, I think I played Dan Gonzales, the now fabled Ironman of Ethnic Studies. He looked real good, but somehow, I won the match. Same strategy.

Then in the finals, George and I met up. He had surprisedly beaten his op-ponents, too. Right away, I knew George was going to win the match. He was a scrapper, like I said, and whenever I would hit the ball back he would scrappily get to it and hit it back to me! I was on the defensive, by my own doing. So he got first place and I second. This story is really George's but then again, it is really my story, too, because even though it's about George, I'm the storyteller. And when a story is told, it is because of the storyteller that the tale got told to begin with.

I remember that day clearly because after the tournament George had invited me to a wedding that night. His sixty something year old father was getting married. I said I couldn't go that day. My aunt was getting married and I had to drive my parents to the wedding. At the wedding that night I saw George again. Unbeknownst to us, till then, that his father was the groom and my aunt Tia Oning, the beautiful bride. Cousin George.

Prelude To A Gig

San Francisco, back in the day, was everyone's favorite city, 'the city that knows how', cosmopolitan city by the bay, where one grew up with musicians and artists and writers walking its steep and windy streets in almost every neighborhood. This is a story of two artists, one very famous and the other quite obscure.

Charles Mingus, the legendary jazz bassist and composer came in from the San Francisco autumn mist for a game of pool because he had a couple of hours to kill before his performance at the Keystone Korner near Chinatown and Manilatown. Big droplets of slanted rain shone in cars' headlights as the vehicles maneuvered the arduous and glistening streets on this particular night during the era of the sixties merging and forging into the seventies. On Kearny Street, the Mabuhay Restaurant was one of the favorite hangouts of the Filipinos. It was owned by the Masonic Brotherhood of the Dimasalang, one of the largest and most influential Filipino organizations at the time, and it is said that writers like Carlos Bulosan, P.C. Morrante, Stanley Garibay, and many others hung out there during their stay in San Francisco when they wrote pieces for the local Filipino papers and journals, as well as their own creative works.

The Mabuhay had a mid-size counter and several tables for eating. In the back, where happens the real action, as in this case, behind a flimsy faded curtain that split in half, were three pool tables, a big brass spittoon on the floor, hat racks and coat racks, benches that lined the walls, tin-can ashtrays spaced evenly over another counter, and a light bulb above each table. In the pool hall, smoke from cigars and cigarettes floated lazily upwards, becoming distinct shapes where the shafts of light pierced the room.

That game of pool was Mr. Mingus' undoing. Mingus wanted to wait out the hard part of the rain before his gig (he had a couple of hours) when he saw the sign "Mabuhay Restaurant, Food and Pool". It would be a perfect combination for his wait in the rain before his gig up the street at The Keystone Korner. But as it turned out, like most seemingly perfect beginnings, it was a disaster. For at the pool hall of the Mabuhay Restaurant, he had the misfortune of playing Yaw-yaw, the Pinoy hustler from Mindanao. Charles Mingus was a large black man compared to Yaw-yaw, a slightly-smaller-than-medium-size Filipino.

Charles Mingus put his big instrument down beside the door as he checked out the place, seeming to take a liking to it right away. He flicked off beads of raindrops from his long, black cashmere coat and hung it on the rack sticking out of a cement wall.

"Hi. How you all doin'?" he smiled. After a while, he said, "The sign outside said food and pool. I see only food tables. Where are the pool tables?"

"They're right behind that curtain, in the back," Manong Al, an old timer who was not that old and who himself dabbled with the jazz piano, volunteered a reply. "Were you gonna eat first? You know Filipino food?"

"I love that stuff," he said. "Can't get enough of it." He lifted his scarf off his neck and hung that with his coat. "But I never eat before I play," he said, opening his hand, palms up, like a preacher blessing his congregation.

Manong Al meanwhile seemed to be in a state of restrained euphoria. He did not know what to do with himself, as if holding his pee in some discomfort, or in delight.

"Anyone for a game of eight ball? Nine ball? Rotation? Whatever." Charles Mingus ambled toward the curtain and parted it, ducking his head in, the footsteps of his big smile still on his face. It was a friendly smile.

Manong Al meanwhile sidled over to answer the stranger, "Why sure. What you wanna play?" And he followed Mingus inside the curtains.

"Well, whatever you want."

"No, no. Not me. I retired. I just bullshit now. Maybe you play Yaw over there. Hey, Yaw-yaw. C'mon over here. Play some pool with this gentleman."

This backroom was a little darker, and the light was not as uniform as it was in the restaurant. Their brightest spots were, of course, the lightbulbs directly over the pool tables.

"Yeah. Just tryin' to kill some time before my gig up the hill," he said, his voice deep, matching what his bass instrument might sound like.

From the smoke-filled room emerged a brown Asian figure, pool stick in hand, tapping the floor with the handle end and chalking the tip, cocksure and five foot five. "Sure ting," said Yaw-yaw. He had on a crumpled, floppy brimmed hat.

"Howdy, friend," said Mingus and extended his hand. The other looked Mingus up and down.

Manong Al turned to Mingus, and gestured towards the newcomer, "This is Yaw-yaw." The old timer then looked at Yaw-yaw "This is Charlie Mingus," and added, whispering with some restraint in Yaw-yaw's ear, "you dumb, ignorant shit."

Yaw-yaw looked Chinese in Chinatown and looked Japanese in Japantown and looked Pinoy in Manilatown. Because of this he frequented these neighborhoods' pool halls with ease and felt at home there, including George's Pool hall on Buchanan street in Japantown where every game was only a dime and one can buy just up the street, a good Chinese meal for seventy-five cents from Soo Chow's Restaurant which was owned by Koreans.

But Yaw-yaw is Pinoy. He got his name for pretty obvious reasons: he talks a lot when he plays. Yaw-yaw ng yaw-yaw.

"What's your pleasure?" asked the big man.

"Let's do some eight ball."

"Sounds good to me."

Charles Mingus was a large man, not only in status, as in the field of jazz, but also in plain physical stature. He looked almost massive to a Filipino like Yaw-yaw. And his huge case for his string bass did not diminish his stature. Yaw-yaw said, "I break." And they played.

It did not take long for Mingus to start losing and losing big. In fact, he lost more than he could pay. The more he lost, it seemed, the more he got into the game. Yaw-yaw always trapped Mingus into dropping all his own balls too quickly in the game of eight ball. Yaw-yaw would still have a lot of his own balls left before having a shot at the eight ball, but those same balls served as obstacles to Mingus' path of shooting. Those balls would always "hook" Mingus so that he would have no clear shot whatsoever. Then he would have a lot of Yaw-yaw's balls to block his shots every time. And when Yaw-yaw would see an opportune moment, he would shoot straight and true. He would run two or three or four balls at a time, talking and yaw-yawing all the while, and then, at the end, take the game. Mingus could not resist shooting his balls into pockets every time he had the opportunity. He did not know that patience was a virtue especially in pool. He did not plan ahead like Yaw-yaw did. Now he was paying for it. Well, not really, as it seemed to be turning out. The question of paying became the problem.

The big black man's head was turning every which way and saying something about him being short of the money he had just lost to Yaw-yaw. "Well, like I said, I don't think I can cover ALL of it, but I got to go to my gig now or I'll be late, see. But I'm coming right back to cover the rest, okay, brother? I mean I'll be just up the street. That's where I'll get the rest of the dough, see."

Yaw-yaw, small as he was, lunged at Mingus. The big man seemed to have almost laughed in astonishment. But Yaw-yaw was not going after the big man, and that laugh provided the gap of distraction for Yaw-yaw to snatch the big cased instrument of Mingus, almost ripping it from the latter's loose grip. As Mingus' head snapped left and right for some explanation, from someone, anyone, Yaw-yaw quickly swept the instrument away, like a bride, to the toilet. Everyone heard the lock click from the inside. "You give me my goddam money, I give you your instrument." He shouted from inside the toilet.

"I got a gig in half an hour, Joe."

"Das your problem. Your word is as good as cash you said. And my name ain't Joe, Joe."

"Name's Charles. My name ain't Joe, either. I'll get the cash for you. Right after the gig. C'mon man. I'm only short 25 dollars. I'll give you the 25 plus another 25 after the gig. Come to the show. Bring whoever you like. I'll give it to you right there."

"He doesn't know you, Mr. Mingus", said Manong Al turning to the musician, trying to explain. "I mean, of you."

Yaw-yaw true to his name shouted from the toilet : "I know him. He gambles without any money! He's gotta pay before he plays"

"He had the money Yaw-yaw. It ran out. Just like everything else."

"Yeah? Why did he keep playing, then?"

"Because he's a stupid gambler like you. I seen you do it lots of times."

For a while there was dead silence. "Do I have to pay?" came the voice weakly from inside the toilet.

"Pay for what?" Asked Manong Al.

"For the show up the street."

"Of course not. I'll take you in myself," Mingus interrupted.

"Nah, you don't' need to do that," came Yaw-yaw's quick reply, his tone slightly softening. "I'll be there, though. I wanna hear you play dat ting. Al says you're good. He's the one who knows music. Hear him play the piano. It'll make you cry." Though not loud, Yaw-yaw's voice rang clear in that toilet acoustic. He opened the toilet door just a wee bit, ever so slowly, and asked, "You really want to go, huh, Manong?"

"Yeah, he's good, Yaw-yaw."

"I hope he's not good like the way he shoots pool."

"He's good, believe me. Angels will be singing to you, Youngblood. And you'll remember your first kiss, man." Manong Al said.

"First kiss? First kiss my fist!" Yaw-yaw snaked his way out of the toilet and appeared tightly hugging the instrument and added: "you sure he's good? I play, too, you know."

"I know. I know you play, Youngblood. I heard you pluck that guitar."

"Come with me, then."

"You bet I will."

The two Pinoys turned to Mingus. "Take it." Said Yaw-yaw. "Go on. I'll just go up the street to the International Hotel and clean up a bit, then we'll be at the joint."

"I'll be waiting. My word is cash."

"You said that before. We'll see," said Yaw-yaw

"Do you guys do 'Prelude to a Kiss'?" asked Manong Al. "I like that."

"You just show up, baby. We'll do it for you."

Yaw-yaw handed Mingus his enormous instrument case until the big man got complete hold of it. "Here," said Yaw-yaw curtly. Mingus grabbed the case and quickly turned to go. Without smiling or saying a word, he lumbered up Kearny Street, then Columbus Avenue, then he was gone.

Beside the famous Hungry-I nightclub, across the street in his room at the International Hotel, as he was quickly getting ready, Yaw-yaw thought of his own guitar playing days as a youth among the vast plantation fields of Dole in Mindanao. Yaw-yaw was a guitar player himself who had a makeshift band in his hometown in the Visayas. It was a rag-tag type of band with a one-string bass grounded on an upside down washbasin, a wash board for some fancy percussion, a guitar and/or a ukulele, and for vocals, whoever was drinking and/or handy at the time. He played guitar with a lot of spontaneity (the way he played pool) all his life so he could be considered a jazzman, only his text was Filipino music with some contemporary mainstream U.S.A. music around the Second World War era. But this Charles Mingus fellow he had never heard of before. He put on a fresh dip of his Three Flowers Brilliantine pomade then placed his floppy-brimmed hat on his head. He was ready to step out.

He met Manong Al waiting at the lobby and the two started walking towards the Keystone Korner. "Are you sure about this Mingus cat, Manong?"

"He's the real McCoy, Youngblood. Ain't you heard of Charlie Mingus, man? That's him!" said Manong Al.

"Mingus, my ass," said Yaw-yaw. "He owes me money and he's gotta pay."

"I told you he's the fucking legendary jazz musician, you idiot!"

"Mingus cunnilingus, my ass." Yaw-yaw mumbled.

"What kind of musician are you? You don't even know the masters of the trade!"

"The kind who can play pool."

When they turned the corner, they saw a line at the ticket booth hidden under the awning, folks smoking and making small talk, their collars turned up against the wind and misty rain. The gig was about to start but there was some commotion at the bar inside. Yaw-yaw spotted Charles Mingus through a crowd of people and he in turn saw Yaw-yaw. Mingus waved and smiled and immediately talked to someone near him, gesturing towards Yaw-yaw near the ticket booth. Before Yaw-yaw and Manong Al got to their turn on the line at the ticket booth, someone from the joint came up to them and whispered something in their ears, whisking them away to a choice seat, front and center.

Then the show began. Mingus, when the music started, seemed to have forgotten about Yaw-yaw altogether. He never looked at him once. First, the notes started hovering around Yaw-yaw's sentimental rememberings. He recognized some of the tunes but it was the notes themselves and their sounds that took Yaw-yaw away. Each note rang crystal clear and the tone that came out of the trumpet player resonated in his brain even when he was not playing anymore. The musicians played independent of, yet essential to, each other. Like smoke from the pool hall lazily drifting into the night, the saxophone came in as subtle as the rain. He was not familiar with any of the players, but Yaw-yaw loved the sounds they orchestrated. The saxophone's silky maneuverings took him away, past remembering, and behind it all persisted the pulse of Mingus's bass. Somewhere, somehow, he heard the rondallas of his hometown in the Philippines. Then they played "Prelude to a Kiss" for Manong Al and they called and mentioned his name and told the audience that he too played some and if he would like to dabble with the piano and play along with them.

"Hell yah, das his paborit!" shouted Yaw-yaw. Al jumped up on stage leveraged by his arm. He played and they all played along with him and Yaw-yaw was carried away into the well-deep days of his childhood in the Visayas and his wandering days in Mindanao.

After the show, Mingus came up to Yaw-yaw and paid off the twenty five plus another twenty five—fifty bucks. "Here," said Mingus. "I got the man to give me the night's pay in advance." This time it was Yaw-yaw who did not look at Mingus. Or the money. He just quickly took it and walked up to the tip jar by the edge of the raised stage area and said to Al, "Godammit," and dropped twenty five dollars in the jar. "You're right. He's good." Then he turned and walked away without saying anything to Mingus.

Walking back to Manilatown in the steady rain that night, Yaw-yaw told Manong Al, "I didn't know music could be played like that."

"This, I think, I have been telling you for years."

"Take you from sad to glad in just seconds. And for real, too! Real sad and real joy, you know. I saw the notes hovering like in the rondallas before when I was young in the Philippines, you know. You tell that Mingus, Manong Al, that next time he comes to town, drop by and get a good ol' fashioned Filipino meal from the Mabuhay Restaurant. My treat. I robbed him of his dinner tonight."

That's Yaw-yaw. Still talking.

Drought

Out my window
The whoosh of tires in the rain

A woman wailing in a foreign language
Echo on the wind-cave corner
Of slanted Columbus and Jackson Streets

Would that I were the earth
today
bathed and quenched by the tempest
of your company.

Dec. 11, 2020

The Fairmont Suite
(Balato)

It was late afternoon and the man stood above and in front of his desk at Bessie Carmichael School staring at the embossed invitation card from the Philippine Consulate, the Indonesian Consulate, and the San Francisco Unified School District, for the event to be held at the San Francisco Fairmont Hotel. The letterings of 'Teacher of the Year Award' were in gold. Lifetime achievements noted. The handwriting was beautiful in fancy penmanship. Please accept. Truly honored. Great and noble profession. Those old cliché's, he thought, were sure to be spoken. The ambassador from Indonesia, a guest of the Consulate, and former beauty queen, was to present the award. The man kept looking out the window, into the city, then at the card lying on his desk. He moved a crystal ball for paper weight and as the snowflakes within the sphere proliferated, he suddenly felt small, and inside the transparent orb, he saw himself 40 years ago, a youth of seventeen.

This tale is one of the many antediluvian stories of the Bay before it was drowned by the Great Flood of the dot.com industry which swept and swallowed the City itself. This was some time ago. And if one were to take a magic carpet ride over the city at that time, one would have seen a stark contrast between two adjacent areas, two aortas, in the heart of the city.

The area south of Market Street, SoMa, was called Central City at the time of this story. Not many folks call it that now. That's what time will do. It can change names. That district Central City was at opposite poles with its next-door neighbor to its north, The Financial District, not just in geography. They differed in almost every aspect, a tale of two districts: in culture, appearance, maintenance, prestige, privilege, and of course, in money.

There was a young girl Triana, who lived in Central City and who was, like many others in that area, not rich, but did not know it, but also very smart, and of course did not know that either, and because of that innocence, became, to some, even more beautiful.

During early mornings, sometimes Roldan, Triana's older brother would hear faint music, jazz music, coming from their sala, living and dining room combined, on Clementina Street and he knew that his father was doodling with his guitar again. He had caught him several times jotting things down by hand, then strumming a rift of some kind on his guitar. He was an early riser, his father, and he hardly missed a note in listening even while writing. Words, too, were notes to him. Pops had told him that the rhythm kept the two together, the words and the notes. "It's like playing 'double-dutch?' jump-rope while singing and rhyming," adding, "like the Harlem Globetrotters do at pregame layups to the music of Sweet Georgia Brown." In the afternoons, sometimes, he would hear Pops do dishes while listening to music. "Music to wash dishes by," his father would turn around with a smile, sensing his presence.

His father, Roldan De la Cruz, worked near the edge of that Financial District as kitchen help and cook's assistant in a posh elegant hotel, the Fairmont, one of the very high class hotels in the City, and was paying for their most expensive Catholic schooling, Jesuit St. Ignatius High School for him, and St. Joseph Elementary for his sister Triana. Nob Hill is the name of the neighborhood upon which the Hotel stood, with cable cars clanging and climbing to the stars, just like the song says. The money here is older than the Financial District money, but of course, the faster money belong to the young. But they are, as the common folks and the Manongs say, 'all same pareho'. Money is money.

Mr. De la Cruz had won at keno in Reno just as he had predicted a thousand times before, that he would be lucky when his armpit started itching that Sunday afternoon at St. Patrick's Church, as the bells were ringing, and where they had Tagalog Mass. Of course, he has had a thousand other excuses or reasons or "signs from above" in the past for being lucky: the itchy palm, the wore-a-shirt-or-underwear inadvertently backwards, *baliktad* (reversed), the discovery of wearing unmatched socks, a vision of something gross and foul (like stepping on dog shit, or dreaming of any kind of shit), so he had naturally concluded for it to be his lucky day...again. But on the one thousand and oneth time of this bullshit, it finally happened. He won in Reno. He struck it. Twelve hundred dollars. He could have won more if he bet the max, but he only bet the minimum because he wanted to cover other bets. So, with this money, as balato, (or gift from a winner) on Triana's birthday, that following Saturday, he decided he would take his son Roldan and his daughter Triana out to dine at the grand Fairmont Hotel where he worked. First class. So, he booked a suite for that Saturday night for the three of them.

"There was a phone call for you earlier, Junyor." Said the father putting down a dish gently on the rack.

"Yeah, I know, Pops. That's what got me up."

"Your friend from the Consulate again?"

"I gotta help him drive around guests of the Consulate. They need drivers." He was dressing up as he was talking to his father. He usually does not get up that early, but that day, that nothing-happening Tuesday, he had to because his friend had asked him to help with driving some diplomats' guests. His friend the Consul's son is a classmate of his in their high school, and is sometimes volunteered by the father to drive guests around, with or without telling his friend beforehand. The specific assignment this time: driving some beauty queens from Asian countries around the city. Miss Philippines, a Margie Moran, of course, was one of them. It would be sort of a tour guide, but not paid, just tips and free food, and driving a fancy car. They needed drivers and his friend had asked Roldan.

"For how long?" The father asked.

"I think they told me about a week. I'll have to work it around school hours"

"A week?" He thought for a while. "Just make sure about Saturday, okay?"

"Of course, Dad. Saturday. You going to work today, Pops?"

"No. Off today. Got errands to do," said the father, still putting dishes down slowly, and winked. "Be at the Fairmont this Saturday, ok, Junyor?"

"Sure thing. That's where they're billeted anyway."

"Who?"

"The beauty queens."

"What beauty queens?"

"The ones that we have to drive around for the Philippine Consulate."

"Ah, the Ambassadors of Love, I see. Don't forget, ha. Saturday night," he whispered looking around, "The Tonga Room." And he put his index finger on his lips.

"Mums the word, Pops," Roldan said.

"Your sister is going to be in and out of the Fairmont kitchen again so make sure she does not get a clue, ok? You know her. *Osiosa yan*, very curious, and will figure things out before you know it."

"Don't worry, Pa."

"Can you take her with you as you drive those people? Not all the time. Just once or twice."

He thought for a while. "Sure. Why not? I'll take her." And added, "when I can." Just before leaving, Roldan said, "Pops, the Tonga Room, ha? Mom would have sure liked that."

"We used to go to the Tonga Room once in a while when we were dating. Couldn't afford to do it often. That woman loved to dance. All night long and into the morning she would still be smiling and dancing on that floating stage that splits on the water," chuckled his father. "And she would sing that 'fifties' song 'I'll Be Tired of You' all the way home. Okay. Remember..." and he put his finger on his lips again.

He was exempt from most of his exams so it was a loose week for him.

That's the best part about the Jesuits, he always thought. They knew how to reward you. His friend, the Consul's son, met him at the Fairmont lobby. He had a car for him to drive, automatic transmission and all.

"Ok, what's the deal, man?" asked Roldan.

"Your dad works at the Fairmont, right?" said the Consul's son.

"Yeah, so."

"So, everything is convenient for you. The beauty queens are billeted here, at the Fairmont. And we'll have the hook-ups from your dad's network of Filipino workers: food, entertainment, The Tonga Room, the works!"

"But what about the pay? No money, huh? Again."

"No money, man. Just tips. They always give, though. My dad sprung this on me again. Listen, I had plans, too, man. Hey, what the hell, free food, fancy car... and expensive places!"

At the lobby of the Fairmont Hotel on California Street, when the two boys were greeting each other, she appeared, no one knew from where, from up the stairs or from the front desk or from the elevator or from the bathroom or wherever, and like his father's favorite tune, *Laura*, she seemed to have come out of a dream. Her gold and scarlet scarf wrapped over her head and onto her shoulders. One bare forearm had a wooden bracelet wrapped around it.

"Roldan, this is Miss Indonesia and Miss Asia Pacific. Yes, she wears two crowns. And her name is Beauty. Miss, this is my friend Roldan. I told you about him. He will be your driver...and guide. You will never see San Francisco like this guy will show you. Whether you've been here before or not, he'll show you San Francisco like you've never seen it before. Every street a story. Amazing, this guy."

"Yeah, right." Roldan retorted.

The Consul's son gave Roldan the keys to the car and disappeared into the revolving door.

"They thought there were two of us, but I had won both titles, so I am the only passenger. Is that okay?" She finally spoke.

"Whatever you say. Your name is Beauty?

"Yes," she laughed a bit. "And my birthday is on Valentine's Day," her laugh trailed to a smile. "No kidding. Hopeless romantic, they say."

"Let's look at what the schedule says here."

He pulled something out from his bag and unfolded a schedule with maps of stops throughout the city. "Let's see. Fisherman's Wharf is here, then, Golden Gate, then the crookedest Street..."

"You know, this is a very famous hotel... for its elegance and all."

"Yes, I heard. I live here so sometimes I forget. Like the cable cars...or the

Golden Gate Bridge. Did you know that the first person who crossed that bridge was a Filipino? Yup. Look it up. The banker who financed it was officially the one on record, but it was really the banker's Filipino driver who test drove the bridge first."

"Really?" She said.

"Yes. Look it up."

"I will. Every landmark a story, as well, huh?" Touching her scarf, she looked at him, "Now, are those the places in that list you yourself would like to go to?"

"Well, no, not really."

"They're recommended, right? Not really compulsory."

"Correct," he said. "I think."

"Let's go to the places you want to see, too. So, it won't be just me who's going to have fun."

"Are you sure you won't get in trouble?"

"Why, who will tell on me? You?"

Her skin was of a cinnamon brown shine, and soft when he brushed by it, gently with his elbow while looking at the map. "Here, take this," and she removed her wooden arm bracelet. "From my country to you."

"Wow, thanks. Let's check our itinerary again. Ok, let's get the outlying sights taken cared of first. Let's head for…Half Moon Bay."

"Is that part of the City?"

"It's part of the family… of cities around the bay, around several bays, really. It's all about family here," he said as he turned away to head for the revolving door.

"How old are you, may I ask?" They both stepped into the opening panel.

"Seventeen," he said, "just like the Sinatra song," and added, "graduating this year." He wanted to ask her age, too, but he knew better.

"I know the tune. Wow. Big year for you, huh? About prom time now, right? Going?"

He handed the car keys that the Consul's son had given him to the valet and waited on the curb with Beauty standing beside him.

"Nah. I don't think so. My dad doesn't believe in spending for those kinds of things."

"*Kuripot* huh. Like me."

"You know Tagalog? I didn't know you could speak."

"What do you mean? I've been speaking to you all this time."

"But you're Indonesian. I mean, speak Tagalog."

"I know what you mean. Pretty much the same people. Besides, I think I am going to end up marrying a Filipino, like you."

"Really?"

"It's all pretty much set up for me. Handsome and quite well to do," she continued. "He is one of the pageant coordinators."

"Oh, I see. Lucky guy."

"That remains to be seen." She said, smiling, and smoothing her skirt from behind, she ducked in one motion onto the seat of the car whose door the valet had just opened.

Inside the car, the youth Roldan said, "There's still plenty of daylight, so I think you'll appreciate this first stop. And remind me to take you to this far-out Indonesian restaurant by Clement Street tomorrow," he said, obviously trying to make some impression.

"Please," she said smiling. "Can we skip that? I eat that thing every day."

"Oh, yeah, huh? Sorry about that. I was thinking of myself."

"You mean you wanted to—"

"It's just that I wanted to try it, having not eaten there before."

"Ok, let's go then."

"It's ok. I wouldn't know what to order anyway."

"Take me there tomorrow and I'll order for us. I did say 'let's go to the places you wanted to go', after all, right?"

The ride took about thirty minutes. She was thoroughly enjoying it, soaking in all the sights and sounds, from the freeway then out through winding roads in Pacifica. They went through treacherous but strikingly beautiful roads through Devil's Slide, and passed the nudist San Gregorio beach. They stopped by Princeton Beach and got some clam chowder with fish and fries. They cruised around Moss Beach, then at Nick's Rockaway Moonraker, in the early approaching sunset, they had a silhouetted conversation. They walked along the water's edge then took a table outside the plaza promenade and sat waiting for their orders in the wind and pounding surf. Beauty ordered white wine, sauvignon blanc; he, a peanut butter shake and a cookie. She insisted on paying for it.

When the lights were just popping on at lamp posts, he drove all the way to the middle of the Bay Bridge, turned into an exit on Treasure Island and drove on a darkening road which looked empty at the end of it, only parking places. At its edge, they had a breathtaking view of both the East Bay and San Francisco, and the glittering city lights in the crisp soft winds of the evening. "It's good to be alive!" she gasped, turned and spread her arms. I guess beauty queens do that all the time, he thought to himself.

"Your Mom?" She asked.

"No more. I was just a boy."

"Sorry."

"That's okay. Just Pops, me and my sister, that little pest. You'll find out for yourself."

On their way back to the Fairmont, they passed through the Financial District, North Beach, Broadway's night lights, and Chinatown. Entering the Fairmont and after getting her room keys for her, he left her at the lobby and went downstairs to the kitchen and said hello to one of his dad's compadres. "He's not here. Took the day off. Busy preparing for you know what."

"Yes, I know, Uncle. He told me. Just wanted to say hello. I had to drop off someone here at the hotel. When do you get off?"

"Soon. I have to get back to the hotel. There's another meeting. They are still demonstrating to oppose the eviction. Lots of action der."

"Is the room taken tonight? I mean, can I look at it now?"

"Oh yeah, no problem, Junyor. We got it all covered. We told Sam the manager, we have it reserved. He gets no more lumpia and adobo, otherwise. Here are the keys. Go check it out. It's beautiful, man. Pirs class. Goodnight."

"Goodnight." He lived down the hill at the International Hotel, where many of his dad's compadres and old timers lived and where recently, the tenants have been given their eviction notices. Roldan remembered as a boy, from Kearny street to downtown, even on rainy days, he never used an umbrella because he knew how to avoid the raindrops by the awnings of buildings he would duck under.

He could not resist it. He went up to the suite that his father had reserved and beheld in awe all the amenities: the bold 360 degrees view of the Bay and the Ocean, the hills of the City, the cable cars, accessibility of various shops, and the first class entertainments inside. It seemed to have had more mirrors in more places and in different sizes than any other item in the room.

When he got home on Clementina Street, his father was sitting down, a table with a lamp in front of him.

"How was it?"

"It was fine, Pops. Which one was kuripot, you or Mom?"

"Who do you think?"

"I think it was her."

"Um hum."

"Why are you still so tight then, in things like the prom?"

"Got to be a habit, I guess. I was just finishing up this letter for my niece back home, your first cousin. She's going to take the medical exams soon. She's a sharp one, that girl."

"Don't put the money in with the letter again, Dad. I'll send it tomorrow. Miss home much?"

"You get used to it. Like arthritis." Stretching and flexing his fingers.

"Is it bad? Does it hurt?"

"Not if I keep playing the guitar." He laughed. "Man, my hands were so good before, Junyor." And he looked at them. "I was the champion at marbles in my neighborhood in Manila." He shook them like he was flicking off beads of water. "And in basketball, here by St. Patrick, all around the City…like wild birds at my bidding, quick and graceful, my fingers then."

"I know, Pops. I heard."

"Ay, sometimes I feel like a man with a baseball bat on a football field, hehe-he. But that was then. Now is now. Enough of that syet."

The second day, Wednesday, was the usual obligatory, designated tour with which he and Beauty had to comply: Fisherman's Wharf, Golden Gate Bridge, Chinatown, North Beach, the usual. That second day was the day that Roldan almost quit. He was discouraged by what he saw when he drove Beauty all around and watched her from a distance being engulfed and enjoyed by all the men, young and old, and she enjoying it all, as well. All he did that day was wait and wait and wait for her. He had to wait nearby, at calling distance, so he was forced to watch the goings-on around her. He could hear a cacophony of various languages. He recognized Filipino, Spanish, Indonesian, Dutch, French, and English among them. She changed outfits about three times, all batik, how-ever. Miss Indonesia was chatting and laughing with the dapper Consulate men of positions, he supposed, even though some of them looked as young as he. He heard her laughter, though faintly from a distance, for he was by the door watching the car, and she, wine glass in her hand, was way in the grand room with a partition half open. He could tell that laugh even though he heard it only a few times. But they were alone when he had heard her laughter so he could remember distinctly. Not like now. Only he was alone. She was being showered by compliments, and stories and conversations galore by all the men, like the proverbial swarming bees buzzing around her. He wondered if the other beauty queens were as popular. But Miss Indonesia was very good with people, he no-ticed. She was enjoying herself thoroughly which made the people around her, both men and women, enjoy themselves thoroughly, too. He tried hard to be happy for her. He almost welcomed and looked forward to the next day when his sister Triana would join them.

When all the festivities had subsided and she had gone to him waiting out-side where the stars were already peeking from the sky, Beauty asked,

"Did you still want to go to that Indonesian restaurant?"

"No, that's all right. Next time. It's getting late."

Triana appeared the next morning, on the third day, at the lobby, when

Roldan and Beauty were sitting down looking at the map. Like Beauty's entrance before her, she came out of nowhere, either from the bathroom or the stairway or the elevator, or the revolving door, or from the street. All of a sudden, she was there.

Roldan rushed towards his sister and was zipping up Triana's backpack because she had it slung awkwardly, and half open. "Girl, can't you even put on a backpack properly?"

"It was all right when I put it on earlier. Here, let me just take it off now." And she unloaded the backpack onto Roldan, her kuya and older brother of five years.

"Hello," she rushed to Miss Indonesia. "So happy to meet you. He's been talking about you. I want you to know that right off."

"I told you about her." He side-eyed Beauty.

"Well, it seems he's been talking about me, too. He's really *tsismoso,* this guy."

"Very pleased to meet you, at last. Yes, he has talked of you. I cannot tell a lie. Well, we can talk about him now."

"Shall I call you your highness, or something? What do they call you?"

She laughed and answered: "*Ateh* will do"

"Hey, you picked up on that Tagalog, too, huh?" She said.

"*Ateh* is Chinese for older sister," said Roldan.

"Yeah, but Filipinos use it more than the Chinese." Said Triana.

"Some people are better with languages than others, I guess," said Miss Indonesia."

"I think that's beautiful," said Roldan. "That's why you're good with people."

"How long have you been on this... tour?" asked the girl.

"Over three weeks now."

"Must miss home. My dad always talks like he misses his home. Indonesia is near the Philippines?"

"Yup. Very close. Yes, I miss home terribly."

"Know what's my favorite part of pageants? The 'if you ruled the world' question. You know, 'what would you do to help the world' question."

"That is mine, too!"

"Know what I'd say? I'd say on any matter of weapons and war, only those 20 years old and younger can vote. They have the most at stake and will live longer. And I'll be one of them. You know, sort of reverse the voting age."

"Wow, what a great idea. You're so smart!"

"It's elementary for us."

"Triana, I forgot to tell you that Miss Indonesia is also Miss Asia Pacific. She wears both crowns. My sister likes crowns."

"You've been telling her a lot, huh? *Tsismoso*."

"He can't help it. He is a storyteller. It's his nature." Beauty reminded her with a smile.

"Hmmm," said the girl. "Who smells nice around here? Like the forest after the rain. Don't tell me that's that 4711 cologne that's been collecting dust on your dresser finally getting some use."

"Classy men use such things selectively, you know. It's not an everyday thing." He turned slightly to Miss Indonesia, "I told you about the pain in the—''

She nodded and touched him, smiling to interrupt.

"She's just proud of you."

"Where does she get such an attitude?" He asked.

"She's a princess. And a smart one. That's where she gets it."

Triana said. "Come with me, your Maj . . . *Ateh*, and I will show you my world." With Roldan behind, she took Beauty down the stairs of the lobby, and into a world of shiny clanging metals, of every equipment imaginable for cooking.

Triana had taken Beauty into the kitchen of the grand Fairmont Hotel, her "palace of pots and pans", where she knew every pot and every pan, every tray of different shape, and every unusual looking utensil because she had hung out there as a kid when she went to school when their mom was alive. Roldan, meanwhile, had gone into another room and greeted and talked to his father's compadres. It took Roldan a good half hour to get everything straight for the surprise and still not everything was set; still negotiating a place to put them for the Tonga Room.

"I have a sister at home in Indonesia and she's fifteen." She was smiling whimsically, not looking at anything or anyone in particular, looking a little hyp-notized by the sparkle on the giant silver pot hanging. Her eyes were looking far away it seemed, but not squinting. Miss Indonesia was still in Indonesia.

"We did not part on good terms when I left." She continued." Then she turned to her, "It was my fault, really. I was advising her to go against her heart. She wanted to be a teacher, and I was against it. She wants to be a teacher. So sweet to see you and your brother together. Is he ever tough on you? Never made you cry?"

"No. never."

"You see. That's what I mean."

"Tough? I know he's soft."

"But he doesn't know that you know that."

"Who knows what boys have in their minds?" said Triana, "are you in love with this guy you're gonna marry?"

Beauty looked at the girl.

"I told you that brother of mine is tsismoso. He told me all about it. Or are you in love with someone else? Or you don't know whether it's love or not?"

"Well, ah...are we supposed to know? Well, it's not quite that melodramatic." She laughed. "I'm really thinking more about my quarrel with my sister. You remind me of her."

When Roldan returned, Triana showed them the way to get from the basement out into the street through a lifter, a sort of an open elevator for workers and deliveries. From that culinary dungeon underground, they emerged outside into California Street, walked out into the sidewalk, greeted by cable cars and sunshine.

They got on the rented new Impala from the Consulate and continued to drive towards the ocean. Just past Lincoln Golf Course clubhouse, late that afternoon, at the Palace of the Legion of Honor, when he came out of the bathroom into the long walkway past the statue of El Cid, he saw her outside seated on the circular stone bench surrounded by the parking spaces that looked out into the city's magnificence. Her head was down, and bare, accented by the absence of her hijab. He felt a veil of sadness draped over her young face. He had to say something...

"A cookie for your thoughts?"

"Oh, it's nothing. Where's your sister?"

"Bathroom inside."

"Here I am gone only three weeks, not even a month, and complaining, while your dad has not been back to his home since he left some thirty years ago!"

"Since his youth, since ... my age. Seventeen, like me!"

"He never told you to go against your heart," she said sadly, "like I did to my sister."

"She'll get over it. You know how kids bounce back. She probably won't even remember," he said. Now, it was the youth's turn to be despondent. They were silent for a while. "Shame should be on me. I saw it quickly in you, but in my own father, whom I've been watching all my life, I did not see till you let me see."

She looked at him and smiled, "But you are still young".

"Well, so are you, right?"

"We are both young; you are right there. *Korek ka dyan.*" And they saw Triana emerge from the Museum building walking towards them.

The next day, Friday, he got up extra early to drop off Triana at school before coming to the Fairmont.

"The Princess will not be joining us today, your highness," he explained to Beauty when he picked her up outside waiting in the blustery winds of the bay. In the open, he liked seeing her feel good. He could see it in the bounce of her walk, in the swing of her arms and expectant face when she was about to see another section of the City. He saw the little girl in her.

"What's next?" She asked eagerly with almost a giggle, and slung her bag back, ready to march off again.

"I gotta get some gas…and cash. Hope you don't mind stopping by this place."

He stopped by Palace Billiards on Market Street where he knew some of his friends would be hanging out. He would get that money that Freddie Egot owed him, or maybe he can borrow from Mando the Eyeball if he's there.

"I'll be right back," he said.

"I want to come," she said, getting out of the car, "Ladies' room," walking up right behind him.

The Palace Billiards' diverse crowds of youths were there. They saw Miss Indonesia enter and their eyes grew wide, even the almond shaped Asian ones got rounded. "I can play pool." She told him.

"That's good," he said. "I'm average, I guess." When she got out of the bathroom, she walked straight to the pool table where Roldan was.

"You ready?"

"Let's go," he touched her lightly to turn to leave.

"Where are you going?"

"Out."

"I meant are you ready to play pool. Let's play first, ok?"

"Why, sure. Nine ball?

"Whatever. You break."

She was wicked on the table. Twice she almost ran the table with the few remaining balls. They played two games. She beat him both times. He had to do some convincing but he got Mando the Eyeball of the Kearny Boys to lend him some money. Freddie Egot wasn't around to pay him back. She came out of the place laughing like a loon onto the sidewalk. "Took about five minutes to beat you in two games of nine ball!"

"I was in a hurry," he retorted. "To lose."

They drove directly to Stow Lake near where the buffalos were in the middle of the Golden Gate Park and there they got on a canoe and rested floating around the lake for a while. It was mid-afternoon, so Roldan paddled to a shade of a willow tree. She looked for something in her bag and pulled out a couple of chicken salad sandwiches that she had bought on the dock. They ate quietly while their canoe sat still on a branch underwater.

"How did you get out of school these last couple of days, ha?"

"J.R.S. The Jesuit Reward System." The sunlight played and shimmered on the water through branches and leaves. "If you have an A going into the finals, you are exempt from finals. I have three such subjects."

"Wow! What about your assignments now?"

"I talked to them already. I'll hand 'em in next week. I'm tight with them."

"You sure?"

"Yes. Mister Tollini, my Latin teacher who spits when he gets passionate about a passage in Vergil's Aeneid, 'hazards of the game' he would say to the ones in front. And there's Father Becker, English teacher, who had arranged a date for me before with a girl from Mercy High School. And then there's Father Ryan, ex-prisoner of (and they say tortured by) the Communists in China, and who always asked me, when I served as an altar boy, for some more wine during Mass. He would extend his venerable arm to me, More, more son. A little more." And they both laughed.

"It's a beautiful city, Roldan, your city."

"And you've seen lots of cities around the world, I bet."

"I've seen a few."

"Well, tomorrow is my sister's big day, so I am getting my friend, the one who introduced us, to drive you. I might not see you, what with all the things planned for that night."

"Of course, I'll see you. We are also guests of the Tonga room that night, remember?"

"Oh, yes, of course. At night. We'll see you then?"

"I would not miss it for the world."

Saturday came and at home Roldan was trying to keep things quiet and not spill the beans. He had talked to Lily's band at the Tonga Room, to spotlight Triana when the time came, but the hotel was giving him trouble in getting a place for hotel workers to have a table in the Tonga Room because it was all fully booked for the Consulates and their guests. They were claiming that those places were reserved for the beauty queens, media, promoters, diplomats and staff, and politicians.

That night, the Tonga room was all decorated quite intimately, with Lily's band on the floating island. When Roldan arrived, a crowd had gathered around a table with his father and his friends discussing something strongly with their white head waiter. From the side entrance, Miss Indonesia was just walking in and quickly came to him and walked him toward the spot of discussion, her arm crooked to his.

"How did you like your driver and the places you went to today?" he asked.

"Fine. We passed by Central City, your sister's Elementary School, St. Patrick's Church, your high school, then the University of San Francisco, Lone Mountain

College. Beautiful, beautiful campus, that one. Your friend talks more than you." She was a natural person not afraid to touch and get close and sometimes when she spoke her face was right in front of him. "But," she continued, "you say more. Listen," and tightened the grip on his arm. "They can't eat in the Tonga Room with the other guests because they are the help. Hotel policy or protocol. The desk just informed me, and I asked to see the manager. Here he is."

"Ms. Asia Pacific, how radiant you look!", the manager commented. "What can I do for you?" She took him aside.

"What seems to be the trouble here, Sam?"

"Well, Miss, the thing is the whole place is taken and there are no seats left, what with all the v.i.p.'s and all…" He was wiping his forehead with a white handkerchief.

"Well, surely you will be watching, Sam, right? Because I had one reserved for you here, is that ok? Next to me?"

"Why yes, of course, your high…I mean, Madam…er Miss."

"Perfect. Well, there you are. Triana's birthday group will sit here, right by your chair, Sam. And mine. I'll reserve your chair while you're busy helping other people. Ok?"

"Okay, Mada…mis. No problem."

In less than a minute, Sam the manager was all smiles and saying 'of course, of course' repeatedly.

Roldan made all the introductions around the table, his father beaming most proudly, Triana at his side, and several of his barkadas.

"Ah, yes, the Ambassadors of Love are always welcome in my world." Mr. De la Cruz said to Beauty.

"I've heard so much about you!" She said, offering her hand.

"I told you, Pops. He's *tsismoso*. You're little boy is *tsismoso*." Triana tried to interject.

The band asked Miss Indonesia to sing a tune with them. She got up and walked gracefully along the aisle into the front and was escorted up the stage. She sang 'I'll Be Tired of You". Afterwards, she got off the stage, signaled the light man like a pro and the spotlight followed her down the stage walking toward Triana. Miss Indonesia removed one arm from behind her and swung it upwards to the front and above to place a tiara of a myriad sparkling colors on Triana's head.

"Fits perfectly; I knew it." said Miss Indonesia. "Because at this table, there is not only a queen, there is also a princess. A princess of Central City." And she kissed the girl like a mother. "Happiest of birthdays, your Majesty," she said. And that night sparkled in everyone's memory.

Indeed, Roldan did not see her anymore after that night. He heard the next day that she had taken an early flight with the rest of the beauty queens to Manila. Miss Philippines, Margie Moran, went on to win the Miss Universe contest that year, and he never saw her again. She had disappeared, like the name Central City, like the City itself, in the days before the great flood of the dot.com industry.

From the table, beside the crystal ball paperweight, he slowly picked up a brown wooden arm-band beside the elegant invitation, slid it into his pocket, and once again looked at the card. Forty years had passed. The janitor of the school who sometimes reminded him of his father was closing up and turning off some of the lights, shutting some doors. He entered his room, looking at him, "It's all right, Sir. You can take your time. I'll close up after you leave. Take your time. After all, you took your time for them."

"Thanks, Pop. I mean. What am I saying? It's been a long day...I'll be right out.".

The night lights outside glittered soft and warm, welcoming him to step forward and, in his retirement years, take his place in a destiny he sensed yet to be played out in the fullness of time. Like a genie coming out of a bottle, he felt the world get bigger. He had heard that the Indonesian restaurant on Clement Street was still there.

Birdman of the I-Hotel

In the early morning,
I see you from my second floor window
Across Jackson Street
Chatting on the corner of a slanted crosswalk
As cars whiz by,
With Ray the Filipino garage man from the basement
And you out again with two bags full
to feed the pigeons
To "deal with the animals", as you
Put it.

Your guitar-strumming fingers
Proffering grains
Of wisdom as well to the hovering doves

Fingers that once untangled
The prurient wires of mainstream media
And let loose the sundry voices of the Bay
From makeshift amplifiers
To KPFA
radio and t.v.
To hold at bay
The corporate claws of darkness
That fell into the abyss
that 26 years later would be the phoenix of
The International Hotel
"We Won't Move!"
We're still here.

Now it is your brain that is tangled
Clouding up those memories
Of pain triumphant
As now you walk the streets
Alone unhealthy and unremembered
By the masses you once helped

I saved some crusts from the

Leftover pizza from the gathering last night.
The dough was so good.
Come by later
And take these crumbs
And put them in one of your bags
For your morning walks,
Manong.

You
Who soar with wild wings
of your own.

May 15, 2021, SF

Norman Jayo feeding I-Hotel birds. ca 2021. Photo credit: Tony Remington.

Ode To A Fire Hydrant

On Columbus and Jackson
you split Chinatown to my left
and North Beach Italian town to my right
and the Financial District below
All three neighborhoods surround you
On your corner
tourists use you
positioning for a good view to take a picture of or with
the TransAmerica Building
Bums use you to lean on,
Short folks looking at their cell phones
sit on you
their feet dangling
Kids and passers-by lift their leg
to tie their shoes on your muzzle
and of course the dogs
also lift their leg on you
but not to tie their shoes
The homeless rest their weary backs on you
Locals use the ATM of East West Bank in front of you.
I sit by my window
at the International Hotel,
and salute, you,
fellow unnoticed noticer

Kapwa tayo

The Asshole of Chinatown

In Chinatown where I live, there was a place called Sam Wo back in the day. I think it is still open now, but it does not have the character it had before. At least not to me. Like a person that is not himself anymore, the place is not the same old place. Sometimes during lunchtime, the height of business, I see chains around its closed gates. Ever since the waiter there died, no more stories emanated from the place. It was the waiter that really made the place. Upon retrospect and posthumously, he was right after all, the asshole. I don't know the name of the waiter. It couldn't have been the name of the restaurant, too, unless he himself owned it. But he never mentioned owning it, so Sam Wo was probably not the waiter's name. But it was the waiter that made the place alive! It was the waiter that was associated with the restaurant's name, so he became known as Sam Wo. A weird turn of business marketing and advertising which became a tribute to the asshole. It was he that the tourists and the locals came to check out when they ate at Sam Wo's at Clay Street in San Francisco's Chinatown.

The food and dishes came up and down a dumbwaiter pulley so that the waiter only stayed upstairs.

He attracted attention and filled the place up because of his assholic behavior. He went against all rules of etiquette and manners and courtesy. Rude would be too kind a word for his attitude. He would not lay your plates individually. He would pass them out quickly like a frisbee on the table. Then he would throw the menu in the middle of the table with the utensils that you were supposed to get yourself. When people asked if he had this dish or that dish, he would cut them off and say, "Order only on the menu. That's why I gave you the menu. That's what the menu is for."

People (mostly tourists) would leave the place saying "Did you get a load of that waiter? What an asshole!"

Yet they would not only be back, they would advertise the place to their friends. Thus, it would be packed all the time. That was the magic of the place, people's unexplainable tendency, attraction, for punishment. The food was excellent so maybe the cook helped bring back the customers, too.

Not only was he a smart ass in action and pantomime, he was pretty snotty with verbal responses, too, with sometimes a surprising vocabulary.

Some would eventually venture to ask very touristy questions like, "Now, are the century eggs really one hundred years old? Is bird's nest soup really bird's puke? Is that the truth? Or is that fiction? Where's the bill?"

"What do you want?" Sam would say. "People who tell lousy stories with biases, or people who tell good stories with biases? Here's your bill. You pay the cook downstairs; you tip the waiter upstairs."

The young tourist couple seemed to be on a date and the girl was quite happy. Her demeanor however changed after reading her fortune cookie. "A storm is coming in your life" said the paper.

"Miss, your purse," said Sam.

Sam saw her upset. She did not act like she heard him because she did not even look at her purse on the table. "Miss, don't forget your purse." He said again. "Want me to help you?"

She showed him the strip of paper from the fortune cookie. Sam read it and looked at her with a shrug. "There's a storm coming in everyone's life, c'mon." Sam told her as they were leaving, "they're only Chinese cookies. They're full of shit. They're not even Chinese! Don't believe them. They're fake. I got the same thing yesterday."

"What an asshole," the girl said, as the couple left.

But for Sam, it turned out to be true. And when he died, not long after, the cook left the place, too.

Ang Lakad ni Rosa Rosal

Ang lakad ni Rosa Rosal
Sa Intramuros ng Anak Dalita
Ay lakad ng Pilipinas sa lansangan ng kasaysayan
Mutya ni Lino Brocka sa Insiang
At mga iba pang daan na gumaya sa kanya
Pagod, mabigat ang damdamin, malalim ang iniisip
Ngunit sarili'y alsa pa rin
Bukhang liwayway na ang kanyang pag uwi sa tirahang Intramuros
At nagaalala pa rin ng mga kapit bahay
Si Rosa Rosal
Maski nakatalikud
Nararamdaman ko ang itsura
Nakikita ko ang mukha
Tulad ng Pilipinas.

Dance is in the DNA of the Universe (and the Filipino)

. . . For every atom belonging to me as good belongs to you

—Song Of Myself, Walt Whitman

Every morning just before dawn from my window of the International Hotel, flights of pigeons descend upon a corner on Kearny and Jackson streets, and soon the dance begins. Older *Manongs* used to ask Filipinos there, "Do they still dance on Kearny Street?" Dancing then was a community builder. Now, it is my addled friend Norman Jayo, fellow tenant, who revives the dance with pigeons. Erstwhile hero, now forgotten by the young, in the '70's, Jayo coordinated the dance of the media that resulted in the human barricade on that fateful night of the fall of the hotel. The "authorities" had been banging on the doors of the hotel for nine years. That's how long the people had been defending and protecting it and its tenants. "We won't move! We won't move!" It was the dance of the I Hotel, the dance of standing your ground, the zen like dance of immobility, when thousands around the Bay from all faiths and non-faiths, and walks of life swooped down like a giant choreographed tsunami into Kearny Street, interlocked arms, and remained steadfast, their energies and forces of resistance reserved inside their own universe. "We won't move! We won't move!"

Dance must have been the first art, the first expression of human experience. We have first of all before any tool, our bodies as our tools. Before words, before language, before drawings and paintings, there were our bodies. Dance is primordial, archetypal, and ancestral. It brings us back, grounds us in our most natural state and inclinations. And of course, our last gesture will be a dance.

Dance and the Warrior

In Kali, a Filipino martial art, the movement, the forms we practice and which we aspire to are called "Sayaw", which literally means, "dance." For a warrior must also be soft. Therein lies the wisdom in the sayaw of the warrior. It is the dance that teaches this principle to the warrior. The essence of a warrior is the essence of a dancer, the poise, the stature, the attitude, the dignity of composure under imminent pressure. Some folks, say, just get a gun, and no need for martial arts. But that belies the dance in the martial arts and its complete absence in the use of a gun. What form will you be in, what stance, means what posture, composure, attitude will you take in the midst of an earthquake, a storm, a hurricane, or a flood? What good is your gun in the face of these disasters? How do you kill the fear inside you? Killing that fear is the beginning of the warrior's dance.

I took to Kali so naturally when I encountered it for the first time in Hawaii. Snooky Sanchez, our legendary teacher, saw it the first day. Dancers see movements right away. He saw what my grandmother and my mother left in me, when I was forced to join folk dances because there were only a few boys participating, as a teenager in San Francisco. And the sword playing of my boyhood in the Philippines emerged in those movements. I used to make swords, not just my own, but for other playmates, too, out of bamboo, as a kid. I even named their weapons. I made them; I got to name them. That was the deal. Mine was "Robin Hood".

Athletes are dancers. All sports, even non-human sports, like horseracing, is poetry in motion, and what is poetry in motion but a dance? All sports is a dance or it's nothing.

The Dance at Work

In my boyhood in the Philippines, the women in the countryside, and some domestic workers in the cities, would wash by a well. They have a dance when they bathe, with just a tabo (hand dipper), a piece of soap, one large pail or bucket of water, or if outside, standing beside a deep and running stream between the trees. They clean themselves not only with their hands, but also with their feet when they have to bend and reach those hard-to-get-at parts of their bodies, like the heels, and the back of the knees.

They rub the back of their knees with their instep, and they clean their insteps with the soles of their feet. Then, (I always had a hard time with this, and I tried it many times), one by one, they rub the narrow part of their heels, the achilles, between the toes of the other foot, and pour water from the tabo little by little, just the right amount to wash and rinse away the day's accumulated dirt there, holding their hair with the other hand as they look down behind them to see the earth wash away from their feet. Then they rub the soles of each foot on top of the opposite instep, and wash that away. Even as they step out of their baths, they skip and hop and turn and, dancers that they are, smile to a new beginning.

In the salmon canneries of Alaska, the unsafe, outdated machines, the Iron Chink, are entangled with the workers. People became adept and even ingenious in adjusting and facilitating. Work, when the fish came, was a 20-hour day on average and on peak days even 24/7. I had a timecard with 26 and a half hours in a day's work. Mathematics be damned if I was not going to get paid for it!

The butchers on the Iron Chink and the Lye Wash Crew danced all hours. I worked in Lye Wash. A partner and I controlled the iron hooked hydraulic hoist (its sound a tempo meter) anchored by a freewheeling moving ball of twenty pounds of iron. We named that moving ball Muhammad Ali. One accident, one hit and you're out! One partner controlled the release and stoppage of the hoist as both swung with the cooler (one square yard of shallow metal strips container filled with 112 shining, gold, one-pound cans of various salmon). The sound of the first click of the hook is important. It set the tempo. Then at the end of each swing, we lay the cooler down in one motion, and on the seventh stack, we added a push so the rail can take away the momentum of the pile stacked seven coolers high. The workers, the weather, the seasons, the river, all flow together with the fishermen's haul of the day and butchers' maneuvering of the Iron Chink.

The Dance at Play

I have watched my first grandchild, before she was even five, dance all day. Throughout her chores, she skips and hops and smiles and waves. I ask her to bring me something and she slides and runs and tosses her hair and exaggerates her movements because it is the dance that propels her. "Papa, you left your tea in the microwave again!" She brings me my baseball cap with a bounce and a leap, and I see my mother and grandmother dancing the Kuratsa in countless fiestas.

I play poker. Gambling is a constant temptress. And to keep gambling at bay, one must perform the dance with Lady Luck. In gambling, one has to feel the pulse of Lady Luck and sway with her, not overpowering, never losing patience, sometimes waiting it out, standing still, giving in, and dancing with your destiny, so that you may take your rightful place in the Great Flow of things. It's bigger than your ego; there is no room for your hubris. Accept. Say yes, like Molly Bloom in James Joyce's Ulysses. Learn humility, or Lady Luck will crush you and toss you out of relevance like yesterday's newspaper.

I am a dancer who had no official lessons, a gambler with no specific training, a traveler with no vehicle, a warrior without a gun, and an athlete without a coach. But I have had mentors, and have had other weapons besides a gun, and have traveled unmapped territories. And I have read and written books as frigates of memory and imagination.

My last memories of the Philippines and my boyhood was a dance, a dance of the streets of Manila. It was Loran's dance on the shores of Manila Bay when all our clothes that he was supposed to have been watching got stolen because of the temptation of ice cream on a hot afternoon. Loran was the sharp-eyed one of our group. When things were lost we always called Loran to find it. Between blades of grass, he would spot a rusty coin or a dull, chipped, battle-wearied marble right away. But that hot afternoon, his talent did not have a chance with the ring-a-ling of an ice cream cart. He was distracted and he gave in and lost his attention, as well as our clothes. All four of us boys ran butt-naked back home and I was in the groove of the dance when a taxi almost hit me crossing the wide Dewey, now Roxas, Boulevard. I wet myself in fear but was quickly relieved to find out that I was naked and had no pants to wet.

My Auntie, my mother's youngest sister, died at 97. She was dancing and swaying and singing on her deathbed. Her mother did the same. I saw them both at it when their turn came. They knew, like Jackson Browne, that the last dance, we do alone.

Carding the Storyteller
(in search of a listener)

He was the ultimate performer...in his own way. On half-assed, make-shift basketball street games, around Manila, he insisted on foul shots being enforced, so he could have a platform, an audience to perform to, to make a speech to, impromptu, improvised extemporaneous. "I dedicate this shot to the one I love whose name I will not mention but is quite known by some of you. For you, sweet one, from an admirer from afar, though I know I'm not the only one," (the guy would actually compose and recite a poem right there on a potholed dirt road where we played while shooting a foul shot) "this foul shot is humbly dedicated to..." He was not really a good basketball player, just average. But he didn't care so much about the game. He never really took it that seriously as we other kids did. Winning or losing was no big thing for him. Having the occasion for having an audience for that foul shot moment gave him the chance to bloom. Theater was in his blood. To spout the caressed words from his mouth about his beloved was the glory of his hour. And he had a certain foul shot pose as he poured his words, a bit akimbo, one elbow sticking out, hand holding waist, the other hand holding ball shot-put pose on his shoulder as he recited to an invisible crowd.

And when Carding told stories, not just the sound effects were given. The international accents of the characters, too! And at times he spoke in their foreign languages. I don't know how he did it. He'd change foreign accents seamlessly from character to character, sometimes, not just accents, but the words themselves. He would make up whole dialogues in what sounded to us like different languages, like when Tonto would speak to the Lone Ranger. "Hamumba meche Tatangka Yotanka, Kimo Sabi," he would flawlessly recount, sounding like he understood every word he was saying. He had a sound for certain noises. He was a precursor of the corny batman camp sounds like "Blammm!", "Splat!", or "Bragoom!" I remember he had a sound for a surprise, an unwanted one. "Ngak!" Droplets of rain on the rooftops ("ploink"), on the river ("platak"), and on the ground ("pak"). I don't know what school he attended. I don't think he was in school. Carding I only saw on the streets. Never in house birthday parties, like our other playmates, Jejomar Binay and Franklin Fontabella, who had regular house parties. I don't remember what neighborhood he came from, either. I know he visited our Teresa Street group quite often.

When going to the movies, because of the many members of our boyhood barkadas, we could not afford to pay for each of us. Some of us did not have the ticket money, all of thirty five centavos at the time. So we took turns physically going to the theaters and seeing the movie. The movie was just related and retold to the rest of the group who did not go by the folks who got to go. Even though Carding rarely had the money, he was almost always the one to go to the movies. He was everyone's choice. Folks would chip in for him. We all knew that Carding got to go more than the rest of us, but no one really complained. Why? He was a good storyteller, a model for us, really, without anyone being conscious of this interplay, and that we are all in need of a listener sometimes. Carding, I dedicate this shot to you.

Suite #4
The Alaskeros

Three *Alaskeros* sitting on a dock near Alaskan cannery. Left to right: Danny Caceres, Narciso Toralba, author. South Naknek, Bristol Bay. Photo credit: Narciso Toralba and Danny Caceres. ca 1978.

Alaskeros were the Filipino workers in Alaska doing seasonal jobs, mostly the salmon run in the summers. There were crab and halibut, too but their seasons are after the summer. There were a few Filipina workers who worked the canneries, as well. Alaskeros were not natives of Alaska, originally. They came from all over the West Coast and some farther, like Elmo the ex-hitman of Al Capone who was from Chicago, but some would eventually take up residences there, like James Bond who they say, was in Alaska 11 months of the year! Alaskeros were not locals, but working seasonal visitors. The same companies that employed them employed the farmworkers who put fruits, as well as fish, in a can. For Filipinos, the same workers that worked the fields of the west coast worked the fish canneries in Alaska. Same foremen for picking fruits and vegetables picked their choice workers to go to Alaska. All the gold in the years of the California Gold Rush does not equal one year of Agribusiness profits. Four months before the now famous grape strike in Delano, union folks led by Larry Itliong were able to negotiate in Coachella a contract in May of 1965. The neighboring Delano farmers knew that Itliong and the farmworkers were coming to their town next and would demand negotiations from the farmers/owners. Agribusiness reared its ugly head, and on September 8, 1965, Larry Itliong and about 1500 Filipino laborers in the farmlands around Delano started day one of a strike and boycott of grapes that would last several more years.

Highway 99 Across Delano, California,

—September 7, 1965

On the eve,
the light from the moon
snagged in the crotch of the old oak tree
flickered through
like fragments of broken glass
above the Filipino
Community Hall
awaiting the morrow's
reckoning.

THE YEAR AFTER I graduated from St Ignatius High School, in the early sixties, I worked two summers in Las Vegas. To my surprise, there were already plenty of Filipinos in Vegas then. In San Francisco, the social worker on Potrero Street was telling us fresh young graduates that Las Vegas was hiring workers left and right. I talked to him about this and the next week I was on a Greyhound bus to Sin City. Two went with me. The next day, three more followed. First night in Vegas, we slept in the announcing booth of the racetracks in the middle of town. A million stars shone brightly above our partial roof and the night air was tinge with horse manure. The Landmark Apartments had just been built and we rented a room there the next day, five of us. Two shifts. Three worked the morning shift (7 am to 3 pm), two the graveyard (11 pm to 7 am). The connection that the San Francisco social worker gave us was a Mr. Yamat in the Riviera Hotel. He was a Kapampangan and almost all his colleagues were also Kapampangan, like Gil and Rolando Santos. There I met some other Kapampangans from California. They were talking about a strike that had just happened in Coachella and the upcoming expected strike in their own town of Delano. I sent all my paychecks to my mother in San Francisco. I lived purely on my tips, some of which were still in silver dollars, minted in the 1880's, just like the Old West I've been reading about. There were so many they were coming out of my ears! Now I do not have a single coin.

Eyes of a Century

(for Truffles, my daughter's tortoise)

You will see my granddaughters' grandchildren at play, oh wise one,
a hundred years from now.
Yours will be the eyes for me then.
You will also see and feel such coming tragedies that I dare not look any further
into the slow turnings of the world
like your aging into the voyeur extraordinaire that you are
look well
when they have parties and come home from parties or are going to parties
and all get-togethers
You will witness it all, the coming and passing of generations,
the unnoticed and mute poet
that you will have become
will carry the fingerprints of memory
lodged deep below your scaly reptile surface,
oh, wise one.

And listen well too.
Perhaps once in a great while someone might mention
the names of the two
who plucked you from destiny
into their living room
and brought you home
in the palm of one hand and in the pulse of a Las Vegas
rainy night

who raised and nurtured you and,
like the cowboy of Red River Valley,
who loved you
so true
though for a mere human lifetime.

San Leandro, 1/1/2013

Alaska

A Filipino contractor of those California farmworkers, Marcelino Divina, top official in the Caballeros de Dimasalang, was also a foreman in an Alaskan fishing cannery. He also regularly got his two bottles of Canadian Club Whisky every six months when the diplomatic pouch arrived at the Philippine Consulate, where my father worked. My father did not drink, and his male acquaintances, who did drink, paid their respects around the time the pouch would arrive. My dad, number three man in the Philippine Consulate in San Francisco, would give all the liquor away, one by one, or in Divina's case, two by two. And in the following summer of '66, this contractor was my father's contact for me to seek out in Seattle where I went to get the job for an Alaskan cannery. "Look for a Marcelino Divina, when you get to Seattle," my father told me. "Pin-striped MacIntosh suit and a big cigar, hehehe."

My father was right. Divina hired me and my two companions, Danny Caceres and Serafin Syquia right there on the spot. But not after three weeks of waiting and not knowing and waiting and contacting connections.

Danny had some relatives in Tacoma. We had contacted them first. We stayed with them for a couple of days. Then, we followed Serafin's connection, Mrs. Sulit, formerly from the Philippine Consulate now an Ambassador someplace. We also stayed partly with my uncle Tio Titing who had friends who worked in Alaska. None of the connections materialized. We had to get a place near the union hall where we must check for daily openings and hire. We went there and waited almost all day, everyday, to get hired, but we did not. Each day waiting, we were looking more and more gaunt, frustrated, angry, critical, bitter and kawawa.

The year was 1966 and the three of us had checked into a hotel near Main Street in Seattle where the union hall was. I was 21. Five dollars a week. (It was condemned the next year we came). We had to get two rooms. One room on the 7th floor which had two beds, and one on the first floor where all the drunks and the rowdies were. We flipped for who would not have to sleep alone on the first floor of that cockroach ridden, flea-infested hotel where half the occupants were drunk and one or two making ruckus in the hallway outside. Danny got the first floor room and I saw the disappointed look on his face right away, so I said, "It's ok. I'll take the first floor."

Around our third week checking with the union hall hirings, I finally said to the other two that I am going to contact this Marcelino Divina that my father told me about. I did not want to use this way of influence thinking that we might get a job on our own. I was 21. Desperate. And wrong.

"Manong," I asked Trinidad Rojo, a union officer whom I had talked with because he was also a writer. He was standing with Chris Mensalvez, a labor leader and good friend of Carlos Bulosan.

"Hey, that Jose in America is in the Heart," said Manong Chris, "that's me!"

"Manong," I asked again. "Do you know a Marcelino Divina?" People were already being dispatched and leaving for their respective canneries in Alaska.

"See that man with a cigar and—"

"MacIntosh suit?"

"Yeah, das him."

I went straight to the man. He was standing with a crowd in the middle of the union hall. One hand holding a cigar, the other on someone's shoulder. "Mr. Divina?" I asked. I knew I interrupted them, but I had to do it.

"Yes?"

"Mr. Divina, I am the son of Florentino Peñaranda from the Philippine Consulate in San Fran"

"'Sannababits! " He coughed out his cigar smoke. "Who are you with?"

"Three of us, po."

"Shit! We are all hired and accounted for. We are all dispatched in my crew. We leave tomorrow. Why the fuck didn't you tell me before?"

"I didn't know who you were."

"So, you ask."

"That's what I did. Finally."

"Wait here." He crossed the wide hall and went into an office. I saw him talking to some people. He came out saying, "I can't put you all in my cannery. Only you. Too pucken late, goddammit!. Tell your friends who are looking kawawa there on that bench that I've never seen a group of boys with that down-and-out kawawa look, hehehe. I can put them both in the same cannery in Peterson Point, not too far from ours. We're going to Bristol Bay."

Overjoyed, I hurried to tell Serafin and Danny. They didn't mind at all being in a different cannery. At least they were together.

"Goddammit. Let me think. You'll be the jitney driver. Our regular one is still in jail here in Seattle and I was going to bail him out, but now I won't. You're his replacement. He's the best jitney driver there is, but an asshole. Never learns."

Thus, the three of us got hired that day.

Every spring after that first salmon season in Alaska, as early as April, I would hear phone calls from Alaskero buddies, stirrings like the salmon anticipating its journey to their spawning grounds in Alaska: from Oregon, Seattle, Delano, all over, asking if I was "going up again" in June. They follow the seasons for work, harvests from the farmlands and of the sea. Alaska is the terminal to the north and the Mexican Border to the south. The path leaves at its wake and includes the San Francisco Bay Area, Vallejo, Vacaville, Fairfield, Putah Creek, Sacramento, Stockton, Suisun Valley, Delano, Portland, Seattle, Wapato, Indio, and Las Vegas. Six of us made a pact the first year that "ip you see my pucking pace here again next year, I give you a hundred pucking bucks!" But they gradually diminished through the years until only I and Slim Gator were left at the end of fifteen consecutive summers, when I suddenly decided to stop coming because of a Union Hall murder in broad daylight on Main Street in Seattle. I knew the victims. I also knew the killers. I am, however, still half expecting Slim Gator to call asking if I'm "going up again" this coming season. Slim and I stopped after 1980. But let me check my messages.

Migrants Roll Call

Manong Blackie from Istockton
Lomboy of Portland Oregon, Mr. Lomboy to you, son,
And Three-fingered Larry of Delano town
Were there three fingers left or three fingers gone?
My Aunt Emma from Shuttel, Alaskera extraordinaire
They are not in the pages of history books
Yet they made history
Like the very grapes they harvested
Bent in burning heat
Sunup to sundown
They put fruits on your table
Yet they themselves could not afford
The fruits of their own labor.
They raised their fists and laid them down again to pave
the paths of justice for our future.

Boy Sige-sige, Freddie Eagle, Slim Gator, and the Wolfman
From fair Santa Clara, ex-Al Capone hit man,
Who wore panties to work. The secret to long hours of work, he told me.
'More comport, more support,' he said.
Who am I to argue? Ex-killer ata yan
Who stayed at the same senior housing my parents lived in
South of Market, Clementina Street, Soma Central City, by Saint Patrick's Church.

No read no write
But work like hell
Drink like hell
And gamble like there was no tomorrow
And for some, there was no tomorrow
They died with their Alaskan cannery boots on.

For my parents and aunties and uncles
and elders who raised me
or tried to
Sacrificed and taught me how to sacrifice
For the good of the many
For the good of loved ones

For the good of the weaker ones
For you, my ancestors from the homeland
For you, my ancestors who have traveled
Far and away from the homeland
And into the loveless fields of the diaspora
I sing these
words of praise
And I ask you all now
For a brief moment
As their obscure lives were
for a brief moment in time
To honor them
By remembering
For memory can be a witness
To their labors and accomplishments.
Their footprints are all over the world
Yet they remain unknown

Vera, the native laundry lady from South Naknek village,
Who had to contend with our sometimes stained underwear,
That brown badge of labor
Every Tuesday, laundry day.
Fancy Pants called the Vagina in Filipino,
Saan si Puki?
Chavacan the Mexican,
Loud-snoring Eng the Chinaman
And Mr. Hollywood of San Francisco
I hear you
I hear you all
Together, we shall pluck you, each by each
out of the dust-bins of history.

If you listen carefully
With a mind thirsty for the truth
And a heart that's pure,
From fields to big cities and small cities and suburbs and towns,
Lakes, rivers, high seas, and bays
From the silences and the noise
From the green grass that blow wild in the meadow,

If you listen carefully
You may hear the wind whisper their names.

Oka of old Frisco town...
Manong Oka now
Yet still a prince of the Island Leyte

All of you
Lay down your sore and aching dreams
At my feet and these hobbled words
Will give them wings
To set us free.

Pieces of the (Midnight) Sun

—Sketches of An *Alaskero*

It was the summers of my youth, itself the summer of life. I started working in Alaska in 1966 when I was just finishing my twenty-first year. When I came home to San Francisco just before the Fall to start school again, I was a father. That was my first year in Alaska. It would be fourteen more consecutive summers before I would see what would become my final trip (up to now) to South Naknek in Bristol Bay, the salmon goldmine of the world.

You took three planes to get there: a big one from Seattle to Anchorage, a 747 sometimes, then a smaller one of about 50 people from Anchorage to King Salmon, a military base. And then a cub plane or a bush plane (which is the most common mode of transportation in Alaska) to the cannery itself. I always liked the ride. It felt like I was in a flying sports car. I could see everything underneath me, and I remember the pilot telling me "Well, there she is...a lot of...nothin'". And true enough, as far as my eye could see, there was nothing but tundra, low bushes of vegetation for miles and miles and miles. Until all of a sudden, some construction made of lumber (for it would contrast with the greens, like a naked part of a hairy anatomy), would jump into view, and we would know that the cannery was nearby, as towns and buildings and ships and boats emerge and take shape. The airport in which we landed sported a sign "South Naknek International Airport". It was nothing but dust and gravel, one hut or shack of a building with just galvanized roofing and a wooden bench. There, one waited to be taken to the cannery by truck and jeeps and all kinds of transportation dispensable by the cannery at that time of arrival. Usually, the fish had not yet started its run, and at that leisurely time there was plenty of transportation available from the cannery. I remembered one flat truck that I was on one summer, early in my years in Alaska. We had stood on the truck, some of us not holding on to anything, hats and bandana scarves blowing in the dusty wind, waving goodbye to the place where planes landed. Even the airport is a character in South Naknek. That's the kind of place it was.

Another place worth noting was of course the lobby of the Filipino bunkhouse. The Indians, Jimmy Walker's crew, were upstairs. In that lobby, which is the first thing you see when you enter the bunkhouse, were benches, two or three big, round, blanketed tables (for gambling), ashtrays and tin cans, and a big window to look out of, though there was really nothing to look out to. It had a view but then again it didn't have a view. But the little view it did have (the young healthy shoots of wild, yellow green grass on a patch of mound about ten feet away) was most welcome at times of severe loneliness and sentimentality and could take one's mind to a journey of a thousand miles. These are the times Filipino songs are heard from all around, haranas, kundiman, love songs of unrequited love.

In that lobby, beside the gamblers, the anglers, the talkers, and the good old fashioned socializers, were the great orators. Great Debaters of the ages. You could tell who did not like whom in these debates. They would participate in bantering and bandying with words, in Tagalog, with some good piece of knowledgeable information as fringe benefits. A *Balagtasan,* Alaska style. A word-war of cleverness and wit and information and inspiration. All extemporaneous. Sometimes the audience would help by calling out topics or issues for discussion. Here you would see year after year "Humpy" (a young, late twenties-early thirties, very dark Pinoy), and "Mr. Exiting", (an Ilocano about 15 years an *Alaskero.* I think he started when they still came by boats,) debate great and minute details in history, language, values, philosophy, common sense, justice, revolution, religion; you name it, they debated it. However, in the Fish House, where they both worked, both put aside their differences. The time for gambling and great debates, however, are numbered; they usually occur in the beginning and end of a season, a time of relative leisure. Or at some other moderately busy time when people only worked till 8 or 9 p.m. Work then would be relatively bearable. We all started at 8 a.m. Breakfast is at seven. But you soon get to realize that breakfast is skippable. For the workers, sleep is what is valued. Sleep, not the salmon, is what is really precious in Alaskan canneries on these days.

Leo, a fellow *Waray,* was bragging again about what had happened in Delano in September of the previous year, when they had the grape strike. Our foreman was from there so the crew had plenty from Delano and Leo was one of them. The union rep in that cannery was actually the leader and organizer of the strike, an experienced and skilled and tough Union man, Larry Itliong. Three-fingered Larry.

"I stood there all alone. Ebriwer police and cops..." continued Leo.

"What's the difference?" Slim Gator interrupted.

"Shuddap. I saw Hubert, one of our Delano Police, chatting and bullshitting with a group of growers when I threw that molotov cocktail. *Madapakas.*"

"Bull shit. I saw you run away looking for a place to hide."

"I was looking for a better bantage point, Pare. Das part of it. Defense offense."

In Delano, the September of the past year, the September before my first summer in Alaska, only months before, the Great Delano grape strike broke out, where one thousand five hundred Filipinos went on strike against the giant agribusiness industry representative, the Grower, the white Grower.

"Besides," continued Leo the Waray, "there was no place to hide. You know dat. It was now or neber."

Leo was the first one of a string of tragic deaths that would follow many of my fellow Alaskeros. They found him floating face down on a nearby swamp in Delano. Throughout the years, I would hear of their passing, one by one, or three by three, dropping out, cashing in, diminishing, fading, going, going...

We would stay in our Alaskan cannery in Bristol Bay about a month and a half to two months on average. You were a "contract worker" until the Salmon season ended, which meant till it became too costly for the company to keep you, and there were no more fish. Eight a.m. to five p.m., the company owned you. You were on company time. But anytime before and after, it was overtime: time and a half and sometimes if it's a holiday like July 4th, double-double time. One could make $500 that day, very big money in those days. They say that the first time you get to Alaska, it's the company's fault; the second time and any time thereafter, it's your fault.

I guess it would have to be the sunsets, if one were to recall what kinds of things one remembers most about South Naknek in the summers. You over-looked a rough-winded bay fed by a widening river, the Naknek River. Some said it meant Snake in Athabascan Indian. Over a cliff behind Cliff Johnson's Bar, one can see all this. And if somehow you have lingered long in this Long Branch Saloon and found yourself wending homewards alone to your bunk-house at near midnight, and looking up to a sunset that spread all across the skies, through ruffles of puffy, thin, wispy technicolor clouds, all across the sky, you knew you would, when, sitting comfortably in your respective abodes down below in the lower forty-eight, remember clearly those spectacular nights. One did not have to look for the sunset. In Bristol Bay, the sunset found you. It came to you like a constant visitor or the voice of the town-crier. Its colors flood-ed and spilled across the whole sky with streaks of rust-red, fire-yellow, and petal-magenta. The sunsets did not last for only five or ten minutes, like the sunsets we know here. The sun lay low in the horizon and lingered for about an hour or two. It seemed to move along the horizon, first to the left and then to the right. The glory of the sunset held the people in awe, with the skies lit up in hues of gold and orange and purple and blood red, the clouds above in streaks of fire and silver. It always seemed a rare sight for us because we were always working. Those sunsets were actually always there. It was we, cannery workers, who were not.

Cliff Johnson's Bar was nicknamed the Long Branch Saloon. Ol' Cliff Johnson is probably still around, still tends to the place at times. Like my Spanish speak-ing Mother always said: "*La mala yerba, nunca muere*" (the bad weed never dies). He has an Aleut wife, Irma, and she has a lot of relatives that help and hang around Ol' Cliff Johnson. He's definitely the richest man in the village, though he looks just like a commoner himself. Some made fun of that, some admired it. "What's the use of having all those millions of dollars if you still smell like fish?" some would say. Yet others would tell "He worked for every penny he has now. Even if some of that money was acquired mysteriously, he risked his ass every time." Cliff Johnson, though in the sunset of his years, himself was one tough white man. A Filipino once shot him, though, back in the forties. He pulled a gun right in front of Johnson and shot him almost point blank. Somehow Johnson was only grazed on the head and when he regained his wits, started coming after the Filipino. But of course, the Pinoy knew when it was time to" fight another day". He was gone before Johnson could clear the bar. The Filipino's close friend, a witness to that event, told me this story himself. He said he did not know how his friend could miss. But then again, he said that his friend had been drinking all night. Something about him buying the groceries while someone else in his hometown down below is eating it now. That song "I Wonder Who's Kissing Her Now" was my boss, our foreman's favorite. He sang that at least once a season. Everybody laughed above their loneliness. The gesture was comic, but the music and lyrics hit too close to home for many whose loved ones down below were loving someone else.

But Cliff Johnson's Bar, christened The Long Branch Saloon by local folklore, was not the only one so christened. In fact, if one really thought about it, there was hardly anything in South Naknek that was not renamed or "christened".

Then there was the mail, the blessings of which droppeth from heaven but once a week . . . usually . . . in a manner of speaking, that is. Depends on the weather, really. If the weather was nice, sometimes twice a week. In fact that was the main consistent characteristic of the mail there, its inconsistency of arrivals. One day, in my rookie year, confounded by this, I set out to find the answer myself. I asked our foreman, and he said once or twice a week. Just to confirm things, I asked the schoolboy-looking store clerks, and they said Mondays, Wednesdays, and Fridays only, "like those classes in college". The mechanics told me Tuesdays and Thursdays. The cooks, weekends only. The carpenters, never on weekends. Only on weekdays. Frustrated, I went to the radio man himself, the one who signals and radios the planes' comings and goings to Bristol Bay. He just shrugged his shoulders and said, "Don't ask me. I just work here."

It was of course the people themselves, the characters, who dominated and perpetuated this christening practice, especially in their nicknames and the rumored stories behind those nicknames. There was Golden Boy Sige-sige and the *"awat"* incident. It was about breaking up a fight that you really did not want to get involved in. Golden Boy Sige-sige was a known killer down below. If he wasn't a killer, he sure looked like one. And who was going to ask or argue? He took on the name Sige-sige after the desperate gangs in Manila in the fifties and sixties. He was one of those few whose nicknames were self-given. He was stocky for a Filipino, and about 5'7". He stood with his boots on almost all the time, his long straggly black and banded hair falling on his vest over his hulking shoulders. And when he smiled, you saw no upper front teeth. And that somehow contrasted sharply with his red bandana wrapped around his neck. I too wore such a bandana. I liked the bandana. For me it was multipurpose, and I had one (store bought, red or blue) for almost all occasions in the canneries. One reason of course, was for the harsh winds that blew hard and mean at a moment's notice. Then just as fast, it would disappear. That neck feels awfully naked in those times. One thing you don't want to be in Alaska is vulnerable.

This particular night of the *awat* incident was cold and the wind was almost howling. In front of the women's bunkhouse, on a patch of moonlit grass, there was a lot of merriment. Junior, the son of the President (and Business Agent) of Local 37, upon which Union all of us Filipinos were enabled to get dispatched to work in Alaska, was there with a couple of white boys. Boy Sige-sige was there with Maybelle, an Athabascan Indian whose family I knew quite well. They were seven siblings and Maybelle was the youngest. They were like brothers and sisters to me, well, not all of them; I liked one of the sisters. Because of this "in-law" situation, Boy called me "Bayaw" jokingly. Maybelle was about sixteen at the time. It was a shitty night as usual, but the moon's light was extraordinarily clear. All of a sudden, I heard the foreman's wife yelling. "Stop them, stop them! Someone stop them!" I was just walking by myself on my merry way from Johnson's Bar, walking home to the bunkhouse. I heard my name being called by the foreman's wife. I had to do something. I looked around and saw a fight going on in front of me, right under the light of the moon, it seemed. This particular midnight, I had no specific memory of seeing the sun. Must have been just another drizzly day when the fish came out by the millions.

In front of me, I saw Junior, the son of our Union president, duking it out with Golden Boy Sige Sige. From where I stood it seemed that Boy was getting the worst of it. Realizing this, Boy's friends—Romeo, Obet, and the Wolfman— jumped on Junior. Junior was one of the few cannery workers who was born here in the States and did not know how to speak Filipino. However, there are even many more who did not speak Filipino but could understand. Junior was one of them. That's when the foreman's wife saw me and looked at me squarely in the eye and screamed again. What could I do? So I jumped in. I don't remember if I said anything or not. I grabbed Boy Sige Sige. He turned around seemingly stunned and paused for a brief fraction of a second then quickly punched me right in the face. I was pretty sure it was the right side of my face. Things went blurred for an instant, but I kept looking at him. When I sensed that he was not going to swing again, I turned around and looked for Boy's friends. They looked stunned, too. When I looked at Boy again, he was sobbing, quite pronouncedly. I went closer and before I could ask anything he said "*Bayaw*, I hit you. I actually hit you! What were you doing there anyway?" And he cried some more. I thought about it later and realized his point. How would he know I was trying to break up the fight? Everything happens quickly in a scuffle.

I got home to the bunkhouse around the same time as Boy and them, but we did not go home together. I headed straight for my room and as usual there were other people there. I recalled my two roommates, and I won the messiest room in the bunkhouse for three years in a row. I greeted everyone there and climbed up the double decker to my bed but found I could not do it. I was losing consciousness; I could feel it. With the metal handle of the bedpost, I pole-vaulted myself quickly with one last effort and I sank onto the bed relieved and very tired all of a sudden. In a moment I was myself again. I felt things were coming back to me. I was feeling comfortable again, that's when I knew I was getting better. People around me were saying, "Oh, are you alright? You passed out trying to climb onto your bunk." Those few moments that I found myself relieved weren't so few after all. They told me I had passed out trying to lie in my bed. Some said they saw me hit the metal pipe frame for the bed with my head. I also found out the next morning that I had lost my right contact lens that night. It was when Golden Boy SigeSige punched me in the face. I knew it was the right side.

Rick Wilson was a white man from New York. People would go to him and say things about New York City like 'how's Broadway', or the Brooklyn Bridge and the Statue of Liberty, and he'll say "Never seen any of 'em. I'm from upstate New York. New York is a state, too. I'm from Troy, New York." and he would smile. Troy, he told me, was near Albany, the capital city of New York State. Rick Wilson was into the drama, the moment, the ridiculousness of existence. He visited me once when he passed by San Francisco before he took the trip back home to New York. Troy, New York. He was somewhat apprehensive. He was to meet his parents (his adopted parents, that is), after being absent, gone from them for about ten years. He stayed with me in San Francisco for several days then he moved on to New York. He took the plane. He left me his M.G. Roadster, a "Triumph" it was, convertible, sporty, but beat up. He told me that if he does not come back in three weeks, "it's yours." And left me the keys. What the hell.

It was the early 70's. And people were into existentialism and Sartre and Camus. He came back before the three weeks was up, though.

One of the most memorable incidents (and there were more than a few) with Rick the Stick was the very first time I met him in Kodiak, and how we lost over six thousand dollars in about half an hour. Men on the boardwalk were playing dice. Rick is the kind that always wants to get involved, participate. I remember in the night clubs of Kodiak that we occasionally visited, he would always call out to the older, over-the-hill entertainers, straining his neck, "You're the one for me, baby. Where have you been all my life? I'd like to kiss your belly button! From the inside out! You drive me to a frenzy of unspeakable desires!" Strangely enough, there was a gentleman about him and his attitude, towards women, especially. In fact he often got taken for a ride by many a young trickster. But the amazing thing about Rick Wilson was that he would forgive in an instant. And he would forgive repeatedly. He was one white man who was a close though brief friend of mine, and one of the very few whom I ended up trusting. Maybe it was because we lost about $6000 once in a crap shoot. We had two hundred each and we (of course it was actually only he) had challenged everybody into taking our money with a quick dice shoot. "We got four hundred dollars right here, gentlemen. Yours for the taking. What do you say? Let's shoot some dice." And right then and there, on the docks and the waterfront boardwalks creaking with the sway of the sea, he took off his jacket and started rolling the dice. "Give me your two hundred, man," and he quickly and confidently stretched his hand out to me. What could I do? The fishermen were in town, fresh from cashing in on their catch. Everybody had big bucks and the money was loose like a long-necked goose, as Rick the Stick liked to quote the Big Bopper of the late fifties. "Here it is Rick." I said. "Go get em." And Rick was hot that late afternoon. His left hand was burning. In about three passes, three winnings, we had close to a thousand. After that, I started to lose count and it didn't matter anymore cause Rick was just throwing one pass after another, getting his number every time, and no sevens were coming out. Surprisingly we were looking at over two thousand dollars in front of us and we, that is Rick, had thrown eight passes already. "I think I'm good for another one," he said. "What do you say pardner?", he would turn to me, confident and ebullient. What can I say? "Let it roll; fuck it." And he rolled and rolled until he got his number again! Rick the Stick asked the pit boss Long Arm Charley for the count. Pit boss Charley was only too glad to accommodate. Anything to stop the flow of luck that has bitten this young white man with a lot of gray hair. Hopefully this will stop the rhythm and change the luck. Long Arm Charley asked his boys to count the money. We had six thousand, four hundred twenty dollars in front of us. "I feel that ten is my number." he said. "We'll let it roll one more time." And the number ten showed up as his point. Though the numbers ten and four are the hardest numbers to get for a point, that's when he got real confident that we were going home with about thirteen thousand dollars. "See the number ten is our number and this is the tenth time. It is all written, pal, all written in our destiny." But it didn't happen. He sevened out, and we watched them rake in all the money that was ours just seconds ago. I wanted to stop at nine passes. I wanted to tell him so, but I couldn't. I didn't want to spoil a quality of experience that he really strove to live for. So we lost all our money that night. It was only really two hundred dollars that we lost. What's 200 dollars? "But what do you think it all means, Stick?" I was forced to ask. "I mean, we had everything, and then, nothing. Gold already, and it somehow turned into shit! Why me? Why us? What is it, Rick? What's it all mean?"

Rick the Stick would give that sudden laugh that abruptly stopped, his eyes widening a bit, but with pleasure. His hawked nose would twitch a bit and the gray streaks on his young head would catch your attention. "What's it all mean? Fuck if I know'" Rick would say and laugh at the same time. "At least", he said "we had something to lose...huh? . . . hehehe. Think of all the fuckers in the world who have nothing to lose, kid! We're lucky for having had so much to lose, even only for a moment. Our whole lives are only for a moment anyway, right?" He would burst into uncontrollable laughter. "Well, you can't win 'em all," he said. I told him he reminded me of my uncle, the boxer who fought one hundred and nineteen fights and lost one hundred and nineteen. And when I asked him why and how, all he said was "you can't win 'em all, son." Yes, two hundred dollars, six thousand dollars, what's the difference? I have squandered more in pettier things, and much more in counter-productive *kalokohans.*

One night, one of the last nights that I saw him, he confided in me. He had been awfully, unusually quiet. He had not been his usual rowdy self. It was his last night on shore for they would be leaving in the morning, fishing, for several days to a couple of weeks.

"Kristen," he told me "is going to be at my place while I'm gone. If it's not too far out of the way, look in on her every now and then."

"Sure," I said, "sure. Don't worry."

"And", he paused quite definitely, "if she'd want to do it with you...well, you know....it's okay with me. I just want to let you know. Really.."

"It's not going to happen, Rick", I said. That young white woman, Kristen, that Rick spoke of was the girlfriend of Bobby Gomez. I don't know exactly when she became the girlfriend of Bobby Gomez. It could have been before, after, or during or all three of the times, that Rick Wilson knew Kristen. This boyfriend was Romeo "Bobby" Gomez of the Philippines. He was a movie star there in the sixties and seventies. But somehow, because of a combination of fate, luck, character, and bad judgments, regrettable decisions were made, and he found himself in the salmon fishing canneries of Alaska and their nearby towns. Bobby Gomez worked as a slimer in the cannery, the Red Salmon Fish Company, across the river from us.

I got a postcard from Rick the Stick one time. Out of the blue. Hadn't heard from him for years, nor since. In the card was a cut-off, folded copy of a poem I wrote and in that poem I had mentioned some shared experiences with Rick. He wrote on it saying, "I was taking a shit in a public restroom one day in Oregon, and I saw this cast aside in a corner and when I looked, it had a poem that you wrote. The poem wasn't worth a fuck, but it's nice to be remembered. Thanks. Rick, the Stick."

There were some you only met in Seattle, before and after each season. They were going to different canneries, too far from each other. One usually has a week, give or take a few days, between being hired (dispatched) and the actual departure to Alaska. Most would hang around Seattle and by the time of leaving, everyone was almost broke and almost everyone was broke. Once a person gets hired, he would sign papers upstairs of the Union Hall, then go on to the other side of downtown on Industrial Street, to take the medical. If you pass, and 95% passed, you get a $50 advance the next morning to tide you over till departure. I have seen people spend that before the day was over. And I have seen many who did not make it to the Airport. Seattle was the seat of Local 37, the Filipino-run Union, and that is where people got hired. They hung around the International District or Chinatown because the Union Building was on Main Street in that district. There were hotels there that my body has known, unreturnable, to be condemned when visited the next year, so you had to find another cheap hotel. The Bush Hotel, a regular alternative, was a pretty steady interim home for many a transient. Lots of Alaskeros stayed there. And the Reynold's, too. I used to invent names when checking into these hotels. Johnny Murder, I remember, was one of them. Also, Shane X. Christmas, who became a character in my play Followers Of the Seasons. He played the town idiot, if I recall correctly. Christopher Sunday was another. I was becoming the fiction I was creating from out of raw life. From memoir to fiction (and back). My friends were complaining that they always had great difficulty in finding me, for a pre-departure get together. I also had family in Seattle. I know, who doesn't have family in Seattle? I wanted to see them. That was one reason why I was glad about the week-long stay in Seattle. In a span of 15 consecutive years, a couple of times, I stayed less than a week, and a couple of times I overstayed up to a month in that city.

My first year of waiting in Seattle was agony. That's another story altogether. My two friends from San Francisco and I waited for about three weeks. We did not know if we were going to get the job. Hanging around the Union Hall every day for those three weeks for possible openings, I was in a good position to view a lot of characters along with the comings and goings of the Union Hall. There was Jacksoon and Dooglas. I had seen them a couple of days before in the Union Hall on Main Street. I never thought they would make the Physical, two very old men in the Medical Exam Building. They were at least 70 years old. I don't know how they passed the exam, but I saw them walk out of the building doors and out into the Seattle winds leaning against each other as they walked and talked, perhaps shielding as well as holding each other up, against those same winds. After a moment, I was sure they passed because I thought I heard them singing Dahil Sa Iyo. I never thought they would make it. In my first year, I have yet to set foot in Alaska and already I had my first lesson. Never underestimate a *Manong*.

In Seattle, there was also Tony Moon. They called him Tony Moon because he had a mustache like Antonio Luna, long and curled up at the ends. He had a snake coiled around his neck, a live snake, in the streets of urban Seattle. The area is now called the International District, but we did not call it that then, just downtown, Chinatown, King Street, Jackson, or the Union Hall (Main Street). He liked to freak people out, this Tony Moon. Believe me, he did not have to have a snake, alive or toy, to freak people out. He was a big Flip. Handsome and loud. Occasionally he would like to test me because I was tall. "Is this guy...who is this guy? " he would say jokingly, pointing at me but looking at the fellow he was asking. But I was not sure whether he was completely joking. "He's Bisayan. Waray," my friend would tell him pointing at me, Waray being one of the subgroups of Bisayan languages. "Oh, Yeah? I'm Bisayan." He would say. And he would test me by talking to me. I don't know what kind of Bisayan he was talking (for there are many), but I would answer in Waray. Somehow that convinced him. Actually, his Bisayan, whatever kind of Bisayan it was, was the shits. But of course, I didn't tell him that. He came up again in a conversation some years later. He had been killed. Murdered. I guess he tested one too many. Or tested the wrong person. Same with Tambok. Tambok was a Tagalog, a great orator. and an ex-jailbird, convicted of larceny and possession ("possession op an ugly pace", his friends would say). He can and would talk about anything without breaking the flow of the music of the words he was saying. And occasionally when he would get stuck he would invent words, but not any old word, but words that sounded like you heard them before. I have tapes of his improvised monologues. I hope I can still find them. I'd let you listen to them. But I guess he fell too in love with words because he bullshitted too much. Abused his gift, as the old folks would say. They say he conned one too many listener. They found Tambok dead in a Reynold's Hotel room, a knife stuck in his throat. He was very good with those Tagalog words but I guess they were not good enough.

I was there 15 consecutive years, fifteen consecutive summers. At about the 7th year, I finally had the discipline to bring a camera and take pictures. I pushed myself to take pictures in as many aspects of cannery life as I could. I took about 20 rolls of film. And I finished those twenty rolls, too. When I got back to Seattle, a friend offered to develop the films for free, all of it, because he had just gotten some grant money for a project. I gave him all 20 rolls and I waited for the film. But I didn't hear a word from him for a while. After about a month had passed, I asked him. He said he had lost it. He said he did not know what happened but the rolls of films along with some other items of his group just did not come back. I was crushed as still I am. But then I said to myself, "This is why you know you must write of them, that is why you hear me now, and that is also why I know that I will once again return to that distant land, though perhaps that might be in a different time, when times have changed, because that's the nature of time, and I not knowing now which is more distant to me, the land or the time.

A Mechanic For the Second Season

Rows and rows of various shipping vessels lined the windy wharf of Kodiak town, Alaska in the late summer of '72. They were all getting ready to ship out again to go fishing and the smell of the last trip of the season was in the air. He was not that down, but he had had no income for ten days now. On his eleventh day in Kodiak, he half decided to look for a job. He figured he'll try for about an hour. He had heard from the Greek at Sid's Pool Hall that skippers were down there and that they were, in fact, hiring deckhands of all sorts. Just walk up and down the docks and ask around, the Greek told him. And that was exactly what he did. When he got to the wharf, it was nearing sunset and its burgeoning brilliance painted the Alaskan skies with splashes of fiery colors, the clouds nearby taking on whatever hues were cast upon them: red, orange, rust or gold. However, one could feel the trespassing of evening. Just three or four stalls down the boardwalk, in a fishing boat, was a stubble-bearded white man with a pinkish face, squatting by the deck, a cluster of his hair standing in the wind, with blue denim overalls and a long-sleeved cream-colored undershirt.

"Are you by any chance in need of a helper?" he asked the white man awkwardly.

"You looking for a job?" the white man stood up.

"That's right, sir."

"What's your name?"

"Chris Sunday," he said.

"Strange name," the man in the long-sleeved undershirt said, "What do you know?"

"About fishing, pretty much nothing." He said, but quickly and confidently added, "but I learn quick."

"Hmm. Pretty much nothing, huh?" He started to scratch his chin and stubbly face. He wasn't really that old, about 50. But he had some gray spread around on that thin, white face. "I'm gonna have to teach you from scratch, do I? Yup. I got me a tinhorn," he was talking to himself, looking down and as he looked up at him he said, 'You're on, son. You're aboard."

"Wow, really?"

"Damn rights. This skipper never says nothin' about work and money unless it's for real. We start tonight. In about an hour and a half."

"What?" The sun was still up. But it was starting the long sunset ritual that would last for hours in this land of the midnight sun. The wind was picking up and he unconsciously sniffed at it. To face it he had to look far into where the sea met the horizon. Then he turned and flipped up the collar of his blue, checkered, woolen, lumberjack shirt. He felt the wind and the fiber on his neck.

"You got a jacket? Let's roll if you're ready. You're ready ain't you? I mean to work."

"Yeah, yeah. I'm ready," he heard himself say.

"You'll be the chief cook and bottle washer and I'll be the skipper. Two-man operation." He laughed.

"Sure thing." He said. The words came reluctantly out of his lips.

"We'll be gone for at least a week."

It was only ten days ago that Christopher Sunday had come to town from Bristol Bay in the north, the season there having just ended. His christened name was Crisostomo Domingo but, as one gets to quickly discover, in Alaska your given name is quickly forgotten and replaced by a name more suited to the times, more associated with Alaskan fishing cannery life. And that was how one eventually became known in these parts. The Indians say the wind has something to do with it. He was twenty-eight years old.

Chris was going for what is called a "second season". There are many ways one can achieve "double season" status and prestige as an elite Alaskero. One way was to work for one company and with your pay look for another on your own. That was how most folks got jobs there, just by looking around on their own. But of course, one would prefer the security of a contract and a union, which is what he had done in Bristol Bay for the Alaska Packers Association. In desperate, neverending, no-sleep-all-work times, the Filipinos called it "Alaska (Mada) Puckers Association". That year was an early short season for the salmon, so he figured he would go visit his friend Andy in Kodiak, maybe put in for double season, although the second season in Kodiak would be entirely on his own. He had sent most of his money home to his wife and two young kids in San Francisco before going to Kodiak from Bristol Bay. He had about five hundred dollars on him when he stepped off the Wein Airline plane that landed on what seemed at first sight to be an endless terrain of mud. Only the wind distracted from the noisy rain. Bristol Bay or Kodiak, it was still Alaska.

He took a well-used cab to town. Five hundred dollars seemed like a lot of money in Kodiak in 1972 so, right out of the airport, leaving his luggage down the lobby, he played poker up the stairs of a building about five doors away from Sid's Pool Hall downtown. He won seven hundred dollars. Twelve hundred dollars seemed even more like a lot of money now. At approximately 4 in the morning, he found a place in town near the Shelikof Hotel, an apartment house on a slope of a hill, among the tall giant figures of pine and fir and oak. Its red and brown dirt and unpaved road rose up into the driveway of the complex. He gave the man at the desk $50 for two nights. It was his first night in Kodiak and he might need both nights to sleep.

His connection in Kodiak, Andy, a fellow San Franciscan, was one of those Pinoys who understood everything in Filipino but did not speak a word of it. Andy would end up in Sid's Pool Hall most times after work and he would always meet him there. After ten days in Kodiak, he thought of getting a job as a hand in a fishing boat off the harbor. They kept saying "it's easy; just look around." Room and board would be free, and he would make some money fishing, too. That would be ideal. Something to wish for. But, as folks say, watch out for what you wish for; you might get it.

He met the Greek there at Sid's Pool Hall. He was about 70 years old with a dark faded coat jacket and a whitish shirt wrinkled a bit and a loose tie around the collar. At Sid's Pool Hall the Greek was always telling him stories. Said he was from Delphi. The old man loved to talk, and Christopher Sunday especially liked the Greek's expressions when he told the stories. He understood them, at least it seemed so. Which was better than anybody else there. No one knew what the hell the Greek was saying. Nobody ever really understood the Greek. There was always something unintelligible in each sentence he uttered. But folks didn't have the heart to keep interrupting him.

"Never can figure out what the hell he's saying." Sid the Pool Hall owner would tell Chris Sunday about the Greek. "He'd be talking to me for hours! And I've been listening to him for years, man," said Sid, who was a middle-aged white man, slow and easy going, and whose wife meant everything to him. "And here you are, just got here, and here he is talking to you right off, and you talking to him like you've been friends for life! I don't get it. What in tarnation is he saying?" The Greek would just look at Chris and laugh.

During those ten days, Chris Sunday got to know the regulars who visited Sid's Pool Hall. One afternoon, Rick the Stick Wilson, the loud-mouthed rowdy was playing Howie the hard core Vietnam Vet an intense game of pool. Howie was a Marine who served 13 months in Vietnam. He had just gotten back. He said after he survived the first three months, it became his mindset that "they just couldn't kill me anymore." Originally, he was a mortician from Missouri. He joined, he said, because he got tired of "making a living out of the dead". It looked like he was losing bad. Maybe he was lucky in Vietnam but here this afternoon at Sid's pool hall, in Kodiak Alaska, he found himself often behind the eight ball. It didn't help his cool any with Rick the Stick mouthing off.

"All right, who'll be next here? I got this guy running and hidin'." Rick however was smart enough not to denigrate big Howie as a Marine just out of Vietnam. Later on, Rick the Stick would tell Chris Sunday that big Howie felt so badly beaten that he kept wanting to play some more and Rick was telling him to just wait till the next time. Luck was not with him that afternoon. But of course, big Howard the Marine Sergeant from Vietnam wouldn't want to quit. Big Howie lost four hundred dollars to Rick Wilson that day.

For seasonal workers, money flowed like water in Alaska. One minute you have it, the next it's all gone. After ten days in Kodiak, and seeing big Howie lose big money big time, Christopher Sunday decided to look for a job, even though he really didn't need one at that moment (yet). One never knew. Following the advice of everyone, he went to the docks and asked around if anyone could use a deckhand or something.

"Are you a mecka-nik?" the white man in the overalls asked.

"A what?"

"A mecka-nik."

"A...a meka what? No. I don't know nothing about machines, engines or motors. Never did. Always been lousy at it," he said, almost laughing. "My wife is the one who carries the hammer around the house."

"I asked Uncle Nick for a meka-nic. But never mind. I guess you'll do fine," he said. "That's all right. You'll learn." He looked Chris Sunday up and down. "You ready now?"

"What?"

"Like I said, I'm taking off in an hour and a half. Before dark starts lingerin'. Thought you were looking for a job?"

"Yeah, I am. I mean I am, but...it takes a long time to get dark this time of year..."

"Well, you want it or not?" The Greek had said that work would be quick to find but he did not realize it would be this quick. He did not want it to be this quick. "Are you in or are you out, kid?" The man turned around to loosen some of the moorings.

"Well yeah, of course—"

"Then hop to it, son! We'll come back for your stuff tomorrow morning."

Chris Sunday did not know what to do, but he heard himself say, "Okay."

"This skiff will take us to my fishing boat. She's waiting there for us and we want to get to the boat before it gets real dark." The blue of the sky was turning deep violet.

"Okay," he said. "You got me," and ducking under a thick and bristly rope, he hopped on board.

"Not here, though. This aint my boat. Like I said she's waiting out in the ocean for us. We'll take the skiff to get where she is." Behind the boat was a small aluminum motorboat where the two boarded, one on each end. "Like I said, you'll be the first cook and bottle washer and I'll be the captain," he said, tucking in the burlap sack that he had taken with him.

"Okay, Skipper. Whatever you say. Let her roll."

By the time the sun had set, well, somewhat set, they had already been riding that skiff over the bay's rough waters for over half an hour. Chris Sunday felt the darkness growing around him, surrounding him. He looked around and saw no one and nothing. He was in the middle of a sea, with barely a tree-speckled horizon to strain his eyes. Then a chill came over him and a hulking, creaking figure began to be visible in the growing dark. In the patchy mist of the high seas, in the vying splashings of the sea and the spurt of the motor-driven skiff, they approached the fishing boat itself, the one who would in essence provide the job. But it was the salmon, of course, that would give almost everyone their livelihood this time of year. The skipper immediately turned off the skiff's engine. In silence, the hull of the boat passed him; slowly the sides of its white panelings emerged squeaking and rocking, the name passing like a ghost in a veil of mist. *Madre Dolorosa,* it slowly spelled out.

The skipper checked the engine and, while Chris was still trying to get his footing on the skiff, jumped on board the *Madre Dolorosa*. Looking down at the skiff, he shouted to Chris Sunday.

"Do you know how to run that thing?" His voice sounded so clear in the still night.

"Of course not. Never had to. How do you operate this thing?"

By the short time that he got his footing, he realized that the skiff had been drifting away from the *Madre Dolorosa*. The skipper from on board the *Madre Dolorosa* went down to the skiff but instead of helping Chris Sunday board the fishing boat, he kicked the skiff (with Christopher Sunday in it), pushing it even further away from the *Madre Dolorosa* and it started drifting into the sea.

"Hey, what do you think you're doing? Why'd you let go of the rope?" The skiff continued drifting away from the boat. "Hey, How'd you work this thing?"

"You figure it out, boy. She's all you got and you're all she's got."

Chris Sunday quickly got his hands on the motor and its string-pull starter. He yanked it hard. It started with no problem. But he was still drifting. The boat was pretty much out of reach. And the young moonlight was not enough to keep him from drifting away into deeper darkness.

"You'll figure it out," and the voice trailed into the sound of lapping water.

Christopher Sunday revved up the engine a bit and started looking for the controls and slowly experimenting with them, and within a minute or so, got the hang of it and could maneuver the skiff left and right, forward and reverse.

He was even starting to like it, playing with it, when the skipper called him in from out of the faint light of the boat. "Come on up here! We got work to do!"

By the time Chris tied the skiff to the *Madre* and had gone to the top deck and looked up, a million stars were starting to glimmer.

"I'm gonna tell it to you straight, son," the skipper said. And from this tone of voice and choice of words, Chris had a gambler's bad feeling that maybe the skipper had not been totally truthful with him before this. Skipper opened the sack he had brought from Kodiak Harbor and pulled out a bottle from it. The clangorous burlap sack betrayed the fact that there were at least two more bottles left in there.

"When are we going out? I mean, fishing? And start making some money, right? Tomorrow?" Christopher Sunday asked directly.

"Now hold on there, tinhorn. First things first. First thing we gotta do is git her running. Are you a mecka-nik?" he asked again as he took a swig at the bottle he had in his hand. After two gulps, he offered the bottle to Christopher Sunday who himself took two gulps.

"What do you mean?"

"This boat ain't going nowhere till that web gets untangled from the propeller."

Christopher Sunday looked at the sky and a million more stars had dotted the velvet dome. He started to get that I'm in the middle of fucking nowhere and if I die, no one will ever know where the hell to find my body, let alone care who the fuck I am . . . feeling inside him again. It was easy for this feeling of insignificance to haunt the traveler far from home, in this case, far from any-where. And this white man of a captain had duped him into doing an unpleas-ant chore. Tinhorn was learning fast.

"What about that propeller?" Chris was afraid to ask.

"You gotta go down and fix it."

"How come you haven't tried?"

"I can't swim."

"What?"

"You heard me. That's why I was expecting a mecka_"

"Yeah, I know. A mecka-nick. Well…, I don't know nothing about engines like I said and…"

"Can you swim?"

"Of course, I can swim. What do you take me for, an idiot? Sorry. I didn't mean that, Skipper." The younger man composed himself. "How can you not know how to swim?"

"Most times knowing how to swim don't matter. The sea will swallow you up anyway, many different ways. Quick, too." He took another swig at the bottle and tried to look at Chris straight in the eye. "It's the web, kid. It's tangled. You gotta cut it off. It's all tangled and knotted up. You gotta go down there and cut it loose, kid."

"In the middle of the night?"

"The sooner you fix it, the sooner we'll be making money, son. Just get that web untangled down there and we'll start making money. There's about a week more fish-permit days left. We don't really have much time to make money but know where to go. Here, take this knife."

Resigned to this piracy in the high seas, Chris replied, "No, thanks. I got my own." The youth was somewhat angry, but he felt powerless. Christopher Sunday bent down and pulled out the mother-of-pearl inlaid handled knife (that his friend Amador Saga had given him from Bristol Bay just last month) from his boot, which he removed. He asked the skipper to keep the room heated.

While still angry, fully clothed, the youth dove into the deep, cold, icy waters of the bay, breaking seawater surface, the crackling of thin ice crystal clear in his imagination. Instantly, he felt his penis recede into unknown crevices of his anatomy. The taste of salt seeped into his mouth and tongue and he remembered for a moment the sea of his boyhood, the very warm sea of his boyhood. There was a largeness to the sea that demanded and took all one's attention. The sea was that way. He gave two kicks underwater and he saw the tangled web right away. He kicked another towards the boat's propeller, a patch of its bronze catching some light from above. He cut two or three knots but the rope from the net was strong. The youth emerged from the water after an interminable time. He blew out some water twice then went down again. He took longer this time. But he came up. Again, he blew water, then, looking around, went down again. When he emerged this time he pulled on the rope that the skipper held on the other end, inside the outer edge of the boat leaning over towards the water.

When he got back up into the boat, he took off his clothes and started to roll and twist them to squeeze and drip out the water.

"Where's the heat, man? I asked you to get the heat going . . ."

"Can't do that, tinhorn. Battery is low or dead. I tried just when you told me. Just now. This here lantern is all we got. Here, let me see. I got two more of these."

He kept reminding himself that this old fart of a drunk is not going to get the better of him. And that after he fixes this problem, there would be nothing but smooth sailing from then on. Smooth fishing, that is, and making money. The big money that he had been promising his wife that he would bring back home to San Francisco. He found the lanterns quick enough. Between three kerosene fueled lanterns, Chris wrung his clothes as dry and warm and as fast as he could while completely naked.

"I gotta go back down there. I didn't get it all cut. There's still some knots left. I gotta go down a few more times. Shit."

"There's a towel hanging right behind you."

Chris put the towel around his neck. "Just let me know when," said the skipper, holding on to his rope.

Chris was turning to go back down when he noticed the skipper slowly sliding from the door handle ready to fall. He put the towel around his waist and caught the skipper in time. Quickly he let him go. "Something bothering you, boss?" It was getting quite obvious to Chris that the skipper was not all there. And that he was getting drunker and drunker.

"Yup. It's an old story, my man." The skipper gulped his bottle. "The wife ran out on me."

"I'm sorry to hear that. I'll have to go down again. Get the lantern going will you?"

"Did you ever get told, I mean right to your face, by your wife that she wants another man, and your friend at that, huh, did you?"

"Let me think on that one," said Chris Sunday. Eying the bottle, he added, "Slow down." He put back the towel to hang adding, "I think that I can finish it in a couple of more dives. Can you save me some, huh?"

"Did you ever watch outside a door expecting your wife and someone else to walk out. Eh, did you? Did you ever..."

"Yeah, I think I got the picture. Look, forget the details. I got the picture. That was a mean and cruel thing she did to you, Skip. And for what, right? For what? A piece of ass? That's all, right? Don't go blaming yourself, too, Skipper, because she's the asshole, remember. "

"Right! Damn rights," slurred the skipper. "Did you ever in the middle of the night hear your wife moan and groan for your friend telling you she can't sleep; she must have him? Huh?"

All of a sudden Christopher Sunday started thinking of his wife. "I...I don't really know. I think I got the idea, Captain...Skipper..."

"Call me whatever you want. It'll probably be pretty close to the truth... which is a loser."

"Don't know about that, Skip. We've all been there."

"Why? Why now? Why me? Why him? 'He's younger', was all she said. Yeah. Guess it was my fault, too. I introduced the two. Yep, he was my friend, all right." He thought for a while. "Used to cooch and coo right in front of me, she was so hard up to have him. Imagine what she did when I wasn't around."

The skipper was drinking that most-likely cheap whiskey all along his tale. His reddish, white face would once in a while glow in the dim of night when the lantern's beam would hit him as the boat pitched and rolled softly, like a lullaby. This reminded Christopher Sunday of the Coleman lantern he had brought back to the Philippines as *pasalubong* to his uncle Prudencio from one of his *balikbayan* trips. His uncle said that he needed it because he (said he) "was a fisherman now". Before that, he (had said he) was a *sabungero*, and before that, a *boksingero*. He probably sold the damn thing while it was still in the box because Chris had never heard his uncle mention it again. That's why he had never thought of it until now.

"Be right back, Skipper," Chris said and jumped down once again into the deep waters. He did this several times, fully clothed, and washed and wrung dry the same blue checkered woolen lumberjack shirt and jeans. Because of the waiting time of drying his clothes by Coleman lantern heat before going down again, between dives, a dialogue ensued between the two. As the youth once more emerged from the sea into the fishing boat like the salmon itself, he found the Captain seemingly awaiting his return.

"This'll be the third year in a row I'll lose money, too," said the white skipper.

"I thought everybody made money fishing." Said Chris, taking off his shirt and wringing it dry once more.

"That's what you think. That's what everybody thinks. You got a lot to learn, tinhorn." And he took a violent swig of his bottle. "I'll learn you some all right."

"You better take it easy with that thing. You ain't learnin' me that. I know how to lift a jug already."

"Why should I? Why should I take it easy? Nobody ever took it easy on me, hah?"

"Better sit it down, Skipper. You don't know what you're saying."

"I know exactly what I'm saying," said the skipper, sitting down. "I know exactly how those bastards cheated me! Fucking assholes!" The skipper's face was turning inside out, sour and slightly slobbery. He was beginning to cry. He tried to stop it but he could not. For a minute it seemed interminable. Finally, he calmed down and composed himself, but he did not stop speaking. "Yup, you got some learning to do, all right, boy," he said and took another swig of the bottle but put it down right away. He took out another bottle from his sack. "You'll learn," the skipper kept on saying. He continued drinking. At times he forgot to wipe his mouth, the liquor still sparkling on his lips. "Every time she smelled him nearby, she started getting itchy."

"Allergies, huh?"

"No. Horniness. In heat, you know."

"I think I got the drift, Skipper…"

"I don't think so. I don't think you get it at all, kid. I mean, what part of ouch don't you get?

"I said I got it."

"You know how much I broke my ass for…never mind."

"That's right, Skipper. Never mind."

Out into the blue darkness that is the water, a sliver of a moon hung like a golden tooth from the deep violet sky. "Maybe you should just concentrate on one thing at a time, Skipper. I mean you've been through a lot. And all at the same time. That's tough. You still got this boat, though."

"This boat ain't no good." the skipper said. "That's why I got you out here. To help me take a look at what's stuck down there. I tricked you." Chris was not surprised. "I thought you would be a mecha…That Uncle Nick…" then the skipper started to mumble and he could not understand him anymore.

As Christopher Sunday surveyed his close quartered surroundings, which was composed of ninety-five percent decomposing red sockeye salmon, he asked the skipper, "Where should I sleep?"

"Wherever you want." was the quick reply. "Just make room for yourself there." The skipper pointed with his bottle.

Where? he thought. There was nothing but fish all around. When he turned around, the skipper had gone down the hole to his bunk and he was left alone in the night with the elements all around him, stark, bleak and terrifyingly beautiful.

He dove down again without thinking, just like when he was a boy. He was always the first to volunteer, not because he was braver than his playmates, as some might have thought, but because he was afraid of the waiting, the anticipation. When he cut the last knot, the net which had enveloped the propeller slid away quietly and quickly like a giant transparent octopus. That night he slept wet; and he slept among a boatload of fish that had been dead for several days.

Morning broke slowly but intensely. He turned off all three lanterns, which had provided him heat throughout the night, one at a time. He squinted at the spot in the horizon where the sun would soon be, glowing in the ruffled clouds. He slowly dusted off his checkered lumberjack shirt as he shook his head into waking. He was sure he stunk like hell but sleeping with the fish all night dulled his sense of smell and for that he, though others might not be, was grateful. He removed the dead battery from the engine and lifted it out. It was heavy. That thing must have been really dead. He briefly checked on the skipper below and found him still asleep, snoring like a bear. He picked up the blanket on the floor and put it over him. Getting on the skiff with the cumbersome battery, he sharply pulled the string and headed straight for shore.

He had no idea where he was when he hit land. He tied the skiff to mangroves, and started walking with the battery.

The black bear, the weakest and 'tamest' of the bears, can kill a horse with one blow. The fiercest is the Grizzly and one of the largest would be right here, the Kodiak Bear. Every now and then he would hear bear sounds but he knew they came from far away because he could still hear the ripple of the streams over them a lot clearer. Christopher Sunday was thinking it might be here that he might find out the prowess, through its claws, of the infamous Kodiak Bear.

The young summer grass, yellow green in their innocence, smelling fresh and vibrant, covered the wooded area and woke him from his stupor of fish stench. He lugged the dead battery across a dense forest. He carried it all sorts of ways. First he put it on his palm with one side of the base closer to his wrist as he lifted it up right above his shoulder. Then, he put more and more weight on his shoulder till he transferred it to the other palm, and then the other shoulder. Then he carried it with one hip. Then the other. He even once put it on top of his head. Then he carried it in front of him, right by his stomach and sort of leaned back a bit as he walked. This slowed him down some but what the hell, at that point he was so tired and angry and filled with conflicting and confusing emotions he was ready to just lie down and await his destiny with that bear he seemed to keep hearing as he walked across the fields of yellow green grass. Then he heard more and more distinct the rush of running water. He spotted clear water trickling off a hollowed limb sticking out of a slope surrounded by mist from a spring somewhere near. He laid down his load slowly and cupped his shaking hand right under the liquid crystals shimmering in the sunlight and dipped his mouth into them, part of the sun reflecting from his sea-dried hair. Sweet. And dizzily delicious. Like nectared rain from the gods! Let the fucking bears come and devour him. He was too resigned to even fend them off. He was already in heaven.

Then he had to get up and walk again. He walked and walked until there seemed no more place to walk. He did not know the direction he was heading (if there was any direction at all to wherever he was heading). He was hoping for a road or a highway to come up through the trees where there would be some vehicles to give him a lift to town. The battery he had been carrying every which way, heavy to begin with, just got heavier and heavier.

Then out of nowhere it seemed, a truck emerged through the line of trees. He did not even hear the highway. Dust puffed from its rear when it braked for him, though it passed him some distance. It had wooden boards for a shell and the rest of it was dirt red.

"Going to town?" The driver shouted turning back toward him trying to catch up with the car.

"Yes, sir," said the youth running towards the vehicle.

The driver pushed the passenger door open, "Hop in", he said. He was a big burly white man with a reddish brown beard and a lumberjack shirt like him, only all red, like his truck, dirt red.

Chris slid right in and with relief, put the battery in between them, lifting his hands slowly, twisting and turning and shaking them. The heater in the truck was intense and the fan was on its maximum. It got a little nauseating, especially during the lull in the conversation. The driver too seemed nauseated. The youngster was sure that it was he and his salmon smell that was making the kind-hearted driver keep makking small talk all throughout the trip to town. Chris thought that the driver scooted away a bit when he first jumped into the vehicle. When he got to town he called his friend Rick the Stick to come pick him up. The battery was not only dead, it was really dead. It was un-rechargeable. He had to buy a new one. Almost a hundred bucks. In the town of Kodiak that night, in his room near the Shelikof Hotel, Christopher Sunday, Crisostomo Domingo, started thinking about things. Only the wind heard his thoughts.

The following day, bright and early, Rick the Stick and Christopher Sunday went back into the mangroves where the skiff was tied to. Chris was plus one battery and minus a hundred bucks. He was going to be frank with the skipper when he saw him. And when he did, the skipper spoke first.

"Well, you got the darned thing right there in your hands. Let me see." And he was still smiling when he took it from Chris, the heavy, new battery for the *Madre Dolorosa*, cradling it in his arms. "Well this is all we really need. We still got a couple of fishing days left. Let's get cracking," he said, still smiling.

"Skipper, I ain't going."

"What?"

"I…I can't," said Chris. "My…my uncle. My Uncle Prudencio is in Anchorage. He wants to see me."

"That's right," said Rick. "I heard them talk on the phone…"

"Is this the Coleman Lantern uncle? Didn't you tell me he was in jail?"

"That's what I thought!" Chris Sunday was like a little boy when he said, "That's why I gotta go. Sorry for leaving you alone with… all this shit."

"Yeah, it's his uncle," Rick seconded again. "He's gotta go. You understand."

The skipper thought for a while, but he did not take long, then said, "Oh, yeah, sure. I understand. Course, I do." It seemed to Chris that the skipper was trying to put on a smile. "Can't say I blame you. Go on, kid. Good luck to ye."

"Will you be okay with all this," he looked around, "this stuff?"

"I'll take care of it," said the skipper, actually smiling. "Got a brand-new battery now, don't I?"

Somehow to Chris Sunday, the skipper sounded like a new man and he felt all right in leaving. But of course, he had to say goodbye to the old timer, the Greek. He had stayed a couple of days at the old man's place in his first days at Kodiak and Chris never forgot that.

He was alone when he came up the road to the Greek's place. The rain made the path muddy and hard to walk on up the trail to the small bungalow. Before Chris got up the path to the door, the old man was already outside with his same faded dark suit jacket and suspenders over his white shirt.

"Came to say goodbye, Greek. I wanted to thank —"

"Did you see my nephew? Did you get a job from him?"

"Your nephew? Was that...Well, yeah...kind of...I mean..."

"I knew you would. I knew you would be good for him, too. How is he? I knew he needed a mechanic."

"But I'm not a mechanic, Greek. I don't know nothing about engines." It seemed the Greek was giving him some more of his usual inscrutability.

"Yes, you are!" He smiled and thumped the young man's chest with his fingertips. "You're a mechanic of the heart," he beamed. "The most important engine of them all!"

He went back to his place near the Shelikof Hotel where the manager had saved a room for him. That's when he suddenly realized that he had not made any money at all. In fact, he lost money! However, Christopher Sunday would come to discover that he had been wrong once again. He got paid all right. He got paid plenty. He stayed at his apartment without going back to Sid's Pool Hall for three more days waiting for his flight for Anchorage. And when he got back to San Francisco, (along with the cases of canned salmon he had sent as gifts around the world, including his hometown in Leyte, as well as the grizzly bear's skin that his Indian friend Mountain from Kotzebue had given him), he unwrapped (like opening an envelope for a paycheck, the paycheck he never had), as payment, the wealth from his *Alaskero's* storybox, this story, and shared it as pasalubong with his wife and two wide-eyed children.

Lust Among the Ruins

—The Alaskero's Sex Life (from memoir to fiction)

You won't read about them in the newspapers. You won't study them in your textbooks. They do not appear in any of your television programs, nor radio, nor films, nor plays. But here on the ground, in Bristol Bay, Alaska, the rocks cry out their follies and glories, the river ebbs and flows with their stories, the tundra tell their tales, and the wind whisper their names.

Just so I won't give sex a bad name, I will include the categories surrounding it, like love, lust, romance, betrayals, and heartbreaks. (There are some of these in my two books Seasons by the Bay and Full Deck, but many more are not there. They would be the ones for storytelling, like this one).

Part of the Alaskero's lore is getting a nickname, or at least being known as having a nickname. Even objects and things get a nickname. The "Iron Chink" was/is named for the butchering machines that cut the salmon for the cannery. They took the place of erstwhile Chinese workers. Most names were given to you. A few, if considered badd enough, gave themselves their own names, like Boy Sige-Sige and James Bond. But first, we come to Johnny Mamayamaya na.

As some may know, there was a practice, not uncommon in those days, maybe still true, of going to the Philippines after the season, as one of the rewards they would give themselves. There would be many reasons for them visiting their homeland. But one was to seek a bride. And for old timers, that find usually ended up in a young bride.

Such was the case with Mang Johnny, a story of passion and patience, with a dash of irony, and paradox. Right after the season, he had gone to the Philippines, Mang Johnny. This story came from two or three different sources and, including mine, you are now getting an amalgamation of all those.

Johnny indeed had met some young thing in the Philippines and had brought her back to the States. He was forewarned of the insatiable energy of youth, should he land an impassioned partner, and end up like Mayor Lacson dying of a heart attack with Susan Roces the movie star by his side...or on top, or bottom, who knows? But surprisingly, it was the old man, in a reversal of expected sexual roles, who was the more energetic. And his bride, well, acted like the sweet young thing that she was, discreet and virginal.

It was Mang Johnny who wanted it all the time and the young bride somehow in her coyness, kept refusing. It was said that they did not have sex on the boat all the way across the Pacific, almost a month. There were speculations why this was so but none was ever confirmed. It would not be rumor anymore if confirmed, would it? She was constantly repulsing him with excuses. What does she think, he thought, that the marriage won't be consummated? She's crazy! But it was not till they were back in the States that he finally worked it in the conversation.

They were just getting up in the morning.

"Haneh, O, ngayon na." He tugged a bit at the side of her duster dress. They were both still lying down. "Let's do it now."

"Ano? Teka. Magluluto pa ko, e. Saka na. Mamayamaya na. [Hold on a second; I still gotta cook. A little later.]"

Then, a little after breakfast,

"Ngayon na? [Now already?]"

"Mamayamaya na. Hugas muna ko ng pinggan, ha. [A little later; let me wash the dishes first, okay?]"

Around lunch, she noticed him approaching her with some urgency. "Now, na."

Again she answered, "lots of errands, you know that. Cook again for lunch, laundry later, then hang up the clothes, lots of errands, so later na, ok? Mamayamaya na."

Frustrated and at the end of his libido's rope, he pulled her to his side, and blurted, "I said ngayon na! . . . At mamiyamaya pa! [Now already!...and then again later!]" And that's how Johnny got his name.

Bad First Impressions

In our cannery of South Naknek, there was a shack that housed all the fishing gear to dry: nets, skeins, tools, ropes, everything. It inspired a scene from "May I Dancing With You" in Seasons By the Bay. It was a good place for a conversation as a prelude to courting since that place had the least smell of salmon because of its open windows that the Alaskan fresh air continuously permeated. It was also convenient because there were many places in that shack for comfort, cover, and concupiscence. It was here that Miss Hollywood (I can't say her name; she might still be around and if she found this out, she would hunt me down), beauty that she was, displayed her fishing prowess and the now famous "skein (sky) hook". This is where Sky King ridiculed himself trying to impress her. Without asking her, he tried to help her by lifting a fishing net (skein) on a pile to dry. He couldn't budge the thing. She stepped across him, picked up the pile with two hands, bent her beautiful knees outlined in those tight jeans, and released the net casting it simultaneously over the beam above with one hand following through, like a Kareem Abdul-Jabar sky hook shot. "You had the wrong footwork from the start," she said. He sure did, he thought.

I too had made the wrong move or uttered the wrong thing trying to impress Miss Hollywood, the beautiful, feisty and mysterious one. She had a page boy cut hair and walked quickly, with her arms hardly swaying, and her hands hardly visible under the overlength sleeves of her jacket.

Up the hill from the cannery, there was one multi-purpose building and that was Johnson's bar. Sunday's it's a church, weekends, it's a dance hall, and weekdays, it's a bar. On a rare moonlit night, at a dance at Johnson's bar, I was sitting alone, and I said "hi" to Miss Hollywood and her two friends as they made their rounds. I sat on a bench, pretty much not moving at all. I noticed her and her friends pass in front of me a couple of more times and greeted them as they passed. I saw the Wolfman dancing away in the middle of the crowd being cheered by the natives and the white guys. "Go Wolfman, go!" Meanwhile, the Wolfman was shouting in Filipino "This is how the white boys dance", mimicking, and flying into contortions of ridiculously awkward positions to the Pinoys' amazement and amusement.

Miss Hollywood and her posse passed by me again and this time she said, "Why aren't you dancing?"

Trying to be flippant and cool-like, I answered, "No one ever asked me." I could not read her reaction, but it was not one that I liked or expected, just like the response from her.

"Well, you're gonna sit there all night," she said. And I did. Outside the dance hall is a cliff overlooking the Naknek river and at night little conclaves have lovers' and lusters' footprints, half-pint, empty whisky bottles, and other remnants or evidences of their activities, with mosquitos as eager participants in the trysts.

Cherchez la Femme

It was really before even coming to Alaska that I had worked in the orchards around Lake Okanagan in British Columbia, where I picked my first fruits of North America. It was partly because of a girl, the sister of the friend I was supposed to visit in Penticton. It was really her I wanted to see. From Vancouver to Penticton at fifteen years old, I and another boy had bought a car for $50, and traveled more than a thousand miles on four bald tires. This inspired my short story: "Baptism: a parable of summer" in Seasons by the Bay.

Some ten years later, in a room at the Reynold's Hotel at the International District of Seattle, James Bond would tell me that he walked the whole city of

Anchorage end to end, downtown to Elmendorf Air Force base, on tight jeans and leather shoes, just to see someone's smile. It was still worth it in those days, he said. There was still room for fools and foolhardiness. I know of what he speaks. From South Naknek in the boondocks to other boondock towns whose names I've now forgotten, I took two bush planes and landed on two makeshift airports in the middle of Lake Iliamna in the Kenai Peninsula, to visit my friend Craig in Nondalton, but it was really to see his cousin, who served as the inspiration for the character of Katherine in "The Visitor".

"Him-la!!!", was one of Eng the Chinaman's few choice utterances. It meant someone got *"him'd"*, (pronoun used as a verb). Back in the day, the old timers used to tell me with malicious delight the origin of this nuanced term. If you were reported to have slept with a native woman, the whole village will know and soon the troopers will know. If you think you will get away Scott free, think again. Many were halted at the South Naknek "International" Airport by authorities, (bosses or troopers). The woman would be brought as the workers boarded their bush planes to King Salmon, then transfer to Anchorage. She would point the accusing finger to the luckless Pinoy waiting in line to board, and say *"Him!" Patay.* Deadball. He then must stay the winter and, if a baby is born, before they let you go, you must make amends by arranging finances for the kid in case you don't intend to stay longer. Where is the Wolfman this year? Not here. He got *"him'd"* last season. I guess folks thought the practice to be an incentive for self-control. It did not work too well with the Alaskero's libido. All the Pinoys reported to have been *"him'd"* willingly stayed, however. To a man, they wanted to see their kid and not staying was not an option for them.

Nostalgic, quickly disappearing, and back in the day, a few signs were still left at the time of this telling. In fact, looking back on things sometimes I would realize that I, like William Faulkner, was looking back into the past as a rider on a moving train with my back to the front, seeing the vista of the past widening but getting further and further away. In hindsight, I was always looking at things disappearing or fading away (e.g. the Alaskero lifestyle, Manilatown in San Francisco) and some things being born in the dying (e.g. Ethnic Studies, the Financial District's Manhattanization of San Francisco), but of course, I was young and I was taken by the lure and romance of adventure, and something more than that, something I did not yet know. I was there for camaraderie but something deeper loomed larger. Though, because of my youth, I didn't notice the full impact of events at the time, I felt a witness to something passing and something coming up on the horizon, a big, brown rolling wonder. I felt the stars starting to align, like Napoleon must have, when he felt the pulse of destiny in his veins.

Location location location

Canneries no matter how big or small will have a fish house, a cannery, and a warehouse. Then there would be buildings for the workers, separated racially, ethnically, and class-wise. Living quarters were bunkhouses and residentials.

The dump yards to watch the bears eat at midnight was the number one date spot for lovers or would be lovers or one night stands. You must hijack a truck or vehicle to do this.

The fishing boats that were docked were good places to start the party. Or end it. But privacy is rare.

Then, there is the warehouse itself: the makeshift, flattened, cardboard boxes thrown on the cold floor, between hot cans of salmon cooling off in the warehouse. In ideal times, one could have a warm and cozy little corner. However, forever at your back you hear coitus interruptus hurrying near. One can even have music playing from a portable machine brought from the bunkhouse.

Women, mostly college age, relatives of white administrators, and of cannery workers, also started coming in significant numbers around 1975, when the male college age white workers started working many Filipino cannery positions. The sex and romance changed too, in leaps and bounds, like the internet.

James Bond was by far the most romantic dreamer in the cannery. He was already a veteran of many canneries in Alaska when I got there and he was not much older than I was. Eleven out of twelve months the cannery folks spoke of his stay in Alaska. It was said that his wife 'down below the lower forty-eight' greeted him by the door with a change of suitcase for the next eleven months. He was the one who named me "Shane". Because I always come back, he said. Kids around the village used to follow me around and sometimes I would promise to be back with some smuggled food or soda pop from the cannery. Funny, salmon is the one that brought us all together with characters from around the world yet with the children of the village, salmon is never sought or even mentioned when looking for something to eat.

One windy night we had some free time. Chavacan the Mexican my bunkmate opened the door and there was James Bond with a guitar slung over his shoulder, a red silk scarf around his neck, and a vest, with no shirt.

"Come on, Shane. Come with me."

"Where the hell are you going?"

"Come on, Shane. You know where. C'mon."

"Hey, there's gonna be lots of fish tomorrow; we better get some shut eye."

"C'mon, Shane. Nobody knows how much fish are coming tomorrow. And so what? Let 'em all come. We'll handle them all. Let's go watch the bears in the dumps. Twyla is going to be there."

Ah, Twyla, the half Russian Indian. I figured something like that.

"I'm gonna serenade the hell out of her, Shane. I'm gonna harana her like nobody's business. I'm gonna sing to her till she says yes! I'm gonna sing to her till I become the song itself! Here, have a shot." And he pulled out a Seagram 7 out of his back pocket. "C'mon, Shane, Let's go."

What can one do? Would you refuse a legend? But then, later, I found out, everybody is a legend in Alaska.

The Crow's Nest Challenge

High above the cannery, atop the company office, sits the Crow's Nest. Supposedly the Penthouse of the Cannery. Only whites, of course, though there are no signs saying so. Sometimes I get a strange notion, a sinister one, an irreverent urge to have sex there just to give a collective "fuck you" to the Mormons and other white evangelicals of the world whom, I see even in the streets of Manila to the country roads of Leyte. But I never got close to that Crow's Nest. Nor to procuring a partner for the literal deed.

Fresh Beginnings

You can reinvent yourself in Alaska. That's what one Romeo Vasquez did. Because of personal and legal troubles at home in the Philippines, the screen idol found himself working on the sliming tables of the Red Salmon Company across the river from its rival the Alaska Packers Association Cannery of South Naknek, where I worked. I was an innocent witness to the age old triangle of betrayal among a threesome. I guess I would make it a foursome, though I, a non-participant in the arrangement. I included this piece into another story of mine. "A Mechanic for the Second Season", I think. Or was it in "Pieces of the (Midnight) Sun"?

In the warehouse where we worked as the Lye Wash Crew, Chavacan The Mexican, spotting a young couple, whispered to me, in Spanish and gestures, "There they are, the skin-and-bones lovers. I don't know but they don't need much room. They can do it practically anywhere, just a little nook is all they need; they are so thin." He smiled. "They are so skinny I bet you when they make love, they make fire!" and he rubbed his two index fingers like two sticks together.

The two lean lovebirds were Nick the foreman's son and his white girlfriend whose name I have forgotten. She had freckles. They had a spot in the warehouse that I always noticed when used because we, the lye wash crew, are the ones to leave work the last of any crew member. We had to wait for the last cans to be cooked and that took 90 minutes. Even the butchers in the fish house who were responsible for cleaning their machines before quitting, had already gone home by then. That Nick could sing the blues like nobody's business. When we had leisure time, it was good to hear and see him do his thing. He would really get into it. Just one of the unappreciated, unheard-of talents of an *Alaskero*. One summer, he did not show up. They found him dead floating on the river in Delano one spring and the foreman grieved for that only son of his, and we felt it all throughout that season.

The Nurse

One year we had a company nurse surprisingly come in during the height of the fishing catch. She was a slender middle aged black woman, very gracious and motherly. Lo and behold, everybody, including me, got mysteriously sick that season, at least once. Just the touch of a woman's soft and tender hand on our bodies was heaven and pleasure enough to warrant a visit to the Nurse. Their tough *Alaskero* machismo veneer melted like ice still clinging to the banks of the Naknek River in summer, and that they used for drinks at every end-of-the-season party.

The Wages of Sin

The foreman, when he saw youngbloods, half-conked out, still groggy from the good times the night before or early morning, would gesture for me to come, and whisper in my ear quite loudly: "The wages of sin. Hehehe. The wages of sin. They were so lively last night at the bar but look at them now. Sleeping like babies during their 15-minute break. Not even bothering with a snack. Shit! *Plastado lahat. Sonamabit*! That one still has food on his lips; that one his coffee still steaming, untouched, the third one, his working gloves still half on, half off. *Sonamabit!* Someone take a picture."

I saw one condom during all the 15 consecutive summers I spent there. It was lying on a windy-edged beach near the water below Johnson's Bar. When I got to my room in the bunkhouse, I quickly scratched out a poem "Looking for Berries" that until now I like. The poem, not the condom.

Their real love and sex lives down below were most likely in tatters, in their ruin as it were. Betrayals of best friends cheating with their wives while they were following the seasons to the tune of "I Wonder Who's Kissing Her

Now" were old stories. Many, of course, were already not getting along; relationships were on the rocks even without Alaska as an excuse. An affair here and there, someone's wife running off with a white pimp, leaving the *Alaskero* with two small kids not knowing what became of her or when she will be back. Scattered around were ruined *Manongs*, ruined cannery buildings, ruined machines, ruined lives, with old men and the boys of summer working and playing in their ruin.

The Visit: At Tess' Place

—On the tundra near a fishing cannery and the village of South Naknek, Alaska.

Tristan enters stage left and takes off his coon hat, feeling very uncomfortable.
Tess: (Opens the door) Come sit down. What took you so long? (She starts making herself busy with her back turned to Tristan).
Tristan: Work. Butcher machine broke in the fish house.
Tess: Want coffee, or do you still have your tea ?
Tristan: Oh . . .whatever.
Tess: (Laughs a little) Same ol' Tristan. Whatever, eh?
Tristan: You can run from your enemies, but you can't hide from a friend . (They laugh and hug).
Tess: Well , what do you want, coffee or tea ?
Tristan: Yeah.
Tess: Yeah what ?
Tristan: Whatever 's easier to fix .
Tess: They 're both easy to fix .
Tristan: Here. (He pulls out a little flask and puts it on the table) Put a little something in 'em if you want. Sit down .
Tess: In a minute .
Tristan: Where 's your little boy ?
Tess: Oh, probably playing around near Johnson 's or something .
Tristan: So you married , uh . . . let's see . . .
Tess: I didn't.
Tristan: Oh .
Tess: That's all right. The little kid's daddy is Mack, if that's what you mean . You remember Mack don't you ?
Tristan: Oh . . . yeah, of course . . . where is he ?
Tess: Who knows ?
Tristan: So you married uh . . . which did you marry again . I'm . . . getting confused here .
Tess: (She starts laughing again) Come on, come on. I never got married. What do you think I am, a glutton for punishment?
Tristan: (Still looking a bit confused) I heard you married...
Tess: Arnold?
Tristan: Yeah, Arnold, that's it.
Tess: Nah. Almost, though. It was close.

Tristan: Well, that's what I heard--

Tess: You got everything twisted again--as usual. (They laugh)

Tristan: I'm sorry about you and Harold, I mean--

Tess: Arnold. Don't be. I should be sorry. But that's okay. It's fixed now. I kicked him out.

Tristan: Oh. (Now he laughs) Same ol' Tess.

Tess: What's that mean?

Tristan: Nothing. Sit down. Relax for a while.

Tess: In a minute. You know my Mom's been asking about you all the time. Shit, you're gonna catch hell if she sees you now.

Tristan: How is she, anyway?

Tess: Not too good, Tris. Kind a sick all the time. My brothers tell me that she asks about you now and then.

Tristan: Well, you know, mothers always loved me, except my own of course. But everybody else's, they adore me--

Tess: I know. And kids, too.

Tristan: It's those in-between age people that can't stand my guts.

Tess: So how are my cousins, those kids; you still babysitting them, I mean are they still bothering the hell out of you? Member that time when we couldn't get rid--

Tristan: Nah. No , you know how they are. Kids will be kids; they just... like to dream a little, I guess.

Tess: Like us, once right?

Tristan: Now, you don't have to talk about that . . .

Tess: Well . . . it's pretty hard . . to resist . . . when the chance is there to dream, you know . . . Most people grab it . Without really looking . . . far and hard . Without really knowing whether you should dream or not . Yeah , well , how 's San Francisco these days?

Tristan: Ok, I guess. I haven't really been there much.

Tess: Oh, you haven't?

Tristan: Nah. How about you? I didn't think you were here. I thought you were in Dillingham or something.

Tess: I was. Till I got sick of the place. Ah , I'd like to go to San Francisco . Get away from here. (Smiling) For a minute, that is .

Tristan: Yeah? What about for an hour or a year ?

Tess: What about you, for an hour or a year here in Alaska, huh ?

Tristan: Nah, I don't know about that. I was young. We were young. I was filled with...wild and crazy notions.

Tess: There's nothing wrong with that.

Tristan: Oh, there is, you know. If you...if you outlive it. You find someday that you have to wake up.

Tess: There's still nothing wrong with that.. Hey, how come you weren't at the village gathering for Ivan the other night.? Old man is turning how old now, one hundred and something?

Tristan: Yup. It varies. Yes, I was there.

Tess I didn't see you there.

Tristan: I passed by. I didn't know--cannery workers were supposed to--

Tess: Oh, cut that out. You're not just a cannery worker, you know that. Somebody mentioned you were there but I didn't see you.

Tristan: Yeah, I just passed by. I had to work.

Tess: And how's Blackie?

Tristan: Oh, he's fine.

Tess: Still working with him?

Tristan: Yeah. I think he's falling in love--finally.

Tess: --at last. (At last and finally are simultaneously spoken) Good for him. How are all those guys, Tris? Are they still around? Those old men. Oh, how I loved them! Lino, how's Lino?

Tristan Oh, Lino died in San Francisco a couple of years ago.

Tess: Oh, I'm sorry. (She finally sits down) What about Alas?

Tristan: Alas is still there. He's ...back there. Sick. He's dying, too.

Tess: I love that man. Can I see him, Tris? I just like to see him. And the fore-man. Is he still--

Tristan: Oh yeah. He's ...very much alive...okay, we'll see 'em. We'll go down there one of these days. Surprise the hell out of 'em. They told me that they thought they saw you. They don't know your name; they forgot. They just called you the princess... "dat injun princess."

Tess: Yup. Same old men, huh... with the flowers in their tongues. What about you? Ain't you married yet?

Tristan: Nnnnuh... I don't know... Too slow. I guess.

Tess: That's for sure. (They both laugh)

Tristan: I heard those girls in the bunkhouse talking about you.

Tess: Oh, really? They're nice. They're sweet. You know, innocent type.

Tristan: I don't know about that.

Tess: Well, maybe you're right there. What do they say about me? (She gets up) Here let me get you some more tea.

Tristan: Oh, nothing much. The usual, you know. You're a regular uh... high point in uh... cannery life here. You're a regular tourist attraction, heh, heh.

Tess: Am I? That's funny. I haven't seen anyone come up here but you. And it took you long enough.

Tristan: I didn't know you were here. Like I said, I thought you were in--

Tess: I know, I know. Just teasin' ya.

Tristan: And I'm not a tourist. Just a stranger.

Tess: You've never been a stranger. (Suddenly up-toned as she sits down again) Hey, you know I waited for you. I kinda waited for you.

Tristan: Let's not get into that. That was my fault, I guess.

Tess: No, let's get into it now. I've never been really clear. In the back of my mind I always wondered about what the hell happened. I wanna know, so let's get into it now, once and for all. I mean, you know, no hard feelings.

Tristan: I don't have any hard feelings.

Tess: Why didn't you show up? That time. In my mother's village where I waited for you.

Tristan: Oh, I was... I almost did... I uh... I don't know, I uh... was 20 miles from it. Then I turned back. I didn't want to make you miserable. I figured you had enough of that.

Tess: Hey, don't make up my mind for me. You're full of shit, you know that. If I wanna be miserable with you, that's... that's up to me.

Tristan: No, it ain't. It's up to me, too... Well, at least, you're not... I don't know... I got scared, I guess, I got... I knew deep down inside, and you did too, that you and I were just from two different worlds... so there was really no use forcing it. So I chickened out... I... I'm sorry. I've always wanted to kind've explain... It felt bad that...

Tess: No, no. No explanations needed. Life. I was just teasin' ya. (She gets up and looks around the cupboard) Relax. I wasn't really waiting for you. Well for a minute, yeah. What I mean is, I stayed for a lot of other reasons, too. For myself, mostly. I stayed longer than usual at the village. For myself first, I mean I hate to disappoint you or anything--

Tristan: You didn't, I mean, wait for--

Tess: Yes, and no, but for me, not just you, got it?

Tristan: This is confusing

Tess: No, it's simple, simple as the truth. So don't feel bad, ok? (She finds a container wrapped in fine cloth or suede)

Tristan: (Mumbling to himself) I don't know if I feel any better, I think I feel worse now

Tess: (Putting down the flask container that Tristan had offered earlier on the table as she sits) Ah, you're full of shit. What are you drinking?

Tristan: Brandy

Tess: What kind is it?

Tristan: Korbel

Tess: Throw that cheap shit away. Let's get down to some serious drinking (She pulls out the cloth wrapping slowly)

Tristan: Couvoisier, VSOP.

Tess: That's French for "Very Special Occasion or Person Only"... or something like that.

Tristan: You ain't even opened it yet.

Tess: It's open now, and I ain't gonna close it.

Tristan: Tess, I gotta get back to work.

Tess: No, you don't. Now, you just relax. (After a long quiet, maybe after a couple of swallows) Hey, thanks... you know... I've never really thanked you... For taking care of my brothers...

Tristan: (Clumsily) Hey, stop it, Tessie. You know... you know me--

Tess: I mean, when I wasn't here I heard... they got in trouble and... you were there--

Tristan: Well, you know... that's family, right?

Tess: Yeah.

Tristan: It was no big thing. It was nothing.

Tess: You alright, my man.

Tristan: (Toasting gesture) You ain't too shabby yourself.

Tess: (After a long silence) You're worried about Karina, huh?

Tristan: (Admittedly) ...I don't know. That girl just-- I can't figure her out. She's just... doomed. Too stubborn or something, too strong. (He looks at her)

Tess: (Curtly, feeling guilty) Don't look at me.

Tristan: I didn't say a word.

Tess: Maybe you can talk to her.

Tristan: Eh, I've done a lot of talking already. Just gotta let 'em go I guess.

Tess: Don't worry too much about it now. You'll just get old fast. Even older than you actually look. Before you know it, you're gonna be just like those old men out there--

Tristan: Oh no!

Tess: --like the Deputy! Or Alas...

Tristan: Lord, no!

Tess: Yeah, you'll be talking all kinds of shit without really knowing what the hell you're talking about and every second word is gonna be a cussword-

Tristan: Yeah that Karina's just too willful... for her own good, you know what I mean?

Tess: Yeah. I think I remember. So were you when you were young.

Tristan: (Smiling defensively) I was being young, too. (Getting up to go)

Tess: Where do you think you're going?

Tristan: Lady, I gotta go to work.

Tess: Well, if you must, you must. (She starts putting things away) Turning a girl down again, huh? (She puts things under the sink) Only man that ever turned me down.

Tristan: C'mon, don't give me a bad time, now. I gotta go. Just regards to you and... you know... everyone else I guess... (Regarding a male jacket, boots, and other male belongings)

Tess: My boyfriend? Yeah, I got a man... I think. He's fishing now.

Tristan: You think you got him, or you think he's fishing, or you think he's a man?

Tess: I think all of the above. I think-- he's fishing now. You come again, all right?

Tristan: Sure. You take good care. (He exits right. From without) Save that bottle!

Tess: I can't promise you that! There's no rainchecks in Alaska! (She puts some more things away and goes towards another direction of stage calling out to her son) Terry! Terry-Boy! Terry! (She exits left).

The Summer of '72

In the summer of '72, Christopher Sunday was imprisoned in Kodiak, Alaska. In the days that followed, strangely enough, it was the officers in their cubicled desks who seemed bored, not him who was in jail. He thought this because one of the younger officers, as Colombo had said describing the troopers in Bristol Bay, ("big, white, and ugly"), had come to him while giving lunch. The big jail room had a couple of shower stalls and toilets on the edge of the room. No curtains, no nothing. There was a cement wall waist high between the showers and a dozen beds.

"You got any books there I might want to read, you think? I've been wanting to read books cuz ...you're Filipino, right?..."

"Yeah. Must really be getting boring out in your cubicles for you guys to be looking into the inmates' files."

"You don't understand. My girlfriend is, too, and she keeps telling me, I should read. But every time I start, I get bored."

"Only the boring get bored, my friend. I commend your girlfriend. Boredom seems to be the general condition or attitude around here. I never get bored."

"And you're the one inside. "

"Don't matter where I am."

"Well, how do you know you won't get bored with a book?"

"I never get bored with anything. If a book doesn't catch my attention, I go to another one. But, like people, I try to give it the benefit of the doubt for twenty or so pages."

"I see. I never gave it much of a chance, I guess."

"Maybe that's part of your incarceration training."

"Well, you sure have a lot of books, let me tell you. The Captain made me carry them all by myself when they emptied your rental trailer. Two trunks-full. And big posters of all them Indian Chiefs on the walls. You Indian, too?"

"You eat Spaghetti?"

"Yeah, of course."

"You Italian?"

The cops were nice enough to give him back all his books. Maybe they had to keep them for evidence, or something, who knows? He was in his last year of his Master's Thesis from San Francisco State College when it was transitioning into a University. He certainly could avail of the time. But the police of Kodiak were looking for drugs, not bards.

"'Intellectual assholes!' the Captain told me." Said the young officer mimicking his Captain. They both laughed. "He hates books! Not me. I'd like to start getting to like reading."

"Well, which topics interest you?"

"I like racial conflicts kinds of shit, you know, there's so much shit happening now a fellow out here in the backwoods can't keep up with things."

"Your girlfriend, you said, was Filipino?"

"And Native. Athabascan. Gonna be a teacher."

"No wonder. She's starting with you, huh? I got one that just might be to your liking." He went to his suitcase under his cot. "Here."

"UHURU, what is that? You got anything in English?"

"It is in English, man. U.S. author. Means freedom, I think, in an African language. Haven't read it since high school. You'll dig it, man." He was twenty eight and the white officer looked barely twenty-one.

"Wow, thanks! You some kind of teacher?"

"Just a student of life, like you"

"Do you want something in return?"

"Of course, I do. I'm in jail, remember? Give me a good hamburger sandwich, the works."

In jail, one eats what one is provided. No outside food. Breakfast: coffee and a pancake. In case the pancake drops, no worries, you don't have to pick it up; it bounces right back up. On his first morning in jail, he had asked this same officer for some cream and sugar for the coffee that had just been brought in by the trustee. Upon his return, the trustee told him, "The Captain said that 'if you can smoke pot, you can drink coffee black!'" It was a small town jail with a family type of atmosphere and feeling to the whole place. The captain was judge, jury, and executioner until the prisoners went to trial for the real judge, jury and god forbid, executioner.

"I'll get you that burger from the best place in town, the Beachcomber."

"That the one by Sid's pool hall?"

"That's the one."

"See if you can get me two, okay?"

The cops had busted into their trailer a week ago in an especially inopportune time. He was deep into listening with brand new headphones the taped music of the Rolling Stones playing "Sympathy for the Devil" intercut with the original story of the Lone Ranger broadcasted decades ago. Just when the Lone Ranger decided to don his identity for the first time, Mick Jagger segued into *"Please, allow me to introduce myself, I'm a man of wealth and taste (Toot to doot). Please to meet you; hope you get my name. Just confusing you is the nature of my game (toot to doot)."*

He heard a loud knock on the trailer door, over the Rolling Stones. "Come in," he said.

The door flung open loudly and three policemen rushed in. One pointed a .357 magnum right at his head. "You Sal Anton?"

Irritated and annoyed more than scared, he did not take full stock of the seriousness of the situation. "No. Must you point that thing at my head?" He had, however, the sense enough not to move an inch. He had invited his white friend Rick Wilson, now in front of him, to have brunch that morning, and Sal, the man the cops were looking for, was actually baking some Alaska salmon at the end of the trailer home they rented.

"Friend," said Rick, to him. "This may be the last time I'll visit you for a while." Rick was dragged along, with the rest of them who lived in the trailer, in hand-cuffs to jail. Rick, however, was released the next day after he told the cops that Rick had just dropped in for coffee that morning and had nothing to do with anything. Sal Anton had been dealing drugs and lived with him in this trailer which was in his name. That is how he got incriminated. Possession was the official charge. 'Possession of an ugly face', as his friends liked to say. The trailer had been under surveillance for a month, the cops told them later.

"I think your starting to read would be what she would want. Let's show her a pile of books that you and she can choose from. These are loans, mind you. I need 'em all back. Only valid in the duration of my stay here, ok?"

"Great. That's still a couple of months away, right?"

"Yeah, thanks. Enjoy."

A week or so later, Sal Anton, his co-inmate, had to get out of jail to see a doc-tor because of his hemorrhoids. He was surprised when his name Crisostomo Domingo was also called, and for him to go with the rest of the prisoners being released that day. He was stunned because he knew he had at least five or six more weeks to go, or according to the officer, "a couple of months". Must be some weird mix-up and a fitting testament to the incompetence of the admin-istration. Immediately, escape entered his mind. What the hell, fate is already giving him an opportunity. The cops themselves ordered his release, though se-cretly he knew it was an error. But hell, it wasn't his error. But then, he thought again. How far can he really go? Kodiak is an island after all. One airport. He'll have to stay the winter, if he got caught. Hell, no. It would be just like being "himmed". He decided to point out the mistake to the authorities and go back to jail to finish his allotted time in peace. Besides, he hated loaning books to people; he was always conflicted between wanting to share and worrying about not getting it back again. Those books grow legs after a while, and he wanted his books back from the young policeman.

Va. Beach

(FANHS Conference, 2000, Virginia, Wesleyan University)

I wished
Sana
I could have gotten to know you better
From a glimpse only
Did I espy you
Who seemed like quite a number.

You could've been
And probably was
And is
A pearl of knowledge
For our sea of ignorance
Or you could've been
A son of a bitch, too.
Or most likely, both.

Sana
Hopefully
Sana
It should've been
Sana
Va.
Beach

7/2/2000

Thursday

I like Thursdays. It creeps up on you, then when you realize it, it's Friday or Saturday already. Its obscurity stands for so many things in life. Wednesday is the "hump" day, the middle of the week. Of course, there's the weekend, and Monday has its notoriety. Tuesdays are when things are closed, but Thursday is not known for anything, except maybe the novel I read as a highschooler when I was starting to devour literature, called The Man Who Was Thursday. It has a sound all its own, too. Its position has a certain out of placeness which reflect many, especially in today's ventures with isolation, vis a vis high tech. And things don't really close on Thursdays. And it has no opposites or counterparts, like weekends and weekdays. Sundays and Fridays have two counter connotations. And if you forget it, by the time you remember, it's almost there again. That's Thursday. Good thing about it, even if it's not Thursday, as long as it's not Wednesday or Friday, things can't be too far from or close to it. And Thursdays are the last open slots in your weekly schedule. It's a meeting-saver and a stress-reliever, an escape, an out. When things are going well, or when a moment of radiance or a flash of beauty or truth comes along, check it. It's probably around a Thursday. Unfortunately, when things are going bad, there's a good chance that it's a Thursday, as well. Thursdays teaches you humility, to take the bad and the good, the vicissitudes in life, as well as the transitoriness of things. What day is it now? Check it.

Suite #5
The Cure

Barugo, Leyte, Philippines. Photo by Tony Remington. ca. 2018

The great writer, National Artist, and mentor NVM Gonzalez once asked me the answer to this riddle.

There was a big mansion on top of a hill. The richest man in town lived there. All his valuable possessions were in that house. The owner always leaves, however, every weekend. And alas, a thief got to observe this. One weekend the thief prepared to rob this rich man. He waited till the rich man would leave. When the owner was completely gone, the thief moved in the house and robbed it clean! Every item was taken, from the biggest to the smallest. Everything! Coming back, as he approached his house, the owner saw the man. He saw the thief filling up his sack of goods. When the owner got there, the thief had gone. But when he went into his mansion and checked for lost items, not one was missing! Everything was still there, intact. How can this be? What container or house can hold a treasure yet when everything is taken from that house or container, everything is still there? Tell me.

You are looking at it. You may be holding it in your hands.

Why, it's a book, of course.

Saved by the Book

Around 2001, right after the 9/11 attacks on the Twin Towers of New York, I was invited to a big writers' conference by the Association of Writing Programs scheduled for Vancouver, Canada. First time I would return to that city of my adolescence. How many years gap, forty? I arrived at night. Ray and Elida Baxter, a couple whom I grew up with in Vancouver, were waiting for me at the airport terminal. However, at the exit lane, I was being hassled by an Indian Canadian immigration/customs officer. I did not bring my passport, just my driver's license. California. That was all that was necessary for travel to Canada and Mexico before 9/11.

"No good," said the guy. "Anybody can make a license for thirty dollars on the internet," he told me. "Especially now," he added. "Especially for people like you and me," his eyes rolled up toward his turban. I tried everything, but the guy would not believe me. "You must show me something to prove that you are indeed this fellow here, Oscar Peñaranda. Look for any documents," he told me. "Otherwise, I can't let you through." I started getting pissed. He started getting pissed. I was thinking my friends must have been waiting for an hour already. He went back to his cubicle again and this time told me that records show that I had been deported in 1976!

"Deported where?" I asked. He started getting annoyed at me and was ready to throw the power trip at me. "I could send you right back, sir. Please don't get curt with me." That's when I thought of showing him the two books' back covers. There was of course a bio on me, the author, and a picture, in a martial artist pose to boot. The guy read it. Slowly. I remember counting to wait. He looked me up and down, then he said, "Okay, sir. You can go." And as I walked out the door, the officer almost shouted at me and said "Your book, sir. You forgot it!" "Keep it." I said. "Then sir," he approached me by the door and held it open with his foot, "can you sign it for me?"

Ibong Adarna

The Tale of Ang Ibong Adarna, NVM Gonzalez once told me, is in the DNA of every Filipino who leaves the homeland to have that bring-back-the-cure mission, starting with the first 15 who went to Hawaii that December in 1906. NVM Gonzalez and I were talking in the flickering light of a Hayward veranda in California. Here is the story.

There was once a king who was very sick and all around the kingdom, healers and seers were sent for and sought, but alas none could find a cure. Until one day, a blind old woman came in and told the king's Council that there is only one thing that can cure the king and that is the song of the bird Adarna that lives seven mountains away, as the king's illness kept getting worse and worse by the day.

"Send me to capture this bird, father, so I can bring home the cure," said the oldest of his three sons.

"Then, go," said the King.

The son went and on his way into the forests, met an old hermit.

"Can you spare some food, sir? I…".

"No!" Get out of the way, you almost frightened my horse. I am on a mission and in a hurry.

Move aside!" And off he went.

When he did not return for a week, the second son said, "Send me, Father. I'll bring back my brother and the bird."

Reluctant and worried, the king again consented.

So, off went the second son. Same thing. He met the hermit at the foot of the mountain and shoved him aside. "Out of my way, old man!" He too did not return.

And the king kept getting sicker and sicker. "Let me go, father," said the youngest son. "NO!" shouted the weak father, his voice breaking. Everyone was surprised. "No more," he said, very tired, "no more. No more will those mountains take my last boy away. Stay home, my bunso."

"But father, you must get well."

"I will not lose my last son."

"But I will be back. I promise. Give me this chance, father."

The father thought for a long time. "Because I have seen that you know your way with strangers, you can go with my blessings."

And off went the youngest son. He was different from his other two brothers. When the hermit appeared on his journey to the seven mountains, this prince did not cast away the old man. Instead, he welcomed him, spread his princely cloak upon the forest floor and asked him to partake of his food.

"I'm very hungry," said the hermit.

"Then eat, and eat well," said the prince.

The old man looked at the prince, a mere boy. "You are but a mere boy, but I will give you the secret to bringing back the beautiful bird of Adarna whose song is the only cure for your father's grave illness." The old man plucked three things from his bag: a knife, a bottle of potion, and some lime (calamansi). "You will need that cage that you brought for the bird, but first you must put the bird in the cage." Then, he quietly explained, "On top of the seventh mountain, you will come upon a tree with two big stones near its base. That is where the bird Adarna lives. You will wait for the bird till he alights on that tree. That is when she sings her spell that makes her listeners drowsy and fall asleep. That is why no one has been able to capture her. In fact it is she and her melodious song that enthrall her listeners. After they've fallen asleep, she poops on them and they turn into stone. The two stones you will see at the foot of the tree trunk are your two brothers. You must pour this magic lotion on those stones to make them come alive and become your brothers again."

"And what do I do with this kalamansi?"

"Ah, yes. Most important. When you hear the song of the bird it will sound so soothing, so calming, so beautiful, so peaceful that you will start to fall asleep. You will try to stay awake, but your drowsiness will get the better of you. That is when you cut your arm with this knife to stay awake and when the stupor becomes unbearable you will squeeze the calamansi onto the cut to keep you up. Then and only then can you stay awake and capture the bird Adarna."

Everything happened as the old man told him. The bird came, beautiful in its majesty and bright colors, alighted and started singing. The song was indeed so beautiful and soothing like a lullaby. And he couldn't stay awake. Falling asleep, he cut his forearm for the pain to wake him. Then he squeezed the kalamansi over the cut to keep on waking him. And when the bird finished her song, it started to fall asleep, as the young prince climbed slowly up the tree and gathered the drowsy bird gently into the cage. He then poured the lotion over the big stones beneath the tree and his brothers came out of them alive again!

The three brothers all alive brought home the bird and the king lived and the people in the kingdom were happy for many many more years.

After a long pause in the stillness of the evening, NVM added: "And the cuts that you must make on your arm to stay awake to overcome sleep are the sacrifices you will make when superficial glitters of the erasers of your memory will lull you to sleep, to make you forget your mission, and that is to find a cure to heal the country, the sick man of Asia represented by family, friends, or the homeland."

There is a path one could trace, a path of many sons and daughters from the homeland who seek that cure for the king, for the town, for the family, for self, only to return home someday and bring back that cure. Mine is that of remembering and telling their stories. From the province, to Manila, to America (U.S. and Canada), a path I found I myself had taken, albeit in another era. I was a dependent of a diplomat because my father worked and pioneered Philippine Consulates in Vancouver, British Columbia, and San Francisco, California. Summer months, no-school months, I was always someplace out of town, away from my two siblings and parents. I don't know the cities in the summers. In the summers, I was always away. The summer months were mine. And those experiences, along with the city of San Francisco herself, helped me find my voice as a writer. Memory is the song of my Ibong Adarna.

WHEN MY GRANDDAUGHTER was born, I started going to the East Bay more often. Heleina of San Leandro, for me, was the face that launched a thousand trains, Bart rides across San Francisco Bay. Always I see, rumbling out of the underwater tunnel, as the train surfaces, like a giant serpent from the sea, from the West Oakland to the Lake Merritt station, the horses of war on watch over the Oakland harbor. Like the Trojan Horse of old, the oil digging, insect looking giant machines in Oakland line the skyline watching over the San Francisco Bay reminding me of my senior year in Saint Ignatius high school where I fell in love with poetry and languages and the epic all at one time. I read, I sang, in Latin, the Aeneid of Vergil when Aeneas the hero was waylaid and distracted by Queen Dido's love temporarily making him forget his destiny, like what the song of the bird Adarna did for many a hapless seeker of the cure.

Marcos Balikbayan Proclamation

In the 1970's, President Ferdinand Marcos of the Philippines sent a decree, a challenge almost, to all Filipinos around the world to return and visit their or their parents' homeland and see for themselves whether his imposed Martial Law is working. Of course, what was not specified was for whom was it really working? To do this, as an incentive, he made affordable the erstwhile steep price of a roundtrip plane fare. Thousands of Filipinos, including myself, became more eager to go back. He named this the Balikbayan Program. Thus, the provenance of that term.

I had mixed feelings. I have always been longing to return to my place of childhood but now I am a grown man with two children, an educator, and a writer. I had left the Philippines when I was only twelve. I never wanted to be a U.S. citizen. When I left for the Philippines for my first visit back nineteen years later as a Balikbayan, I was still a Filipino citizen. Therein lay my dilemma. I did not want the Martial Law government to notice me in any way, so I decided to apply for my U.S. citizenship, just in case I get hassled by Marcos' government while in the Philippines visiting. I was not at the time a vocal, high-profile critic of that government; I was just developing a consciousness. But I had close relatives, friends, and fellow writers who were very active in the anti-Marcos movement in the U.S. So to play it safe, what my father and others could not convince me of in the past, Marcos was able to do; I reluctantly decided to opt for U.S. citizenship.

Ancestors

Part One: A Barugo Reunion

During the Christmas season of 2003-2004, my father's side of the family had a reunion in the Philippines. It was our first official reunion, planned by relatives in the Philippines, as well as abroad.

My paternal first cousins coordinated it and we had at least four generations involved in the planning. We had a hectic, well-planned itinerary for our schedule, but we managed to get through all two weeks of it in one piece. Of course, almost everyone got sick for at least a day. Because of my love for food, I expect to get sick for one or two days. Even the locals got sick. My nephew Miguel who lives in MetroManila got sick in Leyte for a couple of days. I got sick the last few days in Subic. I don't remember ever getting sick in Leyte since I have been coming back as a *balikbayan*, when time and money would permit.

But I do not stay long in Leyte. It was December. It was the rainy season in Leyte. But it was not really a typhoon type of wind. The Hawaiians have many names for rain. This one might be the one they call *malahini*, "little girls' rain", because it just plays tag with the wind and splashes around a bit, becoming annoying at times, then moves on to play somewhere else. So, when we got there, sure enough it was drizzling. Then some sun for a minute or two. Then clouds and rain, then steady rain, until we all finally got resigned to the rhythm of the weather. But when we got to Barugo, our ancestral hometown, the rain almost subsided. The two surviving sisters of my father were there in the ancestral house where we had a get-together with everyone in town who cared to join and, of course, other relatives and friends of relatives. That's almost everybody. My cousin Greg was most influential and represented the U.S. residents. He was very diligent, even way before pa. He had scoped all or most of all the places in our itinerary some months before. My cousin Greg was/is very in tune with the Catholic Church, so we stopped by a few town churches along the way. I heard there were a couple of choice places to visit along other routes, but it had no accessible churches, so we had to forego them.

The People

Of course, we must start with Mana Neny. In Tacloban, a few of us were looking out the terrace of the Leyte Park Hotel where we were not residing. We were quartered at the much-beleaguered MacArthur Hotel, besieged by complaints from everywhere and everyone, 50% of which originated from my "super-Americanized" sister Francisca, (Tita Baby). Looking out wistfully into the ocean, Mana Neny was explaining to Camille and JP (Cousin Greg's kids) why we were not staying here at the Leyte Park Inn instead of the MacArthur Hotel.

"*. . . Sana* we are here but your father wanted the one where we are now, the one where we are having all the troubles. But he said that that hotel is closer to the church so naturally that one won over. Look how nice this is here, o. Wow. Look at the garden. And the view! Out there is the sea! But we are not privy to it. We are not in this hotel. We are in the one where we are now where there are a lot of complaints. Because it is closer to the church. But that's okay. Tuloy ang ligaya. We are having a good time, di ba?"

During the main program at my cousin Nito's house in Sun Valley Subdivision, Mana Neny was overheard in the audience responding to my brother Gil's co-emceeing of the program when he asked whether there were gifts and awards for the participants. "Well, yes, of course," she told him. "You paid for them!"

Not only was Cousin Greg very influential without being overbearing, he literally had a booming exuberance about him that was quickly infectious and one could hear his laughter before entering the room he was in. It would be very difficult for a person to be down and completely depressed, I would imagine, when my cousin Greg (Goly) was in the room.

Seeing the other Peñaranda's, Tio Tibo's and Tia Narsing's tribe, stirred ancestral forces within me. Unexplainable. I really did not know most of my nieces and nephews on that branch, but the minute they spoke to me, everything became natural. So natural and refreshing I did not really think twice about it until later, upon reflection. I wanted to talk to all of them but of course the day was not long enough. That is always the bittersweet part of rare gatherings. Mano Raul, Steve and all their families. And April. Bitsoy's April. She was a baby when I last saw her. Now a young lady, with all her lively cousins around her. Bitsoy (Ruben) and I did a lot of mischievous things when we were boys. We must have, or part of our families, lived together at some time in our childhood. From our generation, our family, Tio Tibo's, Tio Rupin's (Tatay Pino), and later, Tio Namin's were some of the first ones who ventured to Manila from Barugo. I remember vividly the boat rides that we would take to and from Barugo and Manila. During vacation from school times, whole families would go. Cousins and aunts and uncles were all one family. The boat trip took three days then, but only one now.

When these scenes visit my memory, I see in a makeshift canopy of canvas, Tia Lola slowly unwrapping some homemade native torta and roscas, a big smile glowing at me and Bitsoy. I will forget many things in my life (and I have) before I forget Tia Lola's smile that night, she doled out the first portions of her baked goodies to us expectant children. The air was chilly, the ship engine droning, the lanterns swinging under our canvas awning on the deck which in turn was under a canopy of brilliant stars, the ship rocking, lullaby-like, with the natural sway of the sea, and everyone feeling so close.

When I started going back to the Philippines since martial law years, I would always see Bitsoy, except for when he was "in school". I would later find out that that was the code word for "jail". And he was a cop, too! He was a bachelor so I would always pack my toothpaste and toothbrush every time he would pick me up. I never knew where we would end up or how long it would be before I got back home to my cousin Uyen's place, where I was staying.

Once after a party at the Manila Press Club, we were driving away from the place and after about driving for ten minutes on the road at about two in the morning, he stopped the car in the middle of the road and jumped out. There were some road and repair work tools and equipment sticking out of a ditch on the left lane, the lane going the other way. He started shouting, all of a sudden, at the workers who were smoking cigarettes, and scolded them for not having a sign on the road saying WARNING MEN WORKING: SLOW DOWN. "Sino ba kayo?" asked the men working. "Hoy!" shouted Bitsoy again. "Manila Police ako!" He walked towards the two or three men squatting in the faded light of a streetlamp. He flipped his badge at one of the men's faces. "Mali at bawal ang ginagawa ninyo." Years later, when I was already back in San Francisco, I was informed that he had a fatal car accident. I couldn't help but think of that night after the Manila Press Club. He was one year older than me and he liked to tell people, when a little tipsy, that he and I had saved each other's lives at different times when we were boys. And all at the same place—the Pasig River. Tia Lola's upbringing taught us that devils sometimes have to be each other's guardian angels. I overheard Tia Lola say to someone one time of Bitsoy when someone was enumerating the trials and tribulations that he had caused his father Tio Tibo. "*Pasay-lua na la ito kay makipamilya ito.*" We all have our one redeeming trait and for Tia Lola, closeness to family was Bitsoy's. Tio Tibo's story (Bitsoy's father) and how he ended up living as a child until grown with my father in the house of Lito (my father's father) is itself epic. Though both were silent men, even in my boyhood, I saw the closeness of Tio Tibo and my father. My father would not have a brother for twenty years, so Tio Tibo became his younger brother for the duration, and beyond.

We held the Metro Manila ceremonies/programs that the nieces and nephews conjured up for the occasion in my cousin's Nito's house in the aforementioned Sun Valley Subdivision near Bicutan. Where in the year before, almost to the day, my cousin Nito had a sudden and fatal heart attack. In the back of all our minds I am sure that everyone was thinking of him during any given moment of our festive reunion.

Tia Lola was still there. That was one of the providential graces we received as a family because one of our main motivations for the reunion was that all of us, from the oldest to the youngest, had that unmentionable gut feeling that this probably would be the last time we would all be together to see the old folks, Tia Lola and Tia Yeying, my father's two surviving siblings previously mentioned. They were a throwback to the old days. Stories of their impacts in our lives would themselves make several volumes of books. Our collective premonitions turned out to be correct. We lost Tia Lola not long after the reunion. And now, before our even planning of the next/second reunion, Tia Yeying left us.

I had many more things to tell Tia Lola, but I didn't. This is one of my many regrets: that I had several chances, but never took them, to express in words my appreciation and gratitude for her great and silent kindness to me and dozens of other children, throughout her life, but alas, writer though I am, fell short every time. But then, knowing her, she would have stopped me cold and told me to shut up. Maybe she felt uncomfortable talking about emotions, too. Maybe I learned that from her. In the hollowed site of Barugo, during the reunion, she sat on a rocking chair in Tia Yeying's house and welcomed everyone coming to reach for her hand. My niece Camille, ever attentive and observant, told me Tia Lola was looking for me. I finished off my conversation with one of my cousins and hurried to her. I bent down to kiss her and stayed at her side for a while, smiling at her greeters, too. Though a woman of a few words, her silence reached me quicker and sharper than many other authorities' chatter ever did. She taught me to listen to people's silences and I heard her own silence, as well. Sometimes, I still do. And in that silence, I see the steam liner we were on in my childhood, plowing the thick, dark seas, there from our third class cots and lantern-lit gathering of family, Tia Lola's stories echoing from horizon to horizon. It'll be a long time, perhaps a few lifetimes, before I forget that magical night, when Tia Lola under a canopied canvas sky opened up her freshly baked tortas under the lilting lantern amidst our huddled haunches on the deck of a ship adrift under the stars in the middle of the dark Visayan Sea.

Yen, my most understanding and accommodating cousin, was for me a true blessing that I have always thanked my lucky stars for. To be housed by a first cousin who also shared your love of film and literature, and humor, and irony, among other things, not to mention the NBA. To be surrounded by books in his basement library which at times was also my sleeping room was something of a Kafkaesque literary orgasm. The abundance of books represented to me the inexhaustibility of knowledge, and I was ravenous of it, especially in my younger and earlier years of *balikbayaning*. But of course, I could not know till later that the thing that would complement knowledge was wisdom, the wisdom (and folly) of our elders whom I interacted with every day and every time I went anywhere in the Philippines. I found that out gradually as I got to re-know the old folks. Of course, my contemporaries as well, my cousins, facilitated my rediscovery whether they liked it or not, whether they, or I, were conscious of it or not.

Francisca (Tita Baby)

It was well past midnight two days before Christmas. I was waiting, going down the lobby every now and then, for my sister Francisca (Tita Baby) to come into The Presidents Hotel Lobby in Makati Greenbelt. I knew that she was going to be late, but I just did not know how late. When she arrived, Mana Neny and the hotel clerk went to see her to her room. According to Mana Neny, when they walked inside, Tita Baby screamed. Tita Baby swore she saw Mahatma Ghandi himself naked in a very uncompromising position with someone. Instead of darting right out, according to Mana Neny, she (Baby) started explaining that obviously there had been a mistake, and that "goddamn" hotel man gave her the wrong keys and how was she to know that someone is already occupying this room, and she's so sorry. Mana Neny interrupted and whispered loudly "let's go na!" and later would comment, "he was not even cute! Pangit naman, e." But after that, things got relatively settled with her. Pretty soon she was getting her regular almost daily massage for three hours at a time. "I have to work my ass off again when I get back to the States to pay for all this."

The Generations

There were many blurry nights of bar carousing and other misadventures of our nephews and nieces, but of course we must avoid mentioning names, like Miguel and JP and Carlo. Such frolickings will remain a secret. If one's curiosity is bent on more information, then oral literature, or folk literature, (as differentiated from *tsismis*, which carries with it the baggage and connotation of "low class", "uneducated", and "malicious") will have to provide.

I am mindful now, as I leave my thoughts of the reunion, of one of my nieces who was not in our midst, not ever, though she was constantly in my thoughts, and whom I have not seen for three decades at least. She was a small girl the last time I saw her. Eva. In one very real sense, I cannot help but think that it is Eva, who among all of us, is the truest practitioner of Lito's revolutionary legacy, living out the harsh life for her ideals, for she had taken to the hills for her ideals. As I look in the fields and forests of Leyte and Samar—she's out there somewhere—like Lito was, too, between the years of 1899 to 1902, these circumstances upon which I am missing her are again not coincidental but cyclical. I remember you, Eva.

Soon our stay neared its ending. Twilight and dusk of our numbered days rolled in and the stark reality of not having enough time with my nieces and nephews, cousins, aunts and uncles, friends and colleagues, stories of childhood, began to nudge me. But then again, that would be something to look forward to in the next reunion. Would that (*sana*) life be more leisurely and we could have the time and talk a little bit more, and slowly say our long Filipino goodbyes again and again and again.

Ancestors
Part two: El Hijo de Genoveva

Spain was always in the back of my mind. Someday, I'll get there, I always told myself. It would have been great if I got there when my father and mother were still alive. My mother had taken a lot of pictures of their long stay in Spain when they (with my father and 4-year-old sister) went about 50 years ago and I had seen her mount those pictures on respective albums every now and then. They had hardly talked about their trip to us, their two other children, my older brother and I, though I heard them talk about it at some length with others. My mother's father, a Spaniard, had been born in the same hometown of Barugo, Leyte, Philippines, as I was, as had both my parents. They say his father, my maternal great grandfather, was shipwrecked somewhere nearby and remnants of his ship washed ashore, he being one of them. So many such stories circulated around my provincial childhood that this tale became commonplace among partial descendants of Spaniards. The most common narrative, of course, was the Spanish friar from which one's family tree is never quite without.

When I was about eight years old, my parents and my younger only sister left for Spain. My older brother and I were left in the Philippines with relatives. My mother wanted to further her studies. I later learned she had gone to the University of Salamanca. Later, her relatives told me that they remembered her as ‹Genoveva always carrying books!› "Should I change my career, perhaps go in another direction for my studies?" The trip, for my mother fifty years ago, was also, of course, to see her Spanish first cousins who were born in the Philippines and whom she grew up with but had gone to Spain right around the Second World War and have never gone back to the Philippines. My father, mother, and sister lived with these first cousins in Madrid. They did not return until about two years later. My sister returned speaking Spanish completely and had forgotten our Waray language, as well as Tagalog. My older brother and I have never been to Spain. Never even been to Europe. So when I decided after 50 years of my mother's visit to her people that I, too, needed to go, I did a little planning and gave the trip some substantive objectives. One of these goals was to go look for, just in passing maybe, if practical and "not too far out of the way", I was going to look for those second cousins of mine and see if I can find some or any of them. If I didn't, well, that's fine too. I would have seen Spain at least, and I would have seen and enjoyed the country, nonetheless.

My decision to go had many factors. I had a time-share that I wanted to try out. I have been paying for the damn thing for about three years or so and I discovered that I could do a one-week stay in the Mediterranean. We got this place in Benalmadena, Spain, about 10 miles from Malaga on the southern coast of Spain, Costa del Sol. I had only one old phone number that my father gave me about twenty years ago. Both my parents had passed away when I decided on this trip. He had told me that they were still there on that address and phone numbers, these second cousins of mine.

The first ten days we went on a tour, including tours inside cities (read cathedrals), and the not-too verdant countryside. From Madrid to Toledo to the Extremaduras into Portugal and back again into Spain, re-entering it from the south, into Andalusian Spain, towards Sevilla, then back up northward again into Madrid. For the next seventeen days after that, we were on our own. We rented a car, my wife Luisa and my daughter Milena and I. I drove all over Andalusia, southern Spain, stopped by little towns and ate and chatted a bit with the locals. The small, usually family-owned hotels and inns were quite reasonable, about 25 to 40 bucks a day and most of them had a small dining place by the lobby.

I was ready for all the pro-colonial arguments I was expecting from people, relatives or not, in casual or serious conversations, but the common folk disarmed me. In giving directions, old women would put down their bags on the street and walk a ways to point us to the right direction, in some cases, walked with us till we got there, and in one case, asked us to follow his car to the place we were looking for! I once asked my cousin Miguel what they did to all the gold they "took" from their colonies for centuries. He said sadly, doctor that he was, "the same stupid thing all empires do with their loot: use it to supply more wars. It never went to the Spanish people. The poor remained poor." When Miguel took us to the Prado Museum in Madrid, I commented on how young-looking a certain Cardinal was in a portrait. Did they flatter them by painting them looking younger?

"No," he said. He really was young for a Cardinal." and added, "it helps to have the Pope for an uncle."

Sometimes I see Spain and the Philippines as lovers. Then the United States, as a Johnny-come-lately, third-party suitor, as well. Three lovers and I the fourth lover who, in turn, as a result of their lovering, had a lover's quarrel with the world, as Robert Frost expressed.

I called the lone contact my father had given me. Charuko's number. Someone answered but said she was out of town. I tried to explain my situation in Spanish the best I could and left my hotel number, Hotel Mindanao, of all names. Sometime later, a man called and said he was Miguel, Charuko's youngest and only brother, and that he would be there at 8 pm tonight at our hotel. He said the owner of the hotel was his patient.

Genoveva's son. *El hijo* de Genoveva. That's what I overheard them often say as a prelude or an afterthought to awkward introductions with me, a relative never before seen. I was most fortunate that the first one I ever saw was Miguel Ferrer. At about a minute before 8 p.m., the front desk called and said that Mr. Ferrer had arrived. When I came down to the lobby, I saw a gray haired, very animated, active man getting up. And so we met, myself graying around the head. Ferrer's father, we found out later, was my paternal grandfather's verbal sparring mate in Spanish in Barugo when that town was in its heyday. My paternal grandfather (a Filipino) had just been through fighting the U.S.-Philippines War, the second part of the War For Independence in the Philippines, the first was against the Spaniards: one right after the other, in fact one sliding and overlapping right into the other. The Filipinos in their wars for independence, first fought against the Spanish, then against the U.S. Americans. My Uncle Benjamin (my father's youngest sibling and only brother, who also went to Spain and joined my parents in part of their stay in Madrid), had told me that my Spanish grandfather was always chatting and discussing and debating with my Filipino grandfather the "noticias" of the day, when both were still bachelors and did not have a family. Both spoke perfect Spanish.

I was told that my father, perhaps around ten years old then, complained that this Ferrer (Miguel›s father) was always at his father's house having café or tsokolate, with pan y huevos, the way the Spaniards like their eggs, soft boiled to the point of overflowing. My father, as a boy, was responsible for the accounting of eggs in the household. He took care of a certain number of poultry, and he had to make accounts of the egg situation. His father had just given him that charge and this Ferrer guy (Miguel's father) was upsetting all his aspired goals of accounting for all eggs laid in the household. To this day, the old building, though in ruins, which housed a school in Barugo, is still called the Ferrer building. That was Miguel's father who married my aunt or my mother's aunt, Tia Maria. Miguel was the luckiest thing that happened to us in Spain. Miguel's mother and my mother were first cousins, I think. Either that or Miguel and my mother were. I'll figure it all out later, I thought. Not long after, we were at comfortable ease with each other and were on our way to Miguel's house for family introductions.

Under stairways, through trees, along a swimming pool, inside the front door and into the openings of his elegant house, I heard in various introductions "...el hijo de Genoveva. El hijo de Genoveva....de San Francisco..." He had invited as many relatives as he could and was having a sort of a small get together at his place.

I hurriedly pulled out an envelope from my bag and showed Miguel a picture. In the photo, my sister and my parents were with Miguel's parents and extended family, and mine. They were all little children then and Mguel had that fluffy collar and long droopy tie. He went to his room. He came out smiling and showed me in his hand the identical picture.

The next morning, we traveled to Salamanca. Our hotel was right in the middle of Plaza Mayor in Salamanca. When I opened the window curtain overlooking the Plaza that first morning, I could not help but think of my mother's own pilgrimage here in this self-same city fifty years ago, where she attended some classes at the University of Salamanca to add to her repertoire of courses that her Spanish first cousins teased her about and was mounting in accumulation because she constantly was on the verge of changing her major. "Ay, that Genoveva! We remember her bringing home books all the time," her relatives told me.

During our month stay in Spain, we saw Miguel several more times, and more 'family' one more time.

We landed in San Francisco Airport late August. I started getting ready mentally set for the upcoming school year. Then, about two weeks later, on September 11, The World Trade Center's twin towers in New York City fell crashing to the ground with smoke and destruction in its wake.

The next summer, braving the post 9-11 atmosphere of Big Brother, I went again to Spain. I felt I was not finished yet and I had to go again. This time I will go to the place my mother's ancestors came from and ask around if I can find someone to inform me of my mother's last name, Gutierrez. My cousins in Madrid had not gone there much lately. But with more information from them, I could piece clues together to get to the place of my mother's people originally. Santander was one of them. But then, also Reinosa, said Margarita, Miguel's daughter. But it seemed they had all moved to Madrid for generations now and had hardly any contacts with Santander and Reinosa. Maybe I can find out.

On the way to San Sebastian, I drove along beautiful parts of northern Spain. We stopped by a hotel restaurant in Comillas. When I settled in the room, I left my wife and daughter resting to make inquiries downstairs. At the lobby and restaurant, in Spanish, I introduced myself as a guest in the hotel, and politely asked the woman at the desk if she knew of any Gutierrezes around these parts. She almost burst into laughter. I thought I did not pronounce it well enough for her, so I explained that I was from San Francisco curious about looking for Gutierrezes because my mother's father's people came from here and maybe,

"You are so funny," she said.

"Why?"

"You see that man over there by the door standing with a drink, he's a

Gutierrez. See that woman by the window, she's a Gutierrez. Me, I'm a Gutierrez! There are Gutierrezes all over the place here!"

He left for a smoke in the night air and under the street lamp was a merchandise truck with "Gutierrez Bros." printed across its side panels.

The next day we proceeded to San Sebastian. But in the city hall, disappointingly, we were told that the records would be more accurate in Reinosa. Up to the hills in the higher country, I drove to the town of Reinosa. A chill passed through me as we approached the town. I had passed by names of towns, like Ponferrada, which were the last names of some cousins around my hometown in the Philippines!

The town of Reinosa lies on a mountainous path so even though it was late July, it was cold and windy. I imagined those from here basking in the tropical sun of Leyte a century or so ago. When we got there, I was sent to another city building near a city hall, a building containing archives and records. I looked at the documents, hardbound like a book. It was only until 1848. I could not trace Antonio Gutierrez, my mother's grandfather's birth and place date. His parents must have been born before 1848. I was told to go to a chapel nearby in Santillana del Mar where the nuns of the convent kept good records of births and deaths.

The next day, I went to Santillana del Mar, a quaint, tourist-looking town not far from the sea, with restaurant tables on wide lawns under big umbrellas. We ate outside and asked if there was a convent nearby. Why yes, was the immediate reply. Not far from here. The heat was overpowering so I had an ice cream.

When I entered the convent, there was no one inside. It was so hot; I did not notice my surroundings. I saw one nun, but she immediately darted away to another hallway. Then I saw a second nun who saw me and made eye contact and motioned me to the counter while she went inside it. She disappeared inside, and then I heard her voice (presumably) from inside in Spanish. "No one here can talk but me. What can I help you with?" said the voice from the wall, under which was an opening where one can pass documents and other items. I could pretty well communicate in Spanish if I were seeing with whom I was speaking. But it was more challenging when facial expressions and gestures won't be seen to give clues. I explained my mission haltingly. Though I was talking to a wall all the time, she understood right away. She said in a teacher-giving-instruction way: "I will have to go to Santander for this. It will cost you. When are you leaving this area?"

"Tomorrow."

"I will go to Santander tomorrow to do errands and be back in three days.

Ok. Leave me money. Forty dollars to cover fees. Write and leave your address under the slot and I will send you what I can find about your ancestors, okay?"

"Thank you, Sister. Thank you."

"I can't promise you much, but I will try."

I don't remember nuns being that nice and kind in my Catholic experience.

I almost forgot about it but two weeks after I got home from this second trip in Spain, I got a manila envelope letter, stamped "España". In it was a short note and two pages of ancestral bloodline of Antonio Gutierrez going back to the mid sixteenth century! By hand! The dates of births and deaths were diagramed by the Sister's hand. In her note, she said: "This is all I could come up with in such a short time to research, but it is a beginning. I only needed thirty dollars for the documents, so I gave the extra ten dollars to a senior Sister traveling to Cuba who desperately needed eyeglasses." *Sor* Emilia.

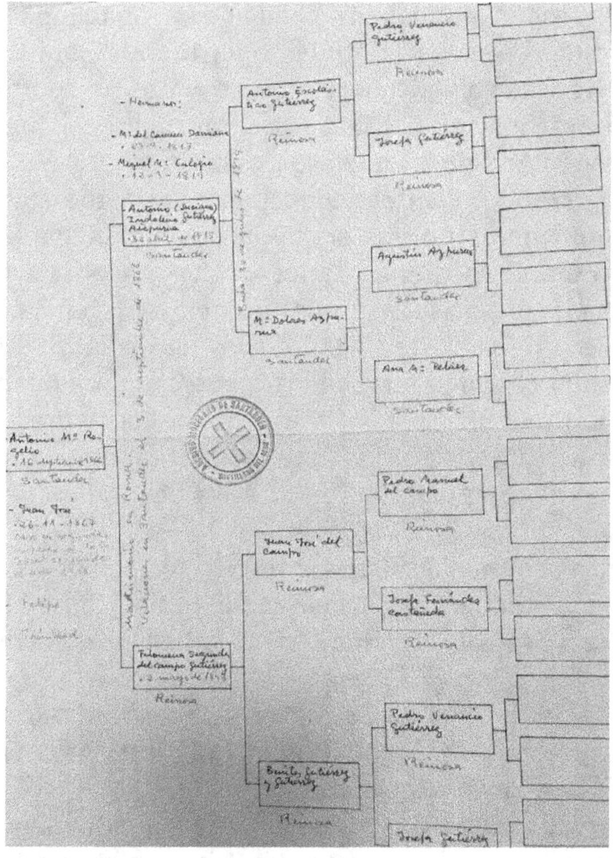

Gutierrez genealogy retrieved by Sor Emila, possession of author

The Believers

There was once a boy who lived near, though not in, the barrios around Magellan's landing, whose name was Tomas though he hardly knew it because people were used to calling him another, Totoy, his nickname, the invention of one being a common practice of the people there, an unwritten and even un-conscious code of originality and ingenuity among Filipinos, and for those living in the Visayan coast towns of Carigara Bay in the Philippines, a heritage almost.

Totoy looked up at the faces of his parents listening to Padre Tunying one hot morning. They never blinked an eye but looked straight toward the priest. Not even when his baby sister's mouth-sore opened anew by the heat, and the flies had gathered around its pus did his mother look down to attend to the infant wailing in her arms. She rocked her arm instinctively and pulled the ba-by's hood over its head to keep the sun away, all the while craning toward the priest. Totoy slowly rolled his eyes and head and began to look for his playmates Amador and Carding. They were both younger than he, but they were still his best playmates. He was going to dart off as soon as he spotted them, but he checked himself. Amador and Carding were not together! They were standing by their own parents. And they too were listening.

Padre Tunying stood on an elevated platform in the sun-baked fields of Magellan's Landing, one of the clusters of barrios huddled around Carigara Bay, the villagers, immutable in the mysteries of the seasons, with their children tugging at their pants or skirts and babies in their arms, encircled the priest.

"All our work have been wasted," Padre Tunying spoke. "If this drought keeps up," he licked his dry chapped lips as his tongue caught a bead of perspiration trickling down the tip of his nose, "if this drought keeps up, all of us will have little to eat or drink..." He looked up at the nauseating sun, then back to his listeners, "...and some of us will starve." The sea beyond the parched land held not a moisture of relief for the townsfolk.

He could hardly see the Padre, so he started to yank at his father's trousers and climb up on his shoulders as he always did. But his father did not mind him. Instead he brushed away his little hands; his father looked irritated though he never looked down.

The Padre was still talking. "An evil eye has scorched our fields and hearts. Our tuba has become poison. Almost all our harvests have withered. It is be-cause of our evil ways, my brothers and sisters!"

Wriggling his way to the front of the circle, Totoy now saw him clearly. The last words of the Padre still rang in his ears. His eyes grew wide. He started to turn back toward his parents, but the Padre's words again had blasted the arid air and he did not dare to move another step.

"We have all become dry and barren like our fields!"

Slowly Totoy turned to face the priest. It seemed like he was the only one there, he and the priest.

"The rainy season will be over in one week and it has not yet rained one drop. Therefore, we must pray." He was talking softer now and Totoy felt relieved. "And pray hard with all our hearts. Pray for forgiveness, and then pray for rain. For only faith can deliver us now. Amen."

"Amen," echoed the villagers.

"'Toy, you like food don't you?" his father asked him when they were back at their small dwelling. His father was laughing. So he laughed in return and answered,

"I love food, Itay."

"Then you watch over your sister Carmen tomorrow, ha? For Inay and I will go to church and pray for some food."

Totoy noticed his father's eyes roam around the room and suddenly stopped at his mother who was busy arranging pictures of saints on the drawer of the living room.

"Don't take that down!" he almost shouted at her. "Don't you know that's San Antonio, my family's patron saint? He's the patron saint of recovery. if you lose something, he's the one to pray to."

She looked around the small house made of bamboo and old wood covered with dry palm leaves, "There is nothing much here to lose," she said. Then she put away the Sacred Heart which was going to replace San Antonio. "I think we should take the children with us," complained his mother. "They might..."

"He's eight years old! He knows what to do with the baby. He'll just be a bother in church again. Besides, Mass is less than an hour at the most."

"But tomorrow is not Sunday 'Tay. It is only Tuesday."

His father looked down at him. "If we are to have food, we must have rain, Totoy. To have rain we must pray to God that He might give it to us," he said.

"Might give it to us 'Tay? You mean even after you pray and do all this, you still do not know if God will give us rain?"

"We know nothing. He knows everything. He does not have to give us anything if He does not want to."

"Yet we do things for him, 'Tay?"

"Well, whatever happens is His will, Totoy, and there's really nothing we can do, well, it's hard to explain son; when you grow a little older, you'll know what I mean..."

When they left, Totoy quickly opened a window and whistled across to the next house. Wonder what heaven's like, he thought. Rainy, I suppose. There was no answer.

"Carding! Carding!" he shouted. "Come on over. We have the whole house to ourselves." There was still no answer. He looked at every opening of Carding's house. It was empty. It was the first time Carding went anywhere without him and not let him know about it. He looked out into the streets of pale brown dust and hard cracked earth. Out there in the distance, he saw two figures moving toward the church and away from him. Running after the familiar silhouettes he called, "Carding! Amador!" He knew that the strange distance they had this morning would not last and he was happy again. "Where are you going? Why didn't you tell me where we should go this morning? Why didn't you answer my whistle?"

Amador and Carding turned to each other and then back again at Totoy.

"We are going to church."

"Going where?"

"To church, Totoy"

"Together? Didn't we plan to play marbles today?"

"Yes, together."

"We don't have much time, Carding," Amador nudged Carding. "Yes, we must go now, 'Toy." There was a pause. For an instant all three were waiting for each other to speak.

"I was going to church, too." Totoy almost shouted.

"You don't have to apologize 'Toy," said Amador. "We understand. Last week all three of us did nothing but have sword fights, roll garbage cans, and play marbles. Now with this drought and all, things are different. We can no longer enjoy playing marbles, Carding and I. It is praying for rain that we must do now."

Amador and Carding started to run away from Totoy, toward church. "Why must you leave?" Totoy wanted to know.

"I told you," Carding said, "so we can be in time for Mass. Everyone has left for church. Your parents, too. Why don't you find someone else to play with or something, 'Toy? It's not really that hard. There are plenty of kids around the other side of the river. There is..."

"You think you're grown up already, don't you? I'm older than both of you, you know."

"No, no, it's not that," Carding said. "Go on, we must leave you. Find some-one else to play with."

"There is no one else," Totoy said, but they had already left. "I wanted to go to church, too," he added. It is true, he thought. Everyone had left. For church.

And every day that week everyone went to church. Totoy, with the aid of his mother, had convinced his father that he too, wanted to go. And so he did. He had joined. Along with everyone else. There he saw Carding and Amador again, though they still preferred Padre Tunying to him.

"Tomorrow is the last day of the rainy season," the priest began, standing at the foot of the altar facing the people, for there was no pulpit. "The Lord has tested us to the last day. Have faith, my brothers and sisters, for we shall be rewarded. Faith will move mountains." He paused. "The rains will come tomorrow."

In an instant the little adobe church became pandemonium. Hats floated up and down the air. Women wept and embraced each other. Carding and Amador dashed towards each other and towards Totoy, grabbed him and started laughing and jumping and shouting. And Totoy did the same.

The morning found the priest already on the platform in the fields directly looking upwards, eyes squinted, and mouth opened. There was not a cloud to be seen. Some of the villagers had started encircling him already, murmuring prayers. But Padre Tunying was waiting for everybody. And everyone indeed came to the platform that morning to see how the Padre would welcome the rain. The villagers began to go down on their knees, singing hymns one after the other.

Totoy was late when he approached the circle. He pushed his way to the front as he had done a week ago. But after a while he did not need to push anymore. Not only could he see the priest from afar, but he had also noticed the Padre's eyes staring at him. For the singing had died down to a hush, and the crowd, with their eyes fixed on Tomas, was making way for him, the only one with an umbrella and a raincoat.

The Lousiest Salesperson in the World

In the late sixties, I worked at a posh San Francisco store, Joseph Magnin's, while taking my master's at San Francisco State College, and keeping up with two toddlers, to boot. But the children were not rowdy, nor boisterous, like the ones you see so many of nowadays. I always felt lucky and thankful to be blessed by having beautiful and levelheaded children while they were children.

I was one of a dozen (when busy and full) shoe salespersons at the store. We worked by rotation. Imelda Marcos, First Lady of the Philippines, closed down the store for the last three hours one time. But my story is not about that one but about one Janis Joplin, rising/risen rock star of the time. Of all the six months or so I worked at that elite shoe store, I had but one, yes, one, day that I earned commission.

We have to sell $200 worth of shoes before getting a fifteen percent commission. I never made a day in which I sold over $200 in the six months or so that I worked at Joseph Magnin's Ladies' Shoe Department, unquestionably the goldmine of the whole store. I stole more shoes for my family than sold to the customers.

She came in almost closing time, Janis. She came in with a sharp looking attorney or secretary-looking companion. In contrast, Miss Joplin looked like something the proverbial cat dragged in. But then, that's how she looked most of the time, anyways. In my young undiscerning eye, I was surprised I wasn't awed. There were a lot of counterculture bands in San Francisco already playing here and there, visiting, doing a love-in, or a teach-in in the many parks of the city, and I couldn't keep up with who's who, so it was not that big of a thing.

My number to assist a customer was called and the manager, a nice Jewish man, introduced the two ladies to me. He knew less of what was going on with the counterculture because he kept asking me why the students at S.F. State were rioting and causing all kinds of trouble.

"Do you have any boots? I want to see some boots." She took off her sunglasses which were almost falling off, anyway, and shook her dirty blond hair. Those boots were the hot items of the era.

"Oh, we got plenty!" I measured her but I did not have to. I'm good at eyeballing their shoe sizes. She was small. I was sure it was no more than 5 and a half. "Ok, sit down here. And you, too, Ma'am. Sit anywhere."

"Yeah, sit down, love." And to me, "I'm going to get ten pairs today, okay dear."

I rushed to the basement to get as much as I could. Two trips. The boot box covers were my favorite pads to write poems on. Sometimes I would write on them and put them back on top of the boxes. I checked to make sure the box covers were not written on. I hurried up the stairs, laid the first bunch in front of her and started to lift her foot, while she was forcing the other foot on, and in her over-earnest engaging and negotiating, with gravity helping out, both her breasts fell out of her one-piece tie-dyed dress. They almost hit my eyes. While she was putting one back in, she said, without skipping a beat, "There," thumping her foot. She finally got one boot firmly on. "Now, put the other shoe on, sweetie." while she deftly and naturally placed the second breast back in her dress.

I used to tell customers the truth all the time and the veteran salespeople would sometimes overhear me and tell me, "No, young man. That's not how you do it. Any questions they ask, always say 'it's the latest thing from Paris'. Even though you mean Paris Street, in the Excelsior District. Even though it was made right here in Oakland. Always say, the latest thing from Paris. And when they ask (Mr. Fishmer, the number one selling salesperson, told me) what's on sale, just say "yeah, this (whatever they're fancying) is on sale. On sale, for sale, same thing."

Kearny Street

Today, walking down Kearny to Market Street, I take the train to the East Bay to see my granddaughter. In the winter when it is bright, at high noon in December, the sun is in your face but soft. You don't want to get away from it; you just don't want to be blinded crossing the street through trees of memory. For a swift moment, a flash, I felt I was my Uncle Angel, inside his body. I don't know why, perhaps from the stories he told us from his gallivanting days on this street during his young manhood, but I suddenly felt I was in his body, my mother's youngest sibling who used to tell me when he stayed with us on 27th Avenue during one or two of his leaves in the Navy before he got kicked out of the Army for being awol in the Philippines because the army could not give him permission to visit his dying mother for a few days while he was stationed in Korea, and who danced and fought and talked stories on the street of Kearny in his heyday. I felt like Uncle Angel from the inside for the first time, totally and physically. But only for a moment. Because if anyone was named wrongly, it would have been him. Though lovable with a kind heart, an angel he was not. RIP, Tio Angel. He said that the dent in my stomach was there because he, gambler that he was, in a dream, had pointed at the number 8, and his sharp guitar finger hit my mother's stomach while I was inside her.

And when my Uncle Angel came to live with us, he brought the music with him. He played the guitar and every day he was with us (my mother was the eldest and he the youngest sibling) the air was filled with music. He didn't just play, he sang. He didn't just sing, he danced, and he told stories, too. Like the one when he got shot in Korea (the war he was on leave from) and how the bullet was still lodged in his palm and once in a while like a muscle, he would move the thing up and down his palm. Then he'd asked us kids to touch it, but only I would volunteer. I moved it around like a pebble in a pillow or in someone's pocket. And when he left to return to war, only my mother sang. And the music, though wounded, was kept alive. But it was Tio Angel who helped me enjoy music and everything associated with it, but most of all, the music itself. One day, at the age of 89, the angels took Tio Angel away. He died in a Las Vegas facility. His name was more a wish than a statement of reality from his parents. Naughtiness and mischievousness seem to have latched onto him like the smile on his face. His father, the Spaniard, they said, named him. Wishful thinking perhaps on a parent's part. The townspeople said he was a very sentimental man and that was his way of saying that that was his baby, his last born. The last picture I saw of my uncle was just months ago, at the latest town fiesta event that we celebrate every year. He was dancing up a storm with his Barong

Tagalog. Last time I saw him was when I visited him at the Las Vegas facility before I left for the Philippines for an event I had to attend, (though I was one day late!). He whispered asking me to collect $200 from a relative. I had wanted to see and check his palm, but when I got there and saw him dying, I forgot all about it.

The times when Tio Angel walked on Kearny Street was a time when Filipino businesses were just opening up around Central City (Soma) and were eagerly supported by the community. I remember Mrs. Rapisura, my mother's friend, one of the original Filipino store owners in San Francisco, climbing up our stairs (Mr. Rapisura stayed in the truck) with a 100 lb of rice, like a cordillera woman with a goat on her shoulders, up the steps of the rice terraces. They themselves delivered in person! Another one, the Evangelista store was just starting to do good, as well. Dr. Borja held his clinic at the Delta Hotel where lots of *kababayans* went, including my father, and once or twice myself, as a teenager. After retiring, my father and mother would live in this area, on Clementina Street, until they died, in the last twenty years of their lives, in one of the first senior housing programs in the city.

We are all children of our times and elders of another. Truly, the child is father to the man and mother to the woman.

A Valediction

at a book launching of Arcadia's publication of Filipinos in San Francisco and ten years later at a commemoration for Carlos Villa, Yerba Buena Gardens, San Francisco

Along the windswept hair
of the Golden Gate Bridge
cables sweeping down
like Mariang Makiling
descending the mountain after a storm

fruits flowers vegetables gathered in the bower of her arms
for the town poor and the playing children,
daylight comes
streaming into the Mission La Mision
then Soma and Central City

Clementina of my father's back yard
St Patrick's with its Tagalog mass
sentinel streets of Lapu-lapu, Bonifacio, Tandang Sora, Rizal and Mabini
La Mision thrusting all the way to the Excelsior and finally emptying into
Top O' the Hill Daly City

Pinoytown Capital of the West
'Prom what part of san prancisco are you? '
'Daly City.'
Serramonte, Mecca of my auntie's shopping appetites

But before that
there were Fosters
Mel's Drive in, Drive-in Movies,
Castle Lanes bowling alley, Palace Billiards, Forbidden City,
Treasure Island's World Fair,

Taxi dance, Ajax, and all-night nightclubs in the tenderloin
From The International Hotel
The I hotel, eye of the Filipino American community
In San Francisco,

To the bonga of the Tonga Room at the Fairmont Hotel

Stockton Monterey Pismo Beach Watsonville
The Delta, Sacramento and back again to Stockton
All our stories rode and echoed
The years away
From 1904 to 2004 and beyond, a century
Of pictures yet just a glimpse into our rich heritage
In this City by the Bay.

Thanks to people like Rachel Lastimosa
whose smile is sunshine
And Raquel Redondiez
both jewels in the crown of Pinayhood
and our community
We thank you one and all.

The Hijacking of America

" The fact that an opinion has been widely held is no evidence that it is not utterly absurd."
—Bertrand Russell

We are one of the most, if not the most, un-homogenous countries in the world. It is one country that is made up of many countries, really. It is in a way a model for "the one-world-one-country" view. Yet, we are the most un-global in our knowledge of, our concerns with, and our attitude towards the rest of this planet.

America is not only NOT just one country, it is a continent, and some say more than one continent, nay, a hemisphere. Half the world is America! It's a loaded word that we take so much for granted.

We are the only country who uses the name of a whole hemisphere as a referent to us, and only us. Sometimes I don't think the word "us" and "U.S." is a coincidence. When we say "Americans", we mean only the citizens of the United States. When the world says "America", we want them to mean (and many indeed do) only the citizens of the United States. Shouldn't we be called "Usans" or "United Statesians" or, what I like to use, "U.S. Americans"?. Some 'revolutionary' activists spell it with a k or kk, 'Amerikka', for its exclusive use. Are the other countries on the rest of the hemisphere then to be relegated a lesser claim to the name "America", even if they are the original inhabitants of America, simply because the United States says so, or can't think of a more accurate name for itself, or that they don't have to, or because the descendants of the Mayflower Anglos and their ilk referred to their land then as "America"? With that seemingly innocent and simple stroke of appellation the word was hijacked to its present exclusive use. More on this later. And throughout history almost everyone (except the other peoples of North, Central, and South America) interchanges these two names substituting one for the other freely. The word America misused over and over becomes standardized and it becomes conventional knowledge and becomes unquestioned. In the process, we have abused our neighbors, confused the population, and conditioned our own minds. Therefore, the use of America equals the United States, and the United States equals America should be exposed as erroneous. Simple geography dictates it.

It is really difficult to explain to a child (or even to one's self) how there is a North America (with several countries) and a South America (with several countries) and a Central America (with several countries) but America is only comprised of one country, the United States. What happened to the rest of the countries that were in North, South and Central America? All of a sudden, they are not Americans? If America were only the U.S., then shouldn't South America be Texas/Louisiana? Shouldn't Chicago be in Central America?

Yet none of the other countries in the western hemisphere has the audacity and the brazenness and the thickness of skin to call itself "America". But we do. It's in the textbooks, in the media (especially in the media), in lofty and subterranean institutions, in literature, in art, in entertainment, education, the sciences, religion, sports, politics of course, and business. Politicians pander to the word America. Notice the frequency of this misuse during election time. Scholars I admire and oppose resound it. Nobel Prize awardees and intellectuals echo it. Working folks claim it. Illiterates boost their egos with it, some members of marginalized groups cling to it for substitute acceptance, media and top-notch newscasters indulge in and propagate its inaccurate usage. Republicans, Independents, Democrats, Progressives, and Revolutionaries all use it, and all ethnicities across the racial divides use the name of the country and the hemisphere interchangeably. That is how pervasive and uncritical is its use. Or misuse. It barely touches, and surfaces to, our cognitive awareness. The use of the word "America" or "American" as being synonymous and exclusive to the United States is pounded into our consciousness steadily and relentlessly. This attitude of exclusivity in the face of something that should be obviously inclusive (like the name of, not only a common continent, but a whole hemisphere) is something quite, dare I say, American. U.S. American. We don't even have the inclination, nor the intent, nor has it ever occurred to most of us, to call ourselves "U.S. Americans". That adjective "American" still belongs, should belong, to everyone living in the whole Western Hemisphere. Claiming and owning America for its own is at the heart of a U. S.-centric worldview.

When the word America is used to stand for the U.S. only, this whole phenomenon of hijacking the word is involved. My ears prick up, especially if a public speaker or a politician uses it. There is usually a subtext, conscious or not; oftentimes, an agenda is being pushed. This exclusive use of America with such uncritical bravado also flatters not just the speaker but the audience. They like the sound, too. This makes it easier for the speaker's agenda to slip right through, like sweetened medicine, like a Trojan horse. The word America (used for the U.S. only) most times serves as a sugar-coater, and many have found its manipulative uses convenient. Politicians won't win unless their speeches are sugar coated with the use of America for the U.S.A. The word to them is a subconscious conjurer of splendor, of glory, of grandness, of goodness, of greatness, and for many, of whiteness. And if you are a group who has been marginalized in spite of being in U.S. society (such as women, people of color), you can feel good and conceited in latching on to this claim of self-flattery, illusory though it is. At least we think we, and the world thinks we, are number one. Though "othered" in their own country of origin, they can "other" other countries now they are in the U.S., in "America". This is tied closely to the attitude of U.S. exceptionalism. Even the sound of the word "America" to them has positive connotations, images of largesse, influence, and power. Then they conclude, consciously or not, from these that the people of the United States are "better" than those who are not, and that not much can be gained by listening to other countries, unless they agree with our U.S. policies. We're number one.

But that word America has also negative connotations, the increasing notice and reporting of which are becoming more and more absorbed and prevalent. Hegemony conveniently exclude or erase the following when conjuring up their U.S. exceptionalism mentality: drone killers of civilians world-wide, corporate-run government, military global control, main polluter of our planet, and unresolved internal legacy of slavery and genocide.

One of the first, if not the first, who practiced this exclusive use of America to refer only to their settlement/community was the generation of the grandchildren of the Mayflower Pilgrims. But it was not a country then yet, so they were referring to their colony in America. The development of a distortion of the truth makes it become a lie with time because parts of the truth become permanently hidden and other parts, reified. The erosion of facts, the deterioration of the truth as the tellers cherry pick their cases for their agenda, like what people do with the bible, make the lie less noticeable until it finally becomes "the truth". Thus, America became the USA. and the USA became America.

The other spinoff of this uncritical use of America is the belief that it is not only identical with the USA, it is also synonymous with the word democracy. Automatic: USA=America=democracy. But the Igorots and many indigenous tribes around the world have, and have had, democracies even longer than from the time of the Greeks! In fact the (U.S.) founding fathers got some of their democratic ideals from the Native nations. The veto power and the check and balances in governing, for instance, came from practices and confederations and constitutions of Indigenous peoples.

America is indigenous, yet they use it in a way that is bereft of any indigenousness at all. America=USA takes away the America of the native Americans— the first nations of this land, the original and real Americans. America, Turtle Island, is, or was, all one before, before the United States usurped and hijacked that name for themselves only. There were no illegal aliens or immigrants in that America, the real America, the correct use of America, the America that applies to all of the Western Hemisphere. If those other peoples who live in America but not in the United States, are not Americans, what are they? No Names? They are not Asians, nor Europeans, nor Australians.

"Are they Martians?" Uruguayan historian Eduardo Galeano sarcastically asked.

But to the indigenous peoples, America was all one. They were all one, though varied, living on one Turtle Island, people living up and down without borders, all free to move about, as long as with respect, and in peace. Today, the same people who refer to America as only the U.S., (those who use America exclusively) are the same people who are bent on building borders (physical, emotional, legal), to keep away the very peoples whose land they have supplanted and which they now claim as their own.

The uncritical, casual, and taken-for-granted use of the word "America" to mean only the United States of America and the words "United States" as a substitute for the word "America" is a grave misnomer, racist, inaccurate geography, arrogant, and exceptionalist, to mention but a few unsavory qualities. The relegation of the word America to mean only the United States, like the relegation of the word "race", is a social construct, not a logical nor a geographical one.

Once I see or hear the word America being used for the United States, I sense a lack of awareness, a crack or failure in critical thinking, or a stealthy, stubborn, and steady conditioning, no matter how much I revile (white supremacists) or admire (Carlos Bulosan) the user. It signals a certain depth, or lack of it, a taste of colonialism, from the thinking behind it. The use of critical thinking, of propagating facts and questioning inaccuracies, are at the core of education. Our educational system is complicit in this unquestioned use and unexamined terminology. Instead, we, especially as educators, should stop such inaccuracy in misnomer especially when it is so easy to fix. If you want to mention the United States of America, mention its correct name, the name that the people of that country gave themselves, The United States . . . of America. "U.S.A." or the "U.S". is not a bad name to call ourselves. It's already used in some circles. Put "U.S." in front of "American" if you want to describe only the United States of America. Add two letters, that's all.

However, the word U.S.A. or the "United States" has no such connotations of (previously mentioned) exceptionalism and grandeur. It has too much of an international ring to it, as if it were just one of the other countries in the world. And we "Americans" prefer the more grandiose connotation to the international one.

There is also, oftentimes, an underlying "patriotism" in this exclusive use of "America" for only the United States of America. This "patriotism" also pervades, usually unconsciously, the mentality of many, displayed by much flag-wavings, God bless America calls, and all the rah-rah's that go with it, which are codes for: "keep it white(ness dominant)". I was never comfortable with associating the worship of that flag and the national anthem as a true demonstration of patriotism. A patriotic thing is to fight, work for change, when the cause is right, including the government at the moment, and mobilize for change if the government, or any other group, is unwilling to follow the constitution of the country. Sometimes, it is to fight for an amendment of the constitution itself! Ironically, like worship of the flag, that process for amendment is in the constitution itself. Peaceful and vigorous dissent is essential in a democracy; that's patriotism. It is not the rah-rah, forcing other people to stand for the anthem-flag-waving crowd majority. The flag is attached to the U.S. constitution, not the present government or powers that be. And it has nothing to do with making the military a special group of citizens. The flag does not belong to the present government, nor the military. The flag belongs to every citizen of the country.

This misnomer finds some sort of sanction because of the lack of dialogue between us (U.S.) and the other countries in America, and what's more, finds reinforcement in dominant U.S. perspectives and policies. How much do we truly know of our neighbors in America? Not much. How many countries are in America, the western hemisphere? If you have to look it up, the point is proven. How much do we expect to know if what we see as America is only us, the U.S.? All the news pundits in the corporate media pounced on the buzz over the book that (the late) Hugo Chavez gave U.S. President Obama as a present to read. Not one of these pundits mentioned ever reading or knowing of the book or its author, Eduardo Galeano. These are the most knowledgeable people in the country, these pundits? That book, *Open Veins of Latin America*, has been around for decades! It just shows how much our media, and our leaders care or know about the peoples of the rest of America.

The uncritical bombardment from everywhere of this exclusive use of America makes the public even more uncritical of its usage. It numbs, lures, dulls, and finally lies to the intellect.

There is no country by the name of America. Look it up anywhere. The Olympics' litany of countries has no America. The United Nations has no America in its membership. The World Cup has no America. Imagine how many countries will have America on their uniforms!

In trade and business, have you seen "made in America"labels? Hardly. Because any country in the western hemisphere can display items that say "Made in America".

In any international official names or lists, the name of this country is not listed as America. So why do we so freely use it, or misuse it? Just like what the U.S. Americans did with the World Series. What World Series? That is a U.S. baseball championship. No other country in the world is participating in it, yet we have had no trouble at all calling it the World Series for over a century!

This appropriation through hegemony seems to be a global phenomenon. Another example is the idea or the image of a holocaust as being only applicable to the Nazi driven Holocaust. Where the Arabs included in Hitler's final solution? In other words, for the Nazis, were Arabs and Jews included in their perception of Jewry? Included in that holocaust were the disabled, mentally challenged, Roma people, queers, and other "unwanted's" in Nazi society. According to Norman Finkelstein (The Holocaust Industry) and other historians, since the Six Day War in June of 1967, if not before, Zionists, some Jews and non-Jews, have increased their literature on that holocaust exponentially to today, and have virtually appropriated the word 'holocaust' for their own only, and made it global. Whatever culture or lifestyle, attitude or beliefs, the dominant one, even if challenged, will appropriate through its hegemony. A holocaust is a devastating, widespread, mass destruction, usually highlighted by burnings, bombings, butcherings, and other forms of heinous humanitarian crimes. Any such devastation is a holocaust. No ethnicity, no country owns that word. Ask the Armenians of their holocaust. Ask the Filipinos of the holocaust of their brutal invasion and occupation by the U.S. Americans in the U.S.-Philippines War of 1898-1915+. Ask the Soviets of the Stalin Cold War Holocaust that cost 20 million lives of his own people. Is it not a Holocaust that the 40 million slaves suffered under the Middle Passage and other cruel genocidal practices of slave owners? Was it not a Holocaust of the American native peoples that the Europeans brought, starting with Columbus, in the course of 500 years decimating 100 million? Was it not a holocaust in the decades of the Inquisition that resulted in witch burnings of 9 million women? Those holocausts, too, should be remembered in our vow of "never again".

Sho'ah is the word the Jews themselves use or give for this event in history. Zionists, and now mainstream, limited the use of that word holocaust to only refer to Nazi Germany's "final solution". But the word holocaust has been around for centuries. Origins are Old English, Latin, Greek origins which meant the burning of the whole or total destruction.

I was taught in school that the meaning of Semite referred to both Arabs and Jews, both children of Shem, Noah's son. The Oxford dictionary states: "a member of any of the peoples who speak or spoke a Semitic language, including in particular the Jews and the Arabs." But now through time and hegemony,

Semite only belongs to the Jews. Some Arabs are even accused of being anti-Semitic! Can they be accused of being anti-semitic to each other? A critic of the present Israeli government is now labeled a hater of Semites, anti-semitic. Yet, the harshest and most thorough critics of the Israeli government are Jews themselves! Norman Finkelstein, Noam Chomsky, Howard Zinn, Amy Goodman, Naomi Klein, Medea Benjamin, and others. They, among others, claim It is not good for Jews, either. Israel and the Jews are not synonymous. Thus, the hegemony of the United States has appropriated America for itself; the hegemony of zionism has appropriated the Holocaust and the word Semite for their own, and only to them. Oftentimes, folks manufacture and manipulate meaning by tampering with definitions to suit their own agenda.

In the Philippines, another example of appropriation through hegemony is the Cebuano = Bisaya language use. Cebuano is Bisaya, but Bisaya does not mean Cebuano only. San Francisco is California, but California is not San Francisco only. It seems simple enough to understand. Yet many insist that Bisaya equals Cebuano only, or derivatives of the Cebuano language. Not at all! Yet its misnomer, its incorrect usage persists. Did I say simple? I take it back. With Filipinos things are simple AND complicated at the same time.

There is a group of islands, in an area, a region in the Philippines known as the Visayas or Bisayas. The "v" and "b" are interchangeable here. There is no specific town, city, island, or province called Visaya per se. It is a region and a people, something like Bicol, or the Balkans in Europe. No specific city or town or municipality called Balkan or Bicol. The same grouping applies to the languages and sub-languages the people in the Visayas speak. There is no language called Visaya per se or Bisaya. Each group has a name for their own language. None was called Bisaya until recently when hegemony set in. Until recently, when Cebuano appropriated the language and interchanged their language's name with Bisaya.

Let's take five languages or sublanguages (there are more) of this Bisayan region. In other words, the word Bisaya covers all these people with their sub-languages. The following names of the people with their corresponding languages are: Aklanon (from Aklan province), Waray (Samar-Leyte), Hiligaynon (Iloilo, Negros Occidental), and Kinaray-a (Antique). These are all in the Bisayan region of the Philippines. Therefore, they are ALL Bisayan languages.

The island of Cebu is also in the Bisayan islands. There, people speak Cebuano. But it is the only language spoken in the area that spread significantly outside, way outside, its provincial adjacent borders.

That's where some of the complications started. The people in Negros Oriental across the island facing Cebu, also speak Cebuano. They would rather call their language Bisaya because they are not really from Cebu. They'd rather settle for Bisaya. Why would they call their language the name of another island, Cebu? They would rather identify as Bisayan than anything Cebuano because they are NOT Cebuano people. Similar is the attitude of the people of Mindanao and Bohol. The Cebuano language has traveled there, too, and they would rather call their language Bisayan because they have no affiliations with the island of Cebu. They claim more ownership of and identification with the language as Bisaya, not Cebuano. But erroneously so.

My non-Cebuano Bisayan friends who speak Cebuano don't really mind the appropriation as much as the other Bisayan peoples who do not speak Cebuano, like Waray, Hiligaynon, Kinaraya.

I first saw the term *Binisaya* used by Waray Bisayan poet and linguist Eduardo Makabenta (1885-1973) of Carigara, Leyte, and he used it to specifically differentiate it from the Cebuano language. Now, even that term Binisaya is being appropriated by the "Cebuano equals Bisaya" powers to mean only Cebuano. This controversy rages until today and there are many perspectives and takes on it, and mine is only one.

The non-Bisayans don't really care about it. The Tagalogs, the Manileños, side with the Cebuano speakers in interchanging Bisaya and Cebuano as languages because Imperial Manila wants to appease them for initially appropriating the Manila-centric but minority Tagalog (then Pilipino, now Filipino) as the national language when more people spoke Cebuano than any other Philippine language at the time.

The Cebuano language has a name, and it is not called Visaya or Bisaya. It is called Cebuano. In the early years of Philippine filmmaking, there were studios called Visayans and Cebuano was spoken in those films around the '30's to the 50's. Around the 1970's, the second golden age of Philippine Cinema, there came a trickle of change. The use of Bisaya for Cebuano was being bandied about by non-Bisayans, and foreigners. In promos and press releases, the promotion of films, independent films, ushered in some movies with Cebuano spoken and once in a while being called Visayan or Bisayan by Manileños, because to them any Bisayan language can be called Bisaya. That trickle is now a river. Unfortunately, this malpractice is spreading like wildfire. Its misuse is being propagated (among others) recently by white men (not from the Philippines) in the internet who are now casually calling Cebuano Bisayan, offhandedly, like it was common knowledge. This way they also feel an "in" with the place and the people by calling Cebuano Visaya/Bisaya.

However, the fact remains that Waray, Kinaray-a, Hiligaynon (Ilonggo), and Aklanon are all Bisayan languages, too. Not just Cebuano.

"America" is not interchangeable with "USA"; "Bisaya" is not interchangeable with "Cebuano". It is not only a gross error by hegemony, but an insult to the other Bisayans who speak other Bisayan languages, languages other than Cebuano. The misuse dismisses, nay erases their own language from the equation. And down the generations, only the Cebuano language will be falsely equated with "Bisayan", and only Cebuano will have a rightful, complete claim to anything "Bisayan", linguistically.

Using America equals the United States, using America as a country, is anti-democratic and ultimately and ironically, anti U.S. American. Yet our leaders use the two interchangeably without a whisper of irony in their statements. The irony of which seems to be lost not only in many of our leaders, but alas, and therefore, many of the masses, as well. Geoffrey Chaucer, lamenting this degeneration of leaders which results in the decay of the masses, as being proven by the U.S. Supreme Court of today, said it way back in the 1300's, "If gold should rust, what will iron do?" I wonder how many of the U.S. Supreme Court Justices use the two terms interchangeably.

America does not belong only to the United States. Bisaya does not belong only to the Cebuanos. Holocausts do not belong only to the Zionists.

If we believe in a republic, then let's respect the other republics with whom we share the continent and the world. We as a country cannot realize our own potential if we do not let other countries (especially neighbors) achieve theirs. If we truly believe in the practice of democracy, then let us remove the trappings of an empire, and start calling our country the name it was given: The United States . . . of America. Not America of America.

The day we reject the word America as solely belonging to the USA, the day we disown their being identical terms, would be the day we stop being an empire and go back to a republic dedicated to a more perfect union. The day the definition of America stands for one hemisphere and not just the United States would be the day the U.S. empire itself begins to unravel yet domestically tighten the fabrics of democracy.

Prayer

In Siquijor where magic blooms,
At Olang Park, one night
I heard the town Maria call my name.
Felt the rush of star showers
Billowing in the velvet night
Of jazz in the forest by
Four local musicians and one Californian guest
And for its audience
the driver, the help, and me

We will all go through those sliding doors
and step into eternity.
Let me cross mine like this night
of nights when the elements weave their spell

While I walk perfectly in stride with the universe

On this island of fire
this island of enchantment
and healing
this island
of no return
for visitors

like me.

Siquijor
ca. 2014

Acquaintances with the Night

I have been one acquainted with the night.
I have walked out in rain—and back in rain.
I have outwalked the furthest city light.
I have looked down the saddest city lane.
I have passed by the watchman on his beat
And dropped my eyes, unwilling to explain.
I have stood still and stopped the sound of feet
When far away an interrupted cry
Came over houses from another street,
But not to call me back or say good-bye;
And further still at an unearthly height,
One luminary clock against the sky
Proclaimed the time was neither wrong nor right.
I have been one acquainted with the night.

—Acquainted With the Night, Robert Frost

He had a friend Archie Reyes who was a drummer in this Brazilian band in a Makati café restaurant called Café Siboney and it was, according to his friend Archie, the biggest money-making restaurant and nightclub in the whole of the Philippines. Its tables were stretched outside the café itself and the outside tables were three times more than the inside tables. There were all sorts of women working and walking and drinking and eating in and around the café. Some did not want to go outside too long because the mosquitos were delighting in the skimpy clothes (or the lack of them) that they wore for their work. The owner of the place, now deceased, was a colorful journalist, a worldly man who struck it rich in the resto business. He had a chain of differently themed restaurants that served different kinds of cuisines. It was known that he gallivanted with Hemingway (photos abound in the café) in Cuba in their heydays in the 50s. Hence the Café's namesake.

There were, according to what he can discern, several types of ladies of the night who frequented Café Siboney. There were what one might call several types or layers or grades of them. One was a straight, no nonsense professional, much like the ones in the U.S., (where he lived since he was 12 years old) and was there almost all the time. The other ladies were sort of semi-pros. They worked part time and were not around all the time. No one he encountered had pimps, like in the States. The money they earned went, not to drugs, like in the States, but to their families because they were most times the single breadwinner. Their prices were different and negotiable, depending on the lady's personality and/or "client". It was a people-oriented country, he was quickly reminded.

Then there were also the non-professionals on a lady's night out adventure, come what may, *bahala na*. These are just the straight ones. Not to mention the gays, lesbians, transvestites, and all sorts of queerness. Only straights were allowed to linger inside. There was an unspoken divide among groups: the lesbians here, the transvestites there, and the straights over there. One look and he realized right away that without the women, this number one money-making club in the country would collapse in a month.

Naturally, the women who saw him seated at a table thought that he, too, was fair game. That's why he was approached not a few times. He told them that the drummer was his friend. The fact that he was a good listener made them linger just a little longer.

More than once he had to remind some ladies that if they wanted some business, they should shut up, get up, leave, and talk to potential and real customers. The women had a very personal, unbusiness-like approach that he found somewhat refreshing. He saw in each one a tragic look when they were not smiling. They had their own stories, their own take on life. He was just an imaginary customer, but he paid for their drinks if he felt they took too much time bullshitting. Some were natural storytellers. Their profession or situation certainly was conducive to it.

But once the women found out that he spoke Filipino, they gracefully and respectfully (some not so) would leave.

"Why do the girls get up and leave once they find out that the man speaks Filipino?"

Because, he was told, they associate Filipino men to what they think, or are what they are used to, as their typical Filipino male: bigoted, jealous, gossiping tightwads who might even know their friends or relatives. And once any of these arise, she's through.

The women also told him of the many tips that came from their own pockets while hanging out at the club.

"*Lugi na kami sa umpisa pa lang*. We are fucked before the night even starts. We need to buy drinks; we tip the waiters depending on whether we get picked up or not. Some even watch and remind those who were making a second pick up. A second tip is required for that. Then, the cab drivers. Some are real assholes and try to get money from us as we get a ride home. They are always asking for an extra *balato* (hand-out), thinking that we girls always make a lot of money when most nights we barely stay afloat. We're fucked before we even get fucked."

"Don't you get scared? I mean going to a hotel room with a complete stranger who could readily get violent, a weirdo who might want to hurt you?"

"No. Scared no. Just careful. If I get bad vibes, he could put a million pesos in my hand and I'll never go anywhere with him. *Pakiramdam yan. Kutuban.* To feel unspoken clues is one of the first things we learn to learn."

He remembered when he was a boy in the Philippines, this very area, he thought, was one of his hangouts, as respite from swimming in Manila Bay. His first cousin, about five years older, once went up to a brothel and he was told to play outside while waiting. But after an hour of playing basketball outside while his cousin was inside, he figured that the latter was taking too long and wanted to know what happened, what was taking his cousin so long. He walked up a hallway where he heard noises and laughter. When he slowly walked in, for the door was a little opened, he saw his cousin and a woman half naked with the sheets still around her, cards strewn on the bed, playing a card game, Lucky Nine, or Baccarat. His cousin told him in Waray to wait a moment longer because he was trying to win his money back from her.

Outside, the sun shone the same for priest and prostitute, sinner and saint. That afternoon and evening, the rain would fall evenly on princes and paupers, and the wind sweep through towers and tombstones, skyscrapers and sepulchers, the loved and the unloved.

Estrellita

Can you turn that thing off for a moment?

Sure, and he turned off the music that he was listening to from the iPhone on the ledge beside the bed. From the worn window curtains on the fourth floor of his pension in Malate, the yellow moon through the dark night settled like a pool on the white sheets. He could taste the ripening fruits of the mango tree that rose even higher in the wind.

Lying face down, he saw her through a half-closed side-eye staring at his face for a long time. He did not move.

She touched him softly and ran her palm along his hair barely touching his temple, then his shoulder. Your skin feels like a baby's. *Ang ganda ng kutis mo, a. Ako araw araw naglo-lotion pero mas makinis pa sa akin ang sayo.*

That's from my father's side of the family.

Like I said in my text. I need your help. My daughter and I are sick. I don›t know if it's the same as my mom's sickness, leukemia. I'm scared. She died at 42. I'm now 33.

Jesus was 33 when he died. He did not know why he said that.

She interrupted with a laugh, Are you saying I am going to die soon?

Bowed down, she started getting out some papers from her purse as she sat on the bed beside his prone body. She was looking down at him, so he sat up to be eye level with her. He saw her eyes reddening though no tears, not even a single one, was visible. Her voice was definitely breaking, the way his mother's did when she knew she could not stop him from going away every summer when school was out. The teardrop was in her voice.

Here are the doctor's receipts. I want you to know I am not lying...

He ignored her show of sincerity completely. I believe you.

Business has been slow at the bar. It's this crack-down and public bombings that have slowed it down.

(There had been a string of bomb threats and one actual bombing around the nightclubs in Manila).

Not too many customers, especially foreigners, are coming to the bars.

What about your Avon job?

That's been really slow. That'll pick up around Christmas pa.

My lawyer for my daughter's custody has said that all the papers have been taken cared of and that it's time that I pay. She has been stalling as long as she could for me. At first she wanted one full payment of 80 thousand, but she is willing to get it in four installments now, so twenty thousand is what I'm asking.

I'll pay for the doctor's check-up and lab tests for my daughter and me. I won't burden you with that.

Ok, he said. I think we can do it. I myself have been lucky enough to have been given a windfall of some money from a lady who wants me to go to bed with her. But I won't.

Why not, naman? she smiled.

I don't want our friendship to get ruined. I told her I have seen it happen time and time again. And that one sexual encounter will be the lock that will imprison the both of us to being tied down. I don't want any more bad feelings with a woman. Already now she is complaining that I don't tell her how beautiful she is and why have I not invited her to some trips and events, and so forth.

Why not do it? Just this once? Maybe it will keep her quiet.

I think it will do the opposite. Once is all you need.

One fuck and your stuck, huh? Why, she's not your type, ba?

I guess not. I don't think I have a type.

Yes, you do. I think we all do. But there are no rules in love and war so it's useless to know such things.

He had always observed her to be sharp and intelligent. If not just for a few bad breaks, she might have been enjoying a less stressful profession.

He watched her walk out the door and looked down the four floors, waiting for her to emerge from the first floor to walk out the gated garden promenade down below. In the still hours of the morning, he shouted in a whisper.

Text me when you get home.

Ok, she said, and he saw a hint of a smile even from that far and from that darkness through the spreading leaves of the giant mango tree that towered over the four floors and the big lighted signboard of Pension Natividad upon which he was looking down at her.

Minutes later, he got her text.

I'm home na. Thanks so much. I really needed that. I will never forget your gesture, ang ginawa mo. You'll see. *Salamat sa pakikipagkapwa mo.* God bless you, po.

He thought that the Filipino in her came out when she mentioned *"Pakikipagkapwa"*. That's deep because it goes to the core of their values. He wanted to text her back these exact words but in the intrusion of daylight, he got all discombobulated and disoriented and had trouble texting the words, so he just gave up, conceding that with the coming dawn, the night, along with his consciousness, was losing its grip.

Estrellita 2

He heard something rapping on his hotel door. It was about mid-day, the time the cleaning staff came, and they rapped on the door. They did not knock. It was a polite gesture, so he got up off the bed and opened the door. He saw no one at first, then a shade of a dress and it was her coming from the room next door.

"Oh, I was knocking on the wrong door. I thought it was here", pointing to the next door.

"Come in," he said, pleasantly surprised. "Wow, a visitor. Visitors," he corrected himself when he saw a little girl of about 7 running ahead of her. "Come in," he said, and the little girl entered first.

They sat on his bed for a while talking. "Did you eat yet? I was just going down. Ok. Go down there and wait for me; I'll be right down." There was a cafe at the lobby of his hotel. Cafe France. Pretty good but of course a limited menu. Small. The daughter, a girl of striking beauty, did not eat much. She was in the talkative age, and she was acting some of the stuff she was talking about. Like most children, she had the makings of a good storyteller.

They were just about finished eating when she broached the subject. "I Have come to ask you for help again. I Know the last time I said it would be the last. But everything seems to pile up one after the other."

"I know. That's how it is. They come in bunches, Shakespeare said that, and everybody else."

"You know it's graduation time and the watcher of my daughter at night, her nanny so to speak, is asking for her end-of-the-month salary in advance because her daughter is graduating sixth grade and she needs to go to the province to be there in person, of course, for her daughter who has not seen her during school time and she really wants to see her and I want to help her, can she have the advance? I know you are thinking I am abusing your kindness but as you know you are all I can turn to and…"

He remembered when he had his sixth-grade graduation. It was his last year in the Philippines because he and his family left for the States after his sixth grade. It's a big thing, he knew. Being there in person mother to daughter would be a big thing for her Nanny, who is giving her a headache with this problem that became her problem, "and now I" she went on, "I'm giving you the headache." They don't see each other much to begin with during most of the year. She, this Nanny, has two jobs in the city and her own child her mother takes care of in the province because the father of the child had abandoned them and has already another family, with problems of their own for sure. He also remembered the time when his own son graduated 8th grade and how big a thing that was for him and how he as a father had disappointed the boy because when called out by the principal and priest at St. James Church in San Francisco where the graduation was, his second wife was arguing with him. So when the priest called his name, he did not respond and he called it two more times, with people turning their heads and his son not knowing how to react on the stage. Hot got there late and the three or four fathers after him had already gone behind their respective sons and he was the last one and he felt like shit to this day about it.

"Why are you quiet again?" She asked.

"Oh, just for a minute." He said.

"You're thinking, huh?"

"Thoughts are rude things. Walang hiya. They come and go as they please."

"I'll pay you back, you'll see. I'm not like that. Ask my friends at the club. They'll tell you I'm the one who helps them out. When times were better."

She and the child went with him to the mall where the ATM was for his bank. The little girl loved the National Bookstore and wanted to stay longer there but the rest of the mall was also okay to explore.

Walking down the hall toward the elevators, walking fast and hop-skipping, the girl went her way but within seeing distance.

"Tall, ha, your daughter?"

"I know. She's only 6. Most people think she's eight or seven. I know I said that the last time was the last time, but this is really the last time. I swear on my daughter's name. Talaga. I am so sorry I have placed this on you, but I have no ..."

"I'll get it back," he smiled. "*Karma...daw...kuno...*so they say. I'll get it back."

Estrellita 3

When Estrellita was banned, kicked out, 86ed out of Siboney, she could not go there to work, indefinitely. She had to decide whether to lower her price and go down to the sleazier clubs in Burgos. She tried it but she could not stomach it. Those were the words she used. She'd rather live frugally for a while and go back up and see whether the big boss would mind if she came back to Siboney. She told him all this because she was giving him the reasons why she needed the money: behind in rent, no electricity, school and medical bills. Her daughter was a sickly thing, and she made sure the girl was monitored medically and regularly. She was a good mother. Most of them were.

She had texted earlier and had asked to come over. She said she had a problem.

He had heard about the ruckus at the Club.

"What the fuck happened now?" He asked.

"This guy. This Filam fat asshole. You seen him before. He is a regular there. Bald, short, ugly. Makes me sick."

"So, what? Lots of bald, short, and ugly people there."

"Well, you know how I don't dance."

"Yeah. (He remembered she told him once she did not dance.

I don't dance, she had said. Not in public. I'm a private dancer.

That's extra?

Of course.)

"I don't think I remember him," he said.

She told his name. It did not ring a bell.

"You've seen him before. Anyway, he asked me to dance. I was on my way to the bathroom. I said I don't dance, and kept going to the CR. Aba, when I got out and on my way back to my seat at the bar, he was on the dance floor and he stopped me saying, Lets dance. I said I don't dance, I told you. Let go of my arm.

He said, why do you come here? Is it not to make money? I have money; c'mon, let's dance. I said no, I don't dance. Then I jerked my arm off, and then he started getting violent and all the employees were telling me, forget it, Yita. He is the owner's friend. I don't give a shit if he's the Pope himself, or Bill Fucking Gates, he is not getting me to dance. That fucking ape. *Binastos nya ako talaga!* You know him when you see him."

"I think I'm getting a picture of him now."

"Yeah, so I have not been there for two months. That's why I'm asking for help."

"I see."

When he went to Club Siboney a few nights later, he purposely looked for the bald headed Filam. He was there, all right. Dancing away. He could dance, though. He saw the Filam as he passed to go to the bathroom and "Baldy" greeted him hello with quite a sincere smile. "Can I buy you a drink?" he asked.

That Estrellita, he thought. Her kutob was right on the money. "Baldy" exuded nothing but bad vibes. But her courage got the better of her. Actually, got the better of him; like she had said, "now I am bringing you the stress." She was right on the money there, too.

Estrellita 4

She met him for a dinner date at Joe Assad's posh restaurant in Rockwell which was in dire financial state. She stood out but not stunningly. She walked through the door, her outfit though creative, could not hide its cheapness. But she was not, so it was ok.

This is very good wine, Estrellita said.

Wow, really! I don't know much about wine.

Yes, this is excellent. She took the bottle and started reading its contents. Yes, from Argentina. I had something like this before. No hangover or after taste. Ummm. Delicious, no?

Yeah, tastes pretty good.

Pretty good? It's exquisitely, buoyantly stimulating!

Yeah, that's what I said, it tastes good. Enjoy.

Yes, we must. For so little time.

And so many wines. Let's toast to fleeting moments of wine and time.

I don't know what you said, but here here. Remember, look, ha? Look at the person you are toasting with.

Korek ka na naman dyan!

And they toasted the night away.

One day, he was not feeling well. And Estrellita knocked on his hotel room. She was carrying a bag. Here, she told him, here are your favorites and finish that sinigang soup, ha. That's what's gonna help you feel better, fishman. It's salmon, not bangus, sinigang. Is it ok?

Wow! He sipped the soup right away while she was still clearing the desk to lay out the rest of the food she had brought. Holy shit, this is good, Estrellita! Man, I didn't know you could cook! Learned from your Mom or Dad? I bet your Dad, huh?

Internet, *po*, she said.

He forgot. She had told him once; she did not know her father and that her Mom died at 42. Of course, she could not have learned to cook from her parents. What parents? She grew up practically an orphan! Then, she was sent to her Aunt's place in Japan. That's where she had her daughter and that whole ordeal which partially resulted in her doing what she was doing now.

Sinigang Queen

Did I forget to thank you
For the dinner (and leftover breakfast)
You paid for last night
As a treat and welcome
to a traveler returning home from distant lands?

That sour sinigang soup woke me
Rising with the morning sun,
Reminding me of how few and far between
beauty and kindness grace one's life.

I am and have been a forgetter of many things
but the taste and tang of your company
always linger

Makati, 8/2023

Queen of the Night

Mara was a working girl, yes, a lady much acquainted with the night, yes, but her elegance, night or day, never left her presence. In motion or at rest, poor though she was, she held that regal stature, that invisible crown of seasoned confidence fit only for a queen, Queen of the Night, and silent warrior during the day against life's harsh realities that had been visiting her without respite all her young life, though never leaving her bitter. She laughed and loved the business of living, raising three children, finally leaving her cruel and abusive partner after three attempts before. But now she had entered another stage and left that night life behind realizing that that was just another phase, as well.

This time, in broad daylight, they walked in front of Café Siboney. Its tables outside sporting a much more conservative clientele of office executives, tourists, visitors, and workers. "*Lumilipas din pala yun,*" she told him. "I didn't realize such things would also pass. *Kaya hindi na ko nag ga-gabi.* I cannot stay out at night anymore. I'm 37 *na.* I can't be doing this all my life."

The first time he saw Mara, her friend Daisy was the one who approached. The two of them were sitting at a corner near the back inside Café Siboney. It was late into the night and the last tunes were being played on the last set. Mara joined us when Daisy motioned for her to come. She would become his first friend from that club.

"Ay, this girl *talaga.* She sent me here first to you because she was too lazy." Daisy said, fanning herself with a little hanky.

"Too tired,' Mara corrected.

"She only softened because I told her you speak Tagalog. I know most of them leave when they find out the man speaks Tagalog. But not my friend."

"Too late at night for nosebleeds. Whew, relieved to know you," she got up and approached him, and said with a smile. "Mara," holding out her hand. They were a pair. Daisy, very forward with her dress, or the lack of it, sending an obvious message, but Mara wore a regular, every day outfit, not seductive at all, though with a certain touch of care. In the hotel room, he told the two the story of the Legend of Maria the *diwata,* or human goddess, of Mt. Makiling, and that is where he learned that Mara was wise and quite perceptive when she articulated the tragic and fateful problem of the male population of the town that the goddess often visited from her abode atop Mt. Makiling. *Hindi marunong tumanggap ng talo*: They didn't know how to accept rejection or losing.

"What is your type *ba*?"

"I don't have any type," she answered. "I don't really care if the man is fat or bald or not good looking. Not at all really. I've been with I don't really want to count them! I don't look at the physical features. I look at the way he treats and talks to people; the way he treats them and himself. *Yung ugali ng tao*. His character, not his looks at all. If I don't like his attitude, not all the money in the world can make me go with him." She meant it.

Sometimes it takes a working girl to point out a shitty and shaky cliche like that. Or ask the question: What really counts in life, what really is important? *"Hindi yung ugly nya kundi yung ugali nya ang pinapansin ko,"* she repeated in Tagalog, punning the words "ugly" and "ugali".

One time she asked him point blank and out of the blue, when she was on top, straddling him, what he thought of her.

"What do you mean?"

"I mean you know. What do you think of me, a working girl?"

"Why, do you feel any difference in how I treat you?"

"That's just it. You're wonderful. Don't you care about what we ladies do? You know what we do, right?"

"Of course."

"Well..."

"Well, what?"

"Well...You know we have to do it, right? No one likes doing what they are doing here."

"Of course not. What are you asking me?"

"Well...nothing. What's wrong with me, anyway? You're wonderful. Gold already and I still want to turn it into shit. Excuse my French." One thing about Mara, she did not use profanities. He heard her say "fuck" in English and its Tagalog counterpart *putang ina* only once, and that was only to mimic him.

When Mara and Archie's friend walked inside Greenbelt Three in Makati during the day, she said, "Wow *ganito pala siya sa aga! Ibang iba ang mukha niya.*" She was talking about a place that she saw and walked around only at night. Café Siboney. She was from Marikina, two or three cities away. She told him that she had been there months before with her kids, briefly during the day, and one of them had asked her "Where around here did you say you worked, Ma?" She had told her family that she worked the night shift at a restaurant. Sometimes she would be gone all night. That's why Mara did not go every night. Basically, she only went when she needed money which is pretty much every other night. She was lucky that her mother sometimes stayed with them, though she'd (Mom) rather go home to Tacloban in Leyte.

Mara could not afford, did not have time and energy, to go every night, anyway, what with three kids and doing housework and being the only breadwinner and all. While walking on this bright day, she took the place in, absorbed the sights and smells with no particular focus, very slowly, smiling once in a while for no apparent reason. Her daughter, the youngest one about 6, she took with her and she was playing and running ahead like most kids do. "*May* heart condition *yan*, the doctor said. Look how she still plays and runs around."

"Just like any kid. She loves life. Must have gotten it from the mother." Mara had two dimples, one more noticeable than the other. That time, he easily saw both.

A few weeks ago, he had asked Mara to accompany him and a friend who needed help in traveling and interpreting in Leyte. His friend was born and bred in the States but needed to locate some relatives in Mayorga and La Paz, Leyte, and Mara was from there. He does not know if she was born there or Manila but he remembers her telling stories of her girlhood in Leyte. *"Dalaga pa ako nun,"* she liked to say, with a smile. "I was still a young maiden then." Her people were from Leyte. He told her his friend would need her for about three days, all on the level, all expenses paid. But she was not really too keen on the idea, he could tell. He thought she would go for it right away. But he was wrong. "I can't leave my kids alone in Marikina. Mom is in Tacloban this time."

Two weeks later he happened to browse a message from Facebook with pictures and images of Mara and her pending trip to Oman, Middle East. He couldn't figure it out. Mara was too worried about leaving her kids because she would be away for three days in Tacloban (about an hour's flight), and then would not hesitate, nay be overjoyed, at the prospect of going thousands of miles away to the Middle East to leave her kids for who knows how many months or years? He tried to contact her on Facebook but all he got was an image sticker of a thumbs up reply. What the hell does that mean?

He remembered when along the potholed streets of Pedro Gil by Robinson's in Malate, Manila, she took his hand to help her step over a puddle. And into the littered streets and stinky sewers and homeless wanderers, she walked and floated, straight-backed and regal, her elegance making her mundane surroundings fit for royalty. Like the flower *Dama de Noche* that releases its fragrance only in the evenings, Mara, quite naturally, transformed into her role as Queen of the Night in Malate, a district in Manila adjacent to the district of Ermita, where he as boy grew up and ran wild. The storyteller in her was one of the things he liked. Someday soon, she'll get that upper right corner tooth fixed or replaced. Only the crown on her head and on that tooth were missing.

They had dinner at Café Adriatico. He noticed she was intently looking out the window at something. He sat across from her looking at the inside of the restaurant, his back to the street.

"Look at that cat across the street."

He turned to see.

The cat was playing by herself, frolicking on the steps outside the nightclub. "She is trying to attract people to give her food."

"How do you know it's a she?"

"You're funny. You know so much, yet so little. There are many signs of her gender." She smiled.

When they finished eating, they walked across Adriatico Street. She went straight to the calico cat and started scratching her head. "He did not know you were a girl," she told the cat. "Wanna come home with me?" The cat walked with them for a bit, then scampered back. She was always a cat person. He did not remember her ever touching a dog or talking about one. She had found a deserted kitten during the Covid epidemic and named her Covid; he remembered her writing him via WhatsApp.

Next time he saw Mara she had just been back in the Philippines from the Middle East. Her stint had ended in disaster...again, so she had to go back home. She said through text she'll tell him all about it when she sees him again. "That could have been a blessing in disguise," she texted, "cuz now, at least, I am here with my kids."

In his room, she explained her failed trip to Oman. She told him the Agency was trying to pull a fast one on her. They were not going to give her fare back to the Philippines because they claimed she did not fulfill her contract, and she retorted that her contract was not even clear to her because she signed no papers relating to her duties, and so on, and so forth. She was glad to have gotten out of there, she said. He told her that he, too, was glad for her to have gotten out of there. Then she gave him a massage and talked about business while she was doing it. He had given her two hundred dollars to start a food truck of some sort. He saw her cousins in Café Siboney and one had said that Ate Mara is very business minded now. Mara told him about the new factory near her place in Marikina and that she intends to put up a stall and sell food.

When he got to California, he got a post from her. She needed a fridge and there's a second-hand fridge someone is selling. "Can I borrow," yes that's the word she used, "a hundred dollars asap before the guy sells it to somebody else? He is holding it only for so long, for me." She again mentioned that near her place in Marikina, there is a factory that was just built and she would like to put up a little food stand near there to catch the workers especially at lunch time. He had "lent" her smaller amounts of money before, around $20, three or four times. He had seen her younger two cousins quite often at Café Siboney, always together. "How's Ate Mara?" One would answer (while she was dancing with a potential customer), "Business minded, that one. What did you do to her? She's selling rabbits now."

"What? I thought it was for a fridge."

"Yes, we got that. Now she's into candles, too, along with the rabbits. All Souls Day coming. She's going to the cemetery and sell candles, too." Sure, enough he saw in one of her posts a picture of the candles and the cemetery and the whole works. She sends pictures of the things she did with the money he had "lent" her.

"Wow. A regular Mrs. Henry Sy, you are." He texted and teased her with a compliment.

"Who's Mrs. Henry Sy?" She texted back.

"Mrs. Shoe Mart, *ano ka ba*? From rags to riches story."

In a few months, he got another post from her with a picture of a tricycle. "I now need a tricycle to deliver goods. *Sayang*, I am turning down so much business. A tricycle for deliveries would be ideal. There's one now for only a hundred dollars (5000 pesos). I get so tired, especially at the end of the day." The money for the tricycle, another hundred dollars, he would have to "lend" her again. "*Sayang*," she said. "It is such a good opportunity to make money. Strike while the iron is hot, right?"

"Whoa, slow down." He posted back right away.

"Timing is of the essence on this one," she said. "Others will inevitably buy it. *Sayang*, that's such a good deal." He saw the trike, the picture that is. It really looked like a good deal. Sturdy, well-kept and durable, and could carry a lot of load. "This deal will not be there forever. The owner is waiting for an answer from me na," she messaged him on WhatsApp. He could not drop the ball on her. He "lent" her another hundred, Western Union, and wondered why she got first pop at all these word-of-mouth great deals.

The Diamond Hotel

From his hotel Pension Natividad, in Malate, adjacent to District Ermita where he grew up and left at thirteen years old, he walked around the corner towards Manila Bay to meet Mara at the Diamond Hotel by Roxas Blvd. It's a five-star hotel and he liked to take a dump there whenever he could. He remembered that was his journalist Uncle Ben's primary use for those five-star hotels. Sometimes he would meet people there. It's only a few buildings from his Pension and it's a good meeting place and landmark. He can use their lobby as a meeting room if there's just a few of them. She texted him and when he got there she was waiting outside where all the dogs and guards were. Evening wear, scarf, layered outfit, with embroidered top clothing, she stood there smiling on top of the driveway to the hotel entrance while he walked up to her. It was their first night of meeting since he got back to the Philippines.

They walked back to Pension Natividad, right turn on the corner of M.H. del Pilar and three buildings away, a big neon sign but dim and not easily seen. While he and Mara were walking in the moonlight, she told him of her Italian boyfriend before. She was such a good storyteller; she held his attention until the next morning.

During breakfast at the lobby, she amused him of the many ups and downs she had with that boyfriend.

This is her story

Naku, I always pissed him off. He did not want me to work in Cafe Siboney anymore. And I lie to him and say okay, but you know I have to make money on my own, too, if I can. I don't like to depend only on him. And sometimes I wanna go gimmicking with my friends and naku, he used to get so angry at me. He would follow and stalk me and sometimes confront me at the weirdest of places and make things really awkward. He'd pop up and start telling me that he heard from his friends who always go to Siboney that they had seen me there again. One time, he slapped me with money bills and they scattered all around the ground.

"I told you not to go there anymore."

"I did not plan to. My friends convinced me. You know, they're my friends and I need to bond with them too. Besides, they were my friends before you."

"Yes, but why there?"

He started to leave huffing and puffing as I picked up the money. Sayang naman.

"Cuz that's where they are. Like what that white guy who wounded up marrying one of my friends here said, 'I don't care where I met her. What's important is that I met her'."

"But I can provide everything you need."

"Sometimes people live not just for things they need," I told him. But I don't think he understood. I think I was a little too mean with him. But you know, I was younger then. More petulant, more wild. And jealousy, though I understand where it comes from, I never could get along with it. That's partly why I fought him every inch of the way. Super Jealous yun! But we had good times. We were together for quite a while, maybe six months". Mara ended there.

"Sorry for all these questions," he said, patting the napkin on his lips, "but I'm a little slow sometimes."

"*Naku, tama ka na!* Come on!" she said. "Your heart is as quick as they come. And you're sharp. *Arte ka pa*, you know all this."

"Oh, you know I know, huh?"

"Yeah. I know you know."

"How?"

"I'm a woman and you're a man. Like that." And as she finished with her knife she took his toast and said, "I'll put you butter," and after giving the bread back, "that's how I know."

He had to admit he was a bit dumbfounded. "How did you know I can't eat toast without butter?"

"That's how I know." She repeated.

"I heard you the first time."

Happy Ending

"May utang ka sa akin. You owe me," she told him after he paid for his massage at Maalikaya outside Heroes Hill in Quezon City where he was staying at his cousin's house. His cousin's house is still there but not Maalikaya. Classic and historical though it was in its heyday, like Club Siboney, it has now disappeared.

"I just paid you."

"It is not money I'm talking about," she said.

He had checked into Maalikaya while getting out of the pressing heat of the city. He had climbed up a spiral stairway and was shown picture albums to choose from. He had picked one from the "Executive Suite", second only to the top tiered "Presidential Suite". No. 147. She was a very nice lady when they got to talking. She had created an instant family, she told him. She had just adopted a kid. She will just be working maybe a year more before she quits the business, though the money is good, she said. She is just working till she saves enough, for what, she did not say. Financially, she was almost there. He had come quickly; that's why she had said, "May utang ka sa akin."

A year later, almost to the day, while at the same cousin's house, curiosity, among other things, got the better of him and he found himself at the "Executive Suite" of Maalikaya again, rummaging through album pages of photos. He could not remember her number. 248? 347? Something Like that. He looked at the pictures like he did before. He found her! Her file was still there. Her number and picture were still the same: 147. He showered and lied down in the dark waiting for her. And then she entered the room. He did not remember what he said but the moment she heard him speak, she stopped what he was saying.

"That voice," she said in the dark "I know that voice."

He could not believe it. "It's been a year!" he said.

"Has it?" she asked.

"How is your instant family?"

"Fine, the boy is fine, And so smart!"

"Must take after the adopted mother."

"You owe me, remember?"

"Amazing," he told her, "the whole country is really amazing!" echoing the voices in the dark of his own debt to the homeland.

Hubert the Hummingbird

In my small backyard and garden
every now and then
a hummingbird I have named Hubert
comes to visit

plain brown against the sun
then as it darts around
its colors change
with the strike of sunlight and shade
from rust-red whirl to
the buzz of midnight blue

Divorce after 27 years late in life
was heavy on my mind

Thank you for the distraction
or was that consolation?
Hubert, the Hummingbird.

The Distant Relative

(novel excerpt)

Chapter One: The Offer

Carmen's was a small restaurant by China Basin right under the Bay Bridge in San Francisco. The place was owned by a Pinay, a strong but very soft-hearted woman. She's had the place since the fifties, way before there was a Pac Bell or an AT&T (or whatever is the corporate owner name at the time) baseball park for the Giants built in that area. Every now and then, there would be music coming out from the joint, whenever some Pinoy musicians got together and jammed. Manny liked it there. He loved the food. He liked looking out the window across the street and checking out the jumping jazz joint restaurant called The Palate of Fine Arts, and then extending his view out into the Bay. Carmen's had mostly mainstream dishes and entrees, but she has some Filipino food, too. And if you're in with her, she might even try your favorite, like...fish or singang. She was one of the very few Filipino restaurant owners in San Francisco who also did the cooking. Carmen's was not a big money-maker, but it got by. Not too many people (though it got full once in a while), but all were friendly and mostly happy. The place never really got jam-packed like the one across the street, The Palate, a renowned jazz joint where the waitress was also the singer of the band. The head of the band was her father, a white guy who played the trumpet like nobody's business. Every break time, the singer would go to the bar, put on an apron, and start waiting on tables.

This is where Manuel Intown was, at The Palate, when two men, black and brown, with some urgency, slithered their way into the ambience of the place. Sugar Pie de Santo, a half Pinay, half black woman was wailing from the jukebox as both men walked and cut into the smoke filled room, rudely penetrating the space of some people. The band was not playing so that meant that the singer was waiting on tables. The men walked straight to Manny sitting intensely, but not completely, caught in the night and the music. This was another of Manny's favorite hangout areas in the City. The Palate of Fine Arts right across Carmen's by the Embarcadero, hosted almost nightly the splash of moonlight by the bay.

The two who walked straight to Manny were familiar figures, so even in the dark, and not directly in view, Manny spotted the two coming towards him seconds after they entered the door at the Palate.

"Trouble, Manny. They sent us to look for you," the black guy said.

"I'm not only off today, I'm off tomorrow, too," was Manny's quick answer.

"Somebody's jumping off the bridge…"

The singer waitress came, a white lady with reddish hair.

"Yeah, what else is new?" said Manny.

The brown man then pulled a chair, turned it towards himself, and sat down with his legs between the backrest in front, and told Manny squarely, "Two things: One, it's the fucking Bay Bridge, Manny, not the Golden Gate bridge. Two: The guy is not speaking English. They think he's talking Filipino."

"I can't talk Filipino."

"You don't have to. Just go over there and show your face. Maybe the guy will soften up if he sees another…," said the brown man.

"Well, in that case, I'll just tell you what to do."

"You gotta go."

"No, I don't. You don't need me there. I can tell you what to do. Find the mother." He added, "I don't feel like being a token this time," and shook his head slowly with his legs outstretched and resting on the table. "Not this time. That's all there is to it, man." Manny slowly took his feet off the table and placed them gently on the floor. The two visitors did not seem to know what else to say. Quite promptly, the three from their seated positions effortlessly and automatically rose and started walking outside heading for a quieter place. Still walking, they continued the conversation under a stark moonlit night, cold and wintry. The branches of trees were dry and bare; the bay winds coming in gusts sliced right into their necks.

Manny flipped up his collar and turned to the brown man, "Look, amigo, here's what you gotta do. Go bring someone from the family there. If the mother is around, that would be a great help. I'm of no use to you. I can't speak Filipino."

"Is that what I should tell the big boss?"

"I would appreciate it, brother." Manny smiled at the two and they parted ways, the two into their car, and Manny crossing the street toward Carmen's. Before he traversed the still-graveled part of the street, framed in the background by the expansive Bay Bridge, he stopped by a flower stand.

"Evening, Dolly." She was getting hefty but she did not lose any of her charms.

"Manuel! So good to see you."

"Dolores, how's business?"

"So-so. What can I do you for?"

"Just two stems. And the boys? Going to college soon, eh?"

"Oh, yes. My boys are smart."

"I know. Take after their mother. Two stems of what do you suggest?"

"Roses this time."

"Roses they are."

Dolly picked two stems and handed them to him. He paid for them and gave one stem back to Dolly, putting it on her lapel-hole. She smiled to a happenstance passerby and said to him, gesturing towards Manny, "I love this man."

Manny continued walking to cross the street. He'll say hello to Carmen if she's there tonight. She should be.

Still in bed, he read about it in the Chronicle the next day. He didn't call the office, nor did he answer any calls that day. It was, after all, still his day off. He was right. The mother being brought to the scene worked. No one was hurt. Some onlookers were quoted as saying that the Filipino guy who was about to jump was convinced, more like threatened, by the mother to change his mind and come back. She even had some baon, food in a container for him. But no one quite solved the mystery of how and why he picked the Bay Bridge where pedestrians were not allowed in the first place. Why didn't he just walk on the Golden Gate Bridge along with the thousands of tourists that walk there everyday, and jump? Why go to all the trouble to avoid detection when it was detection by being conspicuous that he himself had accomplished? He must have driven there, looked for an appropriate place, slowed down, parked his car by the side, amidst everyone's honking, and as the paper said "was practically hanging by one hand, when the mother got there".

Manny slowly got out of his bed. He shook loose his body and started stretching, feeling for aches. He cleaned his glasses and rubbed them with a special cloth he picked up by the lamp. When he put on his glasses, he was already walking away from his bed, grabbing his kali sticks, two long and one short, from a chair, tucking them under one armpit. On the way out across the small living room, he placed the sticks standing up against the wall before entering the kitchen. He pulled a pitcher out of a fridge. He poured his self-made herbal tonic for the morning into a cup and put it in the microwave. He stood looking out the window waiting for the microwave to beep. When he finished drinking his tea, he moved away from the microwave, picking up his sticks. In the living room, as he began his preliminary stretches, every now and then, he would grimace a moan. Maybe it's time to think about retiring. And then he began his dance, his sayaw, of the twelve strikes. (Later, when he would become a fugitive deep in the jungles of the Philippines, a blade would find its way into his possession and his hands would once again be familiar with its handling. Because in moments of emergencies, his hands will do the remembering.)

He was thinking about the offer. All throughout his sayaw he was thinking about the offer, the offer that his boss had laid on him the afternoon before taking his two-week vacation which was now on its last day. He had been thinking about this offer on and off for two weeks. He has to decide. In his sayaw, he incorporated these thoughts, not knowing whether he was supposed to dance clear of thoughts, or dance with one's thoughts, heavy though they might be at the time. Perhaps the sayaw might help him make a good decision. So he danced for a little while. A football game was on t.v. without the sound and while doing his sayaw, he had the music on. About half an hour later, the phone rang. He walked over to it and picked it up from the small table beside the t.v.

"Are you coming tonight? I gotta know. We have eight already." The voice from the other end was that of his friend Danny talking about their Friday night poker games. Manny grew up with most of them in and around San Francisco. This particular time, five of the players including Danny happened to be taxi drivers. Driving cab seemed to be the trend of the day. Sometimes people follow each other and not notice it. There have been numerous occasions their cabs were parked all around Danny's apartment, a Victorian building on the foothills of Twin Peaks. Their names were varied, the cabs: Daly City Cabs, Luxor, Yellow, Sunrise, all kinds of different cabs. The motley colors of the varied cabs under the street lamps decorated many a misty night.

At one time or another, as boys, everyone, including Manny and everyone's second cousin, worked for the St. Francis Yacht Club because Danny's father worked at the Club. Every time they needed a little cash they would work for Danny's father at the St. Francis Yacht Club. Can't get in there any other way. Danny and Manny had gone to Las Vegas one summer and then pretty soon, the rest of his friends all started to check out Vegas in the summers, too, when school was out. Many Filipinos lived in Vegas even then.

"How long is your vacation?" asked Danny over the phone.

"Two weeks," said Manny.

"When is your last day?"

"Today."

"Doing anything special?"

"Naw. I'll have to start work Monday."

"Well, come on over tonight. You got time to lose one more game, right?"

"Right," he said.

Manuel Intawun was his original name. It's Visayan Waray. He has now changed it to Intown because for one thing too many people spelled it that way anyway and he got tired of correcting folks, sometimes almost getting into fights over the damn name. He is working for a corporation of private investigators. He is an ex-cop. Never really got promoted to anything significant. For all his years at the Force, before he quit, he just got up to the rank of Sergeant. But everyone knew he was a good cop. He had instincts, as they say. But that did him no good in his marriage. Things were falling apart. His wife was already seeing someone else. His kids are sometimes strangers to him, and he has taken assignments here and there just to get away. He wanted to get away from his relationship with his wife but he wanted to stay with his children. He, of course, lost both.

There were four taxi cabs, three Yellow's and one Luxor, parked in front of a Victorian building apartment sloped on a triangle corner on 17th Street by Burnett Drive on the west side of Market. Five of Manny's friends, the poker players, were cab drivers working that night, each taking a break from their varied shifts. Of course, all knew that it would not turn out to be a break but an all-nighter because once the lure of poker catches you when you start playing, you are as good as sold. No schedule seems to matter. Priorities get distorted. And one becomes a willing slave to poker's pleasures, most times a willing, losing slave to poker's pleasure. Everyone knew this, yet everyone still persisted on their obsessive inclinations, against, of course, their better judgments, so the gamblers claimed. *"Daw"*, in Filipino.

Manny parked his gray Corolla and walked up the hill to Danny's apartment and then climbed the stairs to the third floor. To the immediate right was the apartment and when Danny opened the door, there were already five people playing. They all greeted each other as Manny was taking his seat and taking off his jacket, the five people's attention, including Danny himself, back to the game. "Who called? Who's still in?"

In the middle of drawing to an inside straight, Danny asked Manny, "You gonna take the job, man?"

"I don't know. It looks pretty good right now, lemme tell you."

"Yeah," one of the players interrupted. "Just let me know what dog taste like when you get back, okay?"

And another, "They'll hang you by the balls there!"

And then Charlie the white friend said, "Take it, man!" Opportunity in disaster...your life (here) being the disaster. I'll be there Christmas time. I'll check you out," said Charlie.

"You? I didn't know you went there."

"I went a couple times. I got business there. And friends, of course.

"You, a white..."

"Yeah, me, a white guy. Hehehe."

When he got to his office downtown on Bryant Street Monday morning, the offer was explained to him by his boss.

"You understand Filipino, right?"

"Understand, yeah, most of it, but I can't speak it."

"Well, that's all right 'cause you're gonna get a lot of practice. You're taking a plane to Manila tomorrow." His boss ran it down.

Manny would go to his assignment, with hazard pay of course, all expenses paid, not much, but all expenses, at least. That assignment would be the Philippines. The objective would be to "find" someone; his boss said the word with some deliberateness. "Insurance completely covered," he added. "That's about all I can tell you. From here you go to Hawaii and there they'll tell you what to do." His boss got up and smiled. "Sound good?"

"It'll sound a lot better if I can have some questions answered right now, like why me? What's the whole picture? Why—"

"Sorry. That's all I can tell you because that's all I know. Here is the order itself. Wanna read it?" His boss tried to hand him the piece of paper, but he did not bother to look.

"Can I let you know from Hawaii? Can I give you my decision then? I mean, I have three days to change my mind, right?"

"I believe that's in the contract."

"Then, like I said, I'll let you know from Hawaii. In three days."

"Right," the Boss said automatically. And thinking about it, he added, "Hey, I like your style. You're alright. You gotta deal. Let me know from Hawaii. Let me know in three days."

Manuel Intown as he now calls himself sometimes has the look of a man whose friends had all moved away. He now works for a private investigator firm. He was with the San Francisco Police force for about 11 years. He was a good cop, they said. *Daw.*

Epilogue

Author at his desk. San Francisco. ca 2018

I did not say I'm right about things; I said I write about things.

In 2012, I retired, and in 2013, I got divorced and found myself in Davao Mindanao, in a cheap hotel room and the horrible t.v. would be the last resort before hitting the sack, so I was browsing through channels (all three of them, two were blurry) and the audio of one caught my attention. The Philippines is truly the mother of small worlds. I heard the names of my friend's two sons, and when the picture cleared, a baseball game was on the screen and sure enough Florentino and Lorenzo, the Ubungen brothers, were playing in a national professional baseball game. It was just finishing, so I switched to another channel. An elderly woman was telling what was the end of a Jewish tale. I did not catch much of the beginning nor middle of her story, but I heard and liked the ending.

It was an allegory or a parable about the story and the truth. And it intrigued me so much and bothered me enough that I could not get the image out of my mind. So, I supplied the beginning and middle parts myself. This is yet another version. L'Chiem!

The Two Strangers (A Jewish Tale)

There was once a village-town that was isolated from all her neighboring towns and cities. No one knew of this town and the people in it were powerless against the grip of this confounding anonymity.

One day a stranger came to town. Tall, ruddy, and handsome he was. He knocked on a villager's door. He was pleasant and attractive and immediately he was welcomed. "Who are you," asked the villager?"

"I am the Story," replied the handsome stranger. In every house that he asked permission to enter, he was greeted with joy and fed and housed and was asked to put his cloak down and stay longer. "But I cannot stay," said the stranger. "I am looking for someone and it is here that I am destined to find that person. It has been my life mission, and my journey has led me to this place."

"Who is that someone?" he was asked.

"I do not know. But I will, when I lay eyes upon that person." And the stranger called the Story was seen walking easily around the village, its paths and road-ways opened up to him, its people accepting of his entertaining ways.

One strange and unexpected day, another stranger came to town. Not handsome or particularly attractive, but simple, yet somehow mysterious. She knocked on a villager's door and right away the villager was struck with her mystery. Unlike the Story who was tall and handsome and pleasing to look at, this one was plain and, in some ways, awkward to be with. Only parts of her were readily acceptable but other parts were not so easy on the eyes. And the villager felt this.

"Who are you?" the villager asked.

"I am the Truth," she said. "May I come in?" She asked.

"No way," said the villager, pushing her aside and away from the children of the house who were curious and already gathering around. So she looked away and turned toward the road that she would travel. And she received the same treatment throughout the town-village. She was not welcomed everywhere she went. Though she was not directly refused by the villagers, she was not let in, either. She was not given passage to their homes. When word went around that there was a second stranger in town, the people went to the Story, for they like the Story and perhaps he could help cast out this disturbance from the second stranger. And they took the Story to the second stranger, the Truth. And when the Story beheld the Truth, he shouted.

"Why, this is she whom I have been looking for, whom I was destined to find here. She is the twin sister whom I have never met. Praise the gods of fate, at last I found you!" and he thanked the village people profusely for helping him fulfill his destiny. The people in turn realized this and gave entrance and passage to the Truth. And the two, the Story and the Truth, walked hand in hand throughout the houses and the roadways and the pathways of the village-town and never again parted.

And as the news spread to the nearby towns, and the cities around, they opened up to this town-village that had been isolated for so long, who now felt like a captive set free, and whose voices were finally heard outside and throughout the region. That is why today, whenever you hear a story, there would be Truth in it; and whenever you discover a Truth in life, why, there you would find a story. For there is no story without the truth and there is no truth without a story.

Author Biography

Norman Jayo and author feeding pigeons on Kearny Street. ca 2023.
Photo Credit: Shirley Ancheta

Oscar Peñaranda is an educator, writer, and culture-bearer for and from both shores of the Pacific and is a recipient of the prestigious *Gawad Alagad ni Balagtas* for lifetime achievement for his writings and endeavors; and the 2023 City of San Francisco Trailblazers Award. He has a Bachelors in Literature and a Masters in Creative Writing from SF State University. While he was working one late summer in Alaska, he was recruited to teach a class in the newly formed Ethnic Studies Department at San Francisco State. Oscar began his teaching career as an assistant of Joaquin Legaspi of the International Hotel and created several classes, one of which was a Survey of Philippine Art and Literature. While at SF State, he created three fourths of those classes which still exist to this day.

www.ingramcontent.com/pod-product-compliance
Lightning Source LLC
Chambersburg PA
CBHW081103300726
48976CB00011B/2704